Dr. Nirit Toshav – Eichner

The Woes of Gender Discrimination
Fired For Being Female

The Woes of Gender Discrimination
Fired For Being Female

Dr. Nirit Toshav – Eichner

Senior Editors & Producers: ContentoNow
Translation: Juliana Starkman
Editor: Melinda Lipkin
Graphics: Talma Asher
Book cover: Benjie Herskowitz
Administrative producer: Herela Hodaya Moise

ISBN: 978-965-550-525-2
International sole distributor: ContentoNow
3 HaBarzel St., Tel Aviv, 6971007, Israel
www.ContentoNow.com
netanel@contentonow.com

Dr. Nirit Toshav – Eichner

The Woes of Gender Discrimination

Fired For Being Female

CONTENTO**NOW**

This book is dedicated to people with
a passion for the fight for equality.

Table of Contents

Acknowledgements

I first wish to thank my dear family—my mother, who was a source of great strength, my father Ephraim of blessed memory, whose optimism was ingrained in me from childhood and accompanied me throughout the difficulties I encountered while writing this study, my partner, Itamar, and my children Ido and Alma, who have in recent years had to grant their mother a lot of "scientific silence" and in return received less mother-time.

Numerous people assisted me in the research of my book over the past few years. This help included grants, which allowed me to take time for my research and to observe, interview, and page through yellowed archive documents. My thanks for this go to the Lafer Centre for Women and Gender Studies, the Minerva Centre for Human Rights, the Shine Centre, the Levi Eshkol Institute, and the Sociology Department—all at the Hebrew University of Jerusalem— as well as the Sapir Foundation at Tel Aviv University.

During these years, I presented sections of the research at conferences and workshops. I would particularly like to thank the members of the Research, Gender, and Politics group at the Van Leer Institute. Within the framework of our meetings, I discovered new directions in thoughts and research for my work.

I would also like to extend my warmest gratitude to the women who participated in the research—those who themselves experienced being made redundant while pregnant. Special thanks go to the supervisors and inspectors of the Ministry of Industry, Trade, and Labour, and to the employers for the cooperation and candour which made this research possible. I'd like to thank Mr. Benny Fefferman, the director of the Bureau of Research and Economics at the Ministry, and the employees of the Bureau, particularly Mr. Eli Levy, for the professional and logistical guidance provided throughout the years. Also, many thanks go to Prof. Tzvi Gilula of the Department of Statistics at the Hebrew University, for his assistance in planning the sampling, and to Mr. Dror Vered of Employment Services for his help in constructing the database. I would also like to thank Prof. Mimi Ajzenstadt for her guidance and support, comments, and insights throughout. I am grateful to the Hebrew University's Media Relations Department, to Ms. Orit Sulitzeanu and Ms. Libi Oz for their care in ensuring that important findings from the research were sent to the media due to their commitment to raise awareness of redundancies during pregnancy. I am deeply grateful to Professor Amos Drori, Rector of the Peres Academic Center, as well as Prof. Reuven Horesh, head of the School of Business Management, without their support, this book could not have come into being.

Finally, my heartfelt thanks to the board that has supported me during the current research, Prof. Barbara Okun, Prof. Daphna Hacker, Prof. Johnny Gal, as well as a particularly big thank-you to the advisors: Prof. Michael Shalev for the unique research directions, the statistical tools, suggestions and encouragement throughout the study, and Prof. Michal Frenkel, who accompanied me to all the conferences in Israel and abroad, supported and encouraged me, and more than anything, made me put in the effort and produce the best I could time after time— all with great patience, guidance, and support. Thank you, dear Michal; more than a guide in research, you have been my guide to a way of life. Fortunate is the person, organisation, or group who has you for support.

I would like to end with the hope that this book will serve as a theoretical and practical foundation for an attempt to initiate change within Israel's fragmented culture with regard to the treatment of pregnant employees, as well as the management of other issues that require constant guidance, coordination, cooperation, and a fight for equality.

Opening Thoughts

The discourse surrounding gender inequality in the workforce deals with, among other things, the imagined character of "the ideal worker" (Acker 1990). This worker is presented as a white male who is available and dedicated to his employers at all times. Nonetheless, in an era in which the meaning of physical work is open to interpretation, many women are able to blur gender lines. However, during pregnancy and after giving birth, the form of the female body and its obvious physical difference from the "ideal worker" model becomes clearer than ever. On the axis upon which the male—whose entire being is dedicated to working as an "ideal" or "natural" employee—is located, the pregnant employee is his polar opposite. She thus becomes less desirable to the employer and is exposed, more than ever, to discrimination on the basis of gender. In order to deal with cases in which equality is breached within the labour market, different countries employ a range of welfare policy schemes, known as Family Policy, containing legislation intended to protect employees during pregnancy. Discrepancies exist nonetheless between written law and its practical implementation, and the consequences are likely to damage the state's objective—to prevent gender-based discrimination.

This book seeks to closely chart the manner in which legislation preventing pregnant women from being dismissed is translated into standard behaviour within institutions, and to examine the layers of mechanisms that generate the level of protection available to women wishing to seek help from the state if and when they are dismissed. Two further questions are considered: to what degree the regulatory system for preventing pregnant women from being made redundant reflects the intent of the legislature, and how the "clients" of said regulation—the women themselves and the employers whose workspace is limited by it—function within it.

In Israel, Family Policy, which seeks to safeguard the positions of pregnant women, is organised through interventional regulation whose aim is to prevent job loss before it occurs. This mechanism functions by way of the state, which examines the employer and the female employee separately, and it is structured according to Section 9a of the Women's Labour Law of 1954, "An employer shall not dismiss a female employee who is pregnant and has not yet begun her maternity leave without permission from the Minister of Labour and Welfare, and the Minister shall not authorise said dismissals if the dismissals are, in his opinion, related to the pregnancy." The language of the law was decided upon at the birth of the State of Israel, which is still considered a pro-birth country today (Berkovitch 1999; Ajzenstadt and Gal 2001). Interventional regulation is meant to act as a universal, equal channel for employers and for women as an alternative to the legal proceedings that occur in most western countries in cases of dismissal during pregnancy. However, despite the intention of the legislature to minimise gender inequality in the labour force, each year more than four thousand pregnant women are dismissed; in some cases, the state turns a blind eye and in others without the state's awareness.

The law itself has undergone numerous reincarnations regarding the length of the protection offered to pregnant employees prior to and after giving birth. The gist of the changes appears in the spirit of the law and its aims, according to the legislatures who designed it, and in the manner of implementation, within the regulatory systems set up to uphold it. In the first three decades of Israel's existence, the law was implemented in the spirit of paternalism[1] and "overprotectiveness", particularly during

---

1   Paternalism is the intervention by the state or by an individual in the affairs of another person, against the wishes of said person, employing the justification that the person for whom

negotiations among employees and the workers' unions in the main labour force, who during that period enjoyed great influence over the structure of employment conditions. Beginning in the late 1970s, with the weakening of the unions and the rise of neoliberalism, the state's regulatory mechanisms were diminished, particularly within the framework of what was then the Ministry of Labour and later became the Ministry of Employment, which is a division of the Ministry of Industry, Trade and Labour (the latter's name was changed in 2013 to the Ministry of the Economy). In the past decade, Israeli legislatures have made a concerted effort to promote human rights and to minimise gender inequality in the labour force.

Along with the legislature and the official regulative bodies, labour courts (or industrial tribunals), employment bureaus, and social security institutions are also working to normalise the status of pregnant women. Further non-governmental players include workers' unions, women's groups and—in cases where the clients can afford it—hired lawyers.

The research presented in the book combines close to one hundred observations from state hearings for employers and female employees within which the strata of interventional regulation were examined. A further source is the integrated data system in which data from

---

they intervened will benefit from the intervention, or will be protected from harm (Dworkin 1972).

over the period of a decade was examined regarding submissions by women and employers to the ministry and the sociodemographic profile of those presenting submissions. This data was compared to the amount of women turning to the social security provided by the National Insurance Institute as well as the Labour Bureau, in relation to human resource survey data from the Central Bureau of Statistics for women actually dismissed during pregnancy. Furthermore, a broad survey was conducted among 101 women who acted according to the regulations, 51 who received protection from the state, and women whose positions the state refused to safeguard during their pregnancies. Further analysis was carried out of the relevant archival documents from the year in which the law was legislated (1954) until the end of the 1970s, and qualitative interviews were done with the women and civil servants, as well as employers who worked within the welfare mechanism of the state and wished to dismiss pregnant employees.

The book focuses on intertwined theoretical and practical aspects. First, the ability to evaluate the effectiveness of the state's actions in defending the positions of pregnant employees; from the cross-section of varied methods at the foundation of the study, it becomes clear that when women receive the protection of the state, their ability to continue integrating into the labour cycle improves. Nonetheless, when the state accepts the claims of the employer and authorises dismissal, the women whose dismissal has been approved have difficulty in returning to and integrating into the labour force. This particularly affects women with no higher education. Therefore, there is great latent potential when the state intervenes to prevent the dismissal of pregnant women, with regard to both the increase in participation by women and mothers in the labour cycle and the need to greatly improve the efficiency of the intervention mechanism. We also learn that a woman acting to prevent dismissal greatly influences her chances of preventing it. Various characteristics of the state welfare mechanism, as well as the worldview of the inspectors who implement it, decide which women will benefit from its protection and impact the type of protection the women will be granted. In this context discrepancies are revealed between the written law and its implementation, along with the significance of the discrepancies. The book seeks to expand the theoretical and practical discourse surrounding the level of the welfare state's contribution through interventional regulation in a neoliberal world that still relies in part on "patriarchal inertia."

Dr. Nirit Toshav - Eichner

Introduction

In recent decades, there has been an upswing in the rate of women's participation in the labour force. As a result, pregnancy has become accepted in the workplace. Concern about the availability of the female employee—from the time the pregnancy is announced, through the pregnancy, and for the next few years that involve mothering small children—may cause many employers to reconsider whether it is worth engaging a female employee, which may lead to them terminating her employment.

Furthermore, though the discourse which seeks to explain gender inequality in the labour market is growing, and within this a fairly broad debate exists concerning the influence of childbirth and parenthood on women's careers,[2] there is still very little research concerning the

2 Izreeli 2000; Herzog 2000; Ben Israel 1998; Frenkel and Hacker 2005; Knijn and Krembher 1997; Rosenfeld et al. 2004;

influence of pregnancy on the work of female employees during pregnancy, as McDonald and Dear explained (McDonald and Dear 2006) in the later study by Russell and Banks (Russell and Banks 2011b):

> There is only a narrow research review of the subject of pregnancy at work that focuses on an empirical study of the phenomena, and even less research on the behaviour of the women experiencing the loss of their jobs as a result of dismissal.[3]

Nonetheless, within this limited framework, there are great similarities between the conclusions of the researchers, which point to many women experiencing negative treatment during pregnancy, for example, delays in promotion, a significant reduction in wages, and occasionally even speedy dismissal once the pregnancy is announced.[4] These conclusions were joined over the past two years by three studies carried out in Ireland, as part of two research programmes within Equality Authority I; the HSE Crisis Pregnancy Programme (CPP), whose aim was to examine pregnancy-based discrimination in the workplace. One study succeeded in locating a link between discriminatory, inflexible, and negative behaviour toward

---

Orloff 1996; Acker 1990, 1995; Williams 2000; Kymlicka 1990; MacKinnon 1984; Kennedy and Mendus 1987; Mill and Mill 1970; Kraamwinkel 1992; Okin 1982; Hernes 1987.

3   Author's translation.

4   Adams et al. 2005; La Valle et al. 2008; James 2004.

pregnant employees and poor health during pregnancy (Russell and Banks 2011b). A further study, carried out with a sampling of 2,300 women who gave birth between 2007–2009, found that 33% suffered a crisis in pregnancy, approximately half (49%) experienced financial worries, and over a quarter (27%) of them claimed that the crisis stemmed from discriminatory responses by the employer or from unequal treatment by work colleagues (Russell et al. 2011). A third study focused on those cases brought before the labour courts and before the equality tribunal, who in cases of pregnancy-based discrimination refer cases to voluntary mediation behind closed doors. This study presents the final results of court decisions, but it criticises the inability to examine either institutional behaviour in mediation hearings or even the decision-making process and its repercussions (Russell and Banks 2011a).

The question of dismissals during pregnancy deeply conflicts with the aim of the legislature—in many countries, including Israel—to reduce gender inequality. We will focus on the "Israeli case"[5] due to its uniqueness compared with western countries, and in Israel, there is an interventional state regulation whose purpose is the prevention of dismissals before they occur. In contrast to the possibility of legal suits—the only action available in other

---

5   The Women's Labour Law is unique to Israel, and a small number of other countries who employ interventional processes.

countries to pregnant women who have been dismissed — Israel's Family Policy, which requires the employer to inform the state of requests to dismiss an employee during pregnancy, does not require that the female employee be aware of the existence of the law or have the financial and social resources needed to manage a suit of this sort. Therefore, the Israeli welfare mechanism seeks to be more universal and egalitarian than those systems which place the onus upon the woman to appeal the courts, and its purpose is to provide equal protection for all women.

The language of the law regarding protection of jobs for pregnant women in Israel was established prior to the founding of the state. During the first decades following legislation, its implementation was based on intra-state negotiations regarding its interpretation. While employers were given a voice in these discussions, female employees were denied any opportunity to present their cases. In the past three decades, separate hearing procedures have been instated for the employee and for the employer; following an investigation, the decision is reached whether to authorise the petition to dismiss during pregnancy or to deny it and instruct the employer to continue engaging the female employee. Nonetheless, despite relatively progressive legislation and the clear intent by the legislature to promote gender equality and prevent the dismissal of pregnant or post-natal women, in 1998–2008 more than 4,000 pregnant women were made redundant in Israel each year. The discrepancy between the legislation and the achieved results raises crucial questions concerning the link between formal policy and its implementation, as well as the ability of the policy to promote significant social change through regulatory means.

We will closely chart the manner in which legislation preventing pregnant women from being dismissed is translated into standard behaviour within institutions, and to examine the layers of mechanisms that generate the level of protection available to women wishing to seek help from the state if and when faced with dismissal.

The first part of the book describes the structure of the state regulatory system. Particular emphasis will be placed on interests, ideologies, public image, and the basic—and occasionally conflicting—premises that characterise the various state players and the negotiators and the power relations within which the regulatory actions take form.

The second part of the book examines the interactions among the players, which occur in the field of research; these players are, in other words, those who implement the "regulation" SLB[6] (street-level bureaucracy), state clients, the employers, the women, and the lawyers involved. In this section, the system's differential accessibility to various population groups is examined. Further, on the

---

6   "Street-level bureaucrats" is an expression that appears in the article by Lipsky (Lipsky 1980), examining the level of influence of civil servants on policy regarding state clients.

basis of interviews and the observations made while investigating pregnant employees and the employers who wished to dismiss them, the day-to-day dynamics were considered: resources available to each of the parties, habitus, background, socioeconomic capital, the reactions of each party, and the effect of these dynamics on the decision in each case. Contrary to the assumption that the decision is based on the legal definition, it emerged that the interpersonal interaction which characterises the investigation itself has an effect on the outcome.

Given that the state regulation intended to address gender-based discrimination is meant to be egalitarian, an understanding of the destructive potential inherent in the fragmented nature of the state's actions in a gender context requires those who research the welfare state to examine not only policy set by the legislature but also the manners of implementation by the various assigned bodies. Particular importance is given in this context to periods of change in policy and the social philosophy at its basis, given that in many cases a shift in social awareness is delayed following a change in formal legislation.

It has already been noted that the state regulation concerning the dismissal of pregnant women in Israel is a particularly interesting case in this sense, given that the State of Israel reserves the right and duty to actively intervene in the dismissal process and even prevent it, as mentioned above, before it occurs.

In keeping with the above, one could assume that most employers would shy away from dismissing pregnant employees. However, the fact is that there are employers who nonetheless wish to do so, whether within the framework of the legal regulations or illegally. The research dilemma, therefore, focuses on a number of subjects, including the following questions: How does the welfare system work? How is the state prepared to protect pregnant employees? How do the various mechanisms addressing the issue work together—i.e. directors at the Ministry of Industry, Trade and Labour, those responsible for enforcement and resolution and those working with the Employment Services and the National Insurance Institute? How does the state's protection influence the ability of women within the labour force in cases where the protective umbrella does not cover them? How long will unprotected women remain outside of the employment market? How does the interaction between the system's clients and its operators affect decisions about whether to accept or deny requests for dismissal? In which ways do the non-state mechanisms, such as women's groups and unions, assist? To what degree does hiring the services of a lawyer increase the likelihood of enjoying the state's protection? Finally, how, if at all, are women able to protect themselves against the state and against employers?

It should be pointed out that the research presented in this book is incapable of estimating the comprehensive influence of state regulation, given that the range of employers who avoid dismissals based on the legal deterrence is impossible to calculate. We are concerned with women whom the employer sought to dismiss and who sought assistance from at least one state mechanism. The study does, however, include an estimate of the number of women dismissed during pregnancy who did not turn to any state institutions. This tool estimates the level of effectiveness of the law as a deterrent.

Over the years, changes have been made in state policy, and at times, we found ourselves following shifts during the research process. Most of these alterations were included in the current study, but some changes may not have been incorporated.

Chapter 1

Theoretical Context

Context for the Creation of Gender Inequality: "The Glass Ceiling," "The Ideal Worker," and "Penalisation" of Mothers

In studies examining workplace discrimination in-depth, it is common to debate the "glass ceiling." This is a concept which first emerged in the 1980s, claiming that women or minority groups were more likely than others to face obstacles and obstruction upon entering the labour market and, more importantly, would be less likely to be recognised for their ability to reach management positions in the workplace.[7] These obstacles stem from the gaps in what is

---

7   Frenkiel 1984; Silberstang 2011; Merlino et al. 2012; Cotter et al. 2001.

known as "personal capital"—a lack of relevant education vis-à-vis other employees, or from the unwillingness of the employer to offer equal opportunities for advancement based on a profile of "the ideal worker," who is available at all times. The image of the "ideal worker," defined as a man who is willing and present whenever his employer demands, is one of the stumbling blocks women encounter in the labour market (Acker 1990). On an axis in which the "ideal worker" is seen as strong and steadfast, a pregnant employee is considered to be his polar opposite and may expect gender discrimination. One further discovers that the varying work methods of different countries may prevent or minimise these obstructions (Glazer-Raymo 1999). Thus, for example, in Israel, there is a specific mechanism in place which seeks to intervene and prevent gender discrimination before it occurs.

It is worth emphasising that beyond the obstacles that form the "glass ceiling," employers are hard-pressed to see mothers as ideal workers, due to pregnancy, maternity leave, and the demands of childcare, as well as regular absences. Thus, even before hitting a "glass ceiling," parenthood creates a "motherhood wall" that appears once an employee has given birth, for example, when rumours abound in the workplace: will she return from maternity leave, and if yes, when? When an employee returns from maternity leave, she must deal with further "punishments for motherhood" (Buding and England 2001), for example, by missing out on bonuses and benefits, and she is liable to see her terms of employment affected, at least in the year following the birth, as her time is no longer solely dedicated to the employer and she is forced to leave earlier than her male counterparts or those females colleagues who do not have children (Porter 2006).

How Does a Welfare State Address Inequality in the Workforce?

In recent decades, several countries began to express an interest in promoting the socioeconomic position of women in society and creating the groundwork for a financial independence in which women do not rely on the family unit. The feminist research discourse has broadly addressed the concept of a woman-friendly welfare state and the ways in which it contributes to minimising or expanding the gender gaps in the labour force.[8] Acknowledgement of the fact that, to a considerable degree, gender gaps stem from women's dual obligations—wage-based work and childrearing—has led to a wide debate regarding support for the work of mothers by the welfare state and the efficacy of the various support systems in this area. While many researchers support extensive aid from the state for working mothers—childcare vacations and other benefits—there are others who claim that special consideration for mothers acts as an obstacle to their entry

---

8   Knjin and Kremer 1997; Hernes 1987; Rosenfeld et al. 2004; Orloff 1996; Kolberg 1991.

into and advancement within the workforce, perpetuating the traditional division of labour that sees women as responsible for "care-based work" in society.[9]

Nevertheless, given that the duty to care for the "family sphere" is still seen as a woman's central responsibility, the built-in tension between the needs of the work world and those of the family are still expressed in women's difficulty to blend into the workforce. Feminist theoretician Joan Williams (Williams 2000) illustrates the importance of separating the "private sphere" from the "public sphere" in reproducing gender inequality in what she called the "domesticity regime." The "domesticity regime" is characterised by the workforce's salary organisation based on the model of the "ideal worker." Although this model does not define the employment demands of all positions currently offered, it defines many of them, including the best—those which provide satisfaction at work, promotion, and financial independence. According to this model, responsibility and production are measured primarily in terms of time; an employee who spends more hours at their workplace is more valued by the employer as a productive and faithful employee (Acker 1995, 2003, 1990, 2006). In order to handle the obstacles created by

---

9   Herzog 2000;Yizreeli 2000; Frenkel and Hacker 2005; Ben Yisrael 1998; Knijn and Krembher 1997; Rosenfeld et al. 2004; Acker 1995; Williams 2000; Kymlicka 1990; MacKinnon 1984; Kennedy and Mendus 1987; Mill and Mill 1970; Kraamwinkel 1992; Okin 1982; Sainsbury 1996.

the domesticity regime and ease the entry of women into the work world, various countries have implemented a series of welfare policies known in the literature as Family Policy. These strategies include "all the compensation and services, including legislation, which are provided by the state to couples with children or to single-parent families" (Esping-Andersen 1999) in order to ensure their participation in the workforce without affecting their parenting responsibilities. According to this school of thought, provision of family services (such as day care, and vacation time to care for children) and the protection of women working at particularly sensitive times, such as during pregnancy and after birth, must form a central core of the welfare policies aimed at preventing gender discrimination.

The difference among those countries that have adopted and implemented the Family Policy blueprint may be described primarily within the framework of the defamilisation debate, the degree to which any policy allows a reduction of a parent's (generally a mother's) dependence on the family unit, and on the workforce as a condition of her welfare and the ability to raise her children. According to this way of thinking, reduction of dependency on the employment market and on family guarantees women's financial independence. In fact, the literature on the family welfare state generally finds a statistical correlation between the formal, family welfare policy and the level of gender inequality present in the workforce.

Esping-Andersen (Esping-Andersen 1990, 1999) distinguished between family policies according to the level of defamilisation they permitted. He claimed that welfare systems were created by social and political powers, and described three types of welfare systems: the "social democratic" model found in Scandinavian countries, which succeeded in removing numerous services from the hands of the family and the workforce, and provided them to all citizens equally; the "liberal" welfare system, characteristic of Anglo-Saxon countries, in which personal and social welfare services are provided mainly through the free market, in accordance with household consumption; and the "conservative" model, which includes most continental European countries, in which the extended family has remained the primary source of social services and treatments. Alongside those characteristics common to countries which share a welfare model, there are also differences that divide the family policies into categories. Studies comparing family policies in different countries (Mandel 2011) focus, for example, on the length of maternity leave and the applicable payments, day care, and length of school days (Gornick et al. 1997; Blau and Kahn 1995), with relatively similar conclusions. Countries where the family policies are most supportive, belong to the group that employs a social-democratic welfare model while less supportive countries belong to the remaining models.

According to Esping-Andersen, the level of defamilisation resulting from family welfare policies in each country determines, in large part, the ability of women to integrate into the workforce. Studies have found that in countries where the Family Policy is more developed, the rate of women in the workforce is highest, and it is only slightly lower than that of men,[10] while in countries where legislation sought to intervene in a more measured manner in the day-to-day work of employers and be less involved in resolving conflicts between work and family life, the level of female participation is somewhat lower. It should be pointed out that the United States is the exception, given that the level of participation of women in the workforce is relatively high, despite the moderate intervention by legislators. In general, however, it is possible to say that countries closer to the social-democratic welfare model will tend to adopt broader family welfare policies and may be characterised by a higher level of gender equality in the workforce (Korpi 2000; Mandel and Shalev 2009). In this context, it is interesting to recall Mandel's research (Mandel 2009, 2011) in which she found that while the Scandinavian social-democratic model helped women balance work and family, it did not help them succeed in salary or status negotiations in the workforce or in seeking management positions. Kricheli-Katz, on the other hand (Kricheli-Katz 2012), found that in more liberal states in the United States women actually faced more discrimination and paid a higher penalty in terms of salary increases and promotions than in states with a more conservative policy.

---

10   Haas 1992; Haas and Hwang 1999; James 2004; Duffield 2002.

In the past decade, the close association between a woman's domestic responsibilities and her situation in the job market has become an integral part of the "gender mainstreaming"[11] being promoted in many countries. Thus, many countries have adopted policies that are externally dictated, without the social logic that would justify this sort of policy having become part of the social discourse surrounding it. The expansion of family welfare policies, which relies on a social-democratic worldview, occasionally clashes with the neoliberal approach in most countries that have been exposed to the process of globalisation (Sassen 2006). In these conditions, the possibility for contradictions within the implementation of family policies increases.

---

11 "Gender mainstreaming" was proposed as a global strategy for the promotion of gender equality, as part of the decisions of the UN International Conference of Women in Beijing in 1995. The proposal was adopted by several countries, but notably it was accepted as guiding policy for governmental and public organizations in EU countries and their institutions, as well as by the UN. The aim is to entrench the gender view within the public discourse, in legislation, in policy by governmental and civic bodies, as well as in research. This positions the gender inequality issue as a society-wide problem and not only as one for women alone. In this study, I will examine how the discourse surrounding gender human rights developed within "gender mainstreaming."

The State in Action

While scientists of the welfare state in general, and researchers of the family welfare state in particular, occasionally view it as a homogenous body—and in order to link formal policy with implementational patterns, they treat it as a strong, positive connection—many researchers point out the possibility of "disconnectedness" (fragmentation, lack of unity, splits, and lack of continuity) in the state's activities. They claim that the state does not necessarily function as a monolithic unit and that its patterns of activity are not cohesive but are instead influenced by political interests, by a varying attitude to public reputation,[12] by goals, and by ideologies. This is almost unavoidable, and it stems from a series of conflicts (O'Connor 1973). This inner fragmentation, as O'Connor argues, is what characterises the capitalist state. On the one hand, the capitalist state is responsible for the cumulative process and systematically increases its expenditure for the infrastructure and support of property owners. On the other hand, though, the state must adhere to its legitimacy, and it must, therefore, maintain a façade of minimal fairness for its citizens and a reputation for caring for those made socially vulnerable by the cumulative process, in particular through maintenance of the unemployed. Therefore, state

---

12 Public reputation is defined as political capital of value, which rational organizations will wish to protect (Carpenter and Krause 2012).

institutions are responsible for the accumulation work in contrast to those responsible for budgeting, with the two powers disrupting one another. Due to the lack of systematic coordination (Pardach 1977; Pressman and Wildavsky 1973) between the various policies,[13] strategies and even goals remain unimplemented. These inherent conflicts are liable to lead to policy failure.

The lack of cohesion in welfare policy, its inherent conflicts, and its occasional fragmentariness, form the basis of a research discourse on "the state in action,"[14] centred on the concept that these inherent conflicts may lead to the failure of policies and to the failure of the family welfare state. The disconnectedness may, therefore, harm women and lead to an increase in inequality in the labour market, even given extensive legislative activity.

State fragmentation[15] also becomes apparent in the coalition model, which focuses on two central, powerful motives—social and economic interests—which design the awareness and behaviour of social players, both in groups and individuals. In other words, the choice of a

---

13 Policy tools are a means of control by civil servants. They include legislation, control over field systems, bureaucratic procedures, budgets, and government decisions (Page 2000).
14 Lein 2000; Martin 1989; Streek and Schmitter 1985; Rosenhek 2002; Evans 1995.
15 Streek and Schmitter 1985; Evans 1995; Rosenhek 2002; Lein 2000.

specific coalition partner may well stem from a public or commercial interest.

The term "state regulation" appears in various contexts, and as with many other key terms, there is a lack of clarity surrounding its precise definition. The broadest common denominator for all uses of the expression is a description of the mechanisms which limit, organise, or minimise the behaviour of the individual—or legal enforcement of expected rules of behaviour as determined by the state. Regulation shall be defined as an act or organisation, control, and enforcement as carried out by an independent, designated state agency. This agency acts based on the legal mandate granting it broad powers of authority for secondary legislation in a specified field, with the aim of regulating (Majone 1994) private activity in the media, banks, consumer protection, sectors in need of state intervention in matters of health, aging, maternity leave, and protection of pregnant employees (Gordon 1988).

The sociological research regarding the manner in which policy is actually implemented is quite limited. Nonetheless, there is extensive literature on this issue in the field of public policy research. This is not the forum to attempt a complete review of the field, but a basic theoretical background will assist in understanding the basis for the development of the study of "upward policy implementation" as is relevant here.

It is common to address policy implementation in the

relevant research discourse as a means to achieve goals and solve problems, against a background of citizen dissatisfaction and a low-functioning civil service.[16] Research addressing policy implementation that focuses on the practical aspect in which the implementation occurs is disseminated and affected.[17] We will concentrate on a definition of the term "policy implementation," which applies to the constant change occurring in women's labour law. Policy implementation in this context is presented as "an unending, constant process of change aimed at constant improvement." This is notwithstanding changes to policy, which may be one-time events (Goffen-Sarig 2004). Researchers define policy change as a result of an extreme, external event that overtakes the regulatory mechanisms of the unit examined (Howlett and Cashore 2009; Howlett 2009). Policy implementation may occur, among other reasons, due to either internal or external pressures.

The study of policy implementation may be divided into two schools of thought. The first argues that implementation takes place at the level of the decision-makers and then moves to the executive level—what is known therefore as a "downward" process. The second approach disagrees with

---

16　Glor 1997; Golden 1997; Merritt and Merritt 1985; Altshuler and Zegans 1997; Lynn 1997.

17　Deutsch 1985; Moore et al. 1997; Altshuler 1997; Merritt and Merritt, 1985.

this premise and argues "upward" control (Elmore 1982). In the critical literature which examines upward policy implementation, several approaches exist:

"Street-level bureaucracy" (SLB) is a theory known for its ties to Lipsky (Lipsky 1980), and it deals with the influence of civil service bureaucrats on the implementation of policies. Lipsky's central argument states that decisions taken by the higher ranks (up) do not affect the implementation of public policy in the same way that those taken by street-level bureaucrats (down) do, insofar as they set the de facto situation through methods for dealing with uncertainties and various work pressures. Further, policy conflicts are manifested not only through arguments among the various interest groups but also in the struggles between individual clerks and those citizens who "challenge" the rules. The clerks work subject to pressures and constraints and are influenced by stereotypes concerning their various clients, which affects their interaction with them. Furthermore, the power of civil servants increases insofar as they are able to influence "control over field evaluation," which is one of the policy tools available to the clerks. Control over field evaluation facilitates "upwards" promotion of policy, and creates facts which will determine change in a particular direction (Page 2006a). Bureaucratic rules—particularly when they are set by clerks with regulatory powers within a particular field—can affect the structure of a system under government control as well as the behaviour and views of the players. A further example is the "management by groping along" model, which occurs in cases where new policies are implemented through a rapid translation of ideas into action and the insertion of changes as required (Goffen-Sarig 2004). The implementation process is not systematic and is not based on planning ahead. It is, instead, dynamic and based on addressing occurrences through trial and error.

In contrasting the differences between an orderly, disciplined process of decision-making that occurs downwards and a process of policy implementation that is affected by actions taking place in the field and a subsequent change in institutional actions, it was found that the success of a public institution in solving complex problems was dependent on its ability to be attentive to voices in the field (Golden 1997).

There are those who argue that the political steadfastness of a regime also determines its level of fragmentation (Li 2002). In order to estimate the level of fragmentation in a state's actions, researchers in recent decades have examined whose political, institutional, or structural interests influence the gaps between formal laws and their de facto implementation. As we have demonstrated, this field of research is not delineated, and it crosses numerous areas of knowledge. A review of the research concerning "state fragmentation" is quite broad, and despite the range of subjects studied, there is agreement that the fragmentation stems from the degree of the government's stability, its nature, and its various interests as they guide the players and clerks (SLB) who directly affect the implementation of legislation.[18]

In these studies, we find discrepancies in interpreting the legislation, along with conflicting institutional interests. Later in the book, we will address these discrepancies and their consequences.

The Law in Action

In order to understand the state's actions in depth, it is important to first examine the stages in the process of the welfare mechanism and its implementation at a daily level. Beyond the wide-ranging heterogeneity in the manners of action by the various state players—in designing and implementing mechanisms to prevent dismissals—there exists a significant difference as well in the ability of citizens to make use of state mechanisms. This issue is central to the study of law in action. The ambiguity expressed in the state systems as well as the differential chances of welfare seekers in receiving appropriate legal representation both explain the failure of legislative interference in preventing forbidden discrimination.[19] According to this approach, differential access to legal aid explains the marginal

---

18   Glenn et al. 1988; Werum and Winders 2001; Panagiotis 2010.
19   Selznick 1961; Silbey 2003; Ewick and Silbey 1998; Silbey 2001; Kritzer and Silbey 2003; Bumiller 1988.

influence of wide-ranging, progressive legislation for the prevention of discrimination in the labour force on the actual minimisation of this discrimination. These studies highlight the importance of state systems that work for the enforcement of laws rather than just the fact of the existence of the laws.[20] In this context, Patricia Ewick and Suzanne Silbey (Ewick and Silbey 1998) claim that the discrepancy between the written law and its implementation is, in fact, a space in which a dynamic of interdependence is created among the policy-makers and its clients.

The Field of Labour Relations: Habitus, Social Capital, Cultural Capital, and Social Exclusion

The term "field" is taken from Bourdieu's fields theory (Bourdieu 1987), according to which each society is constructed of fields. The social field is a tapestry of objective relations between positions located in the field in a hierarchical manner, in keeping with the economic, cultural, and symbolic capital that they provide to institutions and players who possess them. Each field has unique resources for which the players and institutions compete. The rules are agreed upon by the players, contingent upon their participation in the game (Hacker 2008). Researchers of "law in action" argue that examining the law, or in the case of the study, the hearing that takes

---

20 Lofstrom and Gustafsson 1991; Ferber 1991; Bellace 1991; Mendel 2004.

place during an investigation, is an examination of "the arena of inherent practices, which facilitates the study of links among the legal and other fields" (Trubeck 1980). The unrecognised influence of the wide-ranging legislation for the prevention of discrimination in the labour force and its practical reduction is explained in the differential access to legal aid.[21] In this spirit, researchers concur that only studying events beyond the legal field can sharpen the understanding of social reality within the framework of the formal legal process (Hacker 2008; Trubeck 1980).

Thus, the book focuses on the field of labour relations, which functions as a sub-field of the field of the labour market. Bourdieu states that every field is composed of sub-fields—just as within the field of education one finds primary education, secondary education, and higher education—that share the principles of the super-field. Each of these, however, has its specific characteristics and unique goals. Each sub-field has its own logic and patterns of action and functions as a field on its own (Grenfell and James 1998). Within the field, there are sectorial relations among people, institutions, and bodies which establish and repeat social actions. The ability to obtain resources is influenced by the habitus of the players in the field. Bourdieu defined "habitus" as the tendencies and patterns of behaviour that organise the manners of action and

---

21 Bellace 1991; Ferber 1991; Lofstrom and Gustafsson 1991; Mendel 2004.

behaviour of the individual (Bourdieu and Passeron 1990). People behave in accordance with their understanding and desires and in keeping with their interests; these, however, are submerged within and designed according to social norms and arrangements. Therefore, he argues that the habitus and the field are mutually established, and the ability of the influencing bodyto enter a field and successfully complete for its prizes is influenced by the habitus of said players (Bourdieu 1986).

Within this context, it is helpful to recall the term "agency," which is defined as the ability to act and initiate. This approach is supported by some sociologists, who claim that agency is not absolute, and changes in resources and the acquisition of new capital are easier[22] than what is portrayed by Bourdieu—that man is trapped within a habitus that is influenced and negotiated by sociocultural capital. Bourdieu defines social and cultural capital as not solely economic or material. He explains that sociocultural capital divides those who are born in a financially fortunate position from those who become rich during the course of their lives. One may acquire cultural capital only if one is armed with the "appropriate" mental value mechanisms and with an understanding of these properties. Bourdieu distinguishes among internalised cultural capital, which is inherent in people and represents their knowledge, ability,

---

22 Eisenhardt 1989; Burt 2000; Blau 1964; Gambetta 2000; Giddens 1976.

values and cultural tastes, and institutionalised cultural capital, which documents "institutionalised" cultural ability, something that grants a fixed, conventional, legal value with a relation to power, such as academic degrees. In its institutionalised state, cultural capital overcomes limitations inherent in the characteristics of internalized cultural capital, such as its ties to the person who possesses it. The institutionalised form of capital has a relative autonomy from its owners and is even relative to internalised cultural capital.

Researchers of "law in action" who analyse the implementation of laws use terms of this sort when addressing the difficulty inherent in the need to appeal the courts in order to receive aid for the protection of equal opportunities for women, in cases in which the employer breaks the law. The high cost of using the courts, along with the physical and emotional effort required by the process, creates a further mechanism that leads to status inequality, given that the women who succeed in realising their rights are usually middle class and educated.[23] In Bourdieu's terms, it would appear that everyone has the same opportunity to receive the state's protection according to the law; however, in practice, the ability to contend is reliant upon the habitus required to cope with the fallout (permission for/protection from dismissal) that

---

23 Bumiller 1988; Selznick 1961; Silbey 2001, 2003; Ewick and
    Silbey 1998; Kritzer and Silbey 2003.

the field allows. This ability acts as an influencing body which reproduces inequality, the social superiority of specific groups, and the diminution and exclusion of others (Bourdieu 2005a). The expression "social exclusion" is defined as removal from the group, distancing, prevention, and prohibition. The term is often used in stratified, feminist, social discourse in order to note unequal social structure that excludes members of certain groups within it and is therefore directly and indirectly responsible for their location on the margins of society, for their sense of deprivation and for their inability to blend into a social system and participate in it. The exclusion may occur in the political, economic, social, or cultural fields. Those responsible are highly influential, powerful players, who determine the policy and execute it. Reasons for exclusion may include their desire to maintain the hegemony, a hierarchical view of reality, and the creation of identity and power that is based on oppression of the "other." This situation leads to the separation of the excluded person from support mechanisms that would permit them the ability to cope, such as tribunals and courts, or as in the case addressed in the current study, from the mechanism providing welfare protection from dismissal during pregnancy (Estivill 2003; Hill 2004).

Given that the state welfare system is meant to be universal and egalitarian for everyone—for our purposes, for all women—the book seeks to address the following: whether access to the system is, in fact, equal for women from different habitus; which of the women have "agency," in other words, the ability to mould their destiny and resist dismissal during pregnancy; and whether there are women who from the start are excluded from entering the field due to their position in the social structure. I further wish to examine the practice and logic of the action of players in the field, and how the web of powers in the field shapes the patterns of its actions.

Pregnancy, Work, and Discrimination

Although there is limited literature that focuses on dismissal during pregnancy, there are three central, identifiable, waves in this field of research. The first began in the early 1980s, with the increased entry of women into the labour market (Rodmell and Smart 1982). Studies focus on the attempt to provide a response to the physiological questions—whether employment during pregnancy is likely to physically harm the employee or the foetus, if pregnancy is an illness, and how productivity is liable to be affected (Saurel and Kaminski 1983). The second wave began in the 1990s and dealt primarily with legislative questions, with the institutionalisation of the blending of home and work, as well as with the degree to which organisations were supportive of women during pregnancy and after giving birth.[24] During the past decade

---

24 Desai and Waite 1991; Calloway 1995; Grover and Crooker 1995; Houston and Marks 2003; McRae 1991, 1993.

a third wave has emerged, dealing with empirical research based on various aspects of the discourse on gender rights and discrimination.[25] One unusual study touched upon the influence pregnancy and birth have on productivity, work, and family, and found that on the one hand mothers pay the price of harm to the family and on the other they themselves are affected vis-à-vis their promotional path and wage conditions, and they find themselves constantly concerned about dismissal (Del Bono et al. 2012).

Studies from the past decade found that pregnant women and postpartum mothers experienced poor treatment from their employer, which manifested as a lack of flexibility and withholding of benefits, and in some cases they suffered inappropriate behaviour from colleagues. Furthermore, it was shown that female management-level employees suffered from more blatant inequality than other groups of female employees, and they were more likely to suffer because of pregnancy.[26]

The European Union has begun to initiate empirical studies that examine diverse aspects of the issue (Adams

25 Gatrell 2011; Kohl et al. 2005; Tahmincioglu 2007; Benko and Weisberg 2007; Blair-Loy 2003; Edwards 1996; EOC 2005; Equalities Review 2007; Haynes 2010; James 2007; Padavic and Reskin 2002; Rouse and Sappleton 2009.
26 Buzzanell and Liu 2007; El-Sawad et al. 2004; Collinson 2000; Gatrell 2007a; Haynes 2006a, 2008a, b; Mäkelä 2005, 2009; Russell and Banks 2011b.

et al. 2005; James 2004). Participants in the surveys are mothers of small children who were requested to describe the treatment they received in the workplace once they had announced their pregnancies. Findings showed that most were not dismissed; however, their treatment by employers and colleagues included humiliation, contempt, comments on their physiological state, and even being prevented from participating in long-term projects that, due to the birth, they would not be able to complete (on-site). Further studies present the opinions of employers regarding pregnant employees or those with small children. The overall conclusion from all these studies is that many women are discriminated against in the workplace—from comments about their pregnancies to behaviour that leads them to want to resign, as well as clear dismissals. Those studies that examine the opinions of employers explain the background to the unequal treatment women are forced to suffer in the workplace. Thus, for example, 70% of those who participated in a survey of employers in Britain (Mori 2002) consider the employment of pregnant women or mothers of small children to be a financial burden, due to constant absences. Close to 40% of the employers stated that, due to their desire to care for their children, women do not return to work following their maternity leave. Reasons given by employers for the discrimination against women due to pregnancy focused mainly on the woman's responsibilities in the home as a central aspect of her life. This leads employers to feel that the workplace is seen by women as of secondary importance.

Given that this book focuses on the "Israeli case," it should be emphasised that the range of research in this specific area is small.[27] Studies performed in this field in Israel thus far have concentrated on it as part of a wider framework; they examine the matter in research literature and, for the most part, focus on presenting the formal data provided by the Ministry of Industry, Trade, and Labour.

Dismissals during Pregnancy in Welfare States

The relatively limited discourse concerning the role of the welfare state in protecting pregnant employees emerged in the early 2000s (Adams et al. 2005; James 2004). Researchers emphasise the need to expand existing knowledge about the employment of women during pregnancy and after giving birth, as well as the long-term repercussions of dismissal during pregnancy (James et al. 2005). Studies exist that concentrate on the link between the existence of a developed Family Policy and the rate of participation of women in the labour market.[28] Empirical research comparing two different welfare regimes with defamilisation policies (Evertson and Grunow 2012) found that among German employees there was more concern regarding dismissal and unemployment—as expressed in early return from maternity leave—than among female

---

27 Toshav-Eichner and Frenkel 2011; Almagor-Lotan 2012; Alfassi 2008; Toshav-Eichner 2003, 2006.

28 Haas 1992; Haas and Hwang 1999; James 2004; Duffield 2002.

employees in Sweden. The apprehension among female employees in Germany was based on the phenomenon of dismissal during pregnancy, which is described as widespread and cross-sectorial. Discriminatory behaviour by the employer during pregnancy is so common that in one article (Mäkelä 2005) it is described as "routine."

Researchers in the United States and in Europe claim that concern about the matter is common to both academics and to policy-makers (EOC 2005). They argue that dismissal and discrimination based on pregnancy are among the most unjust, damaging, and "hidden" phenomena in places of work, and despite broad-based legal protection for pregnant employees, it is insufficient (James 2004, 2009, 2011; Duffield 2002).

The attempt to estimate the extent of dismissals during pregnancy runs into difficulties, due both to the bureaucratic wall of hearings behind closed doors and to the lack of willingness by women to sue employers for illegal dismissal (Russell and Banks 2011a; Russell et al. 2008). In Britain, for example, findings show that tens of thousands of women sought to clarify their rights following the intention of employers to dismiss them during pregnancy (Dunstan 2001). Further research found that thousands of women experienced workplace discrimination due to pregnancy, however, only a small percentage of them faced their employer in court (James 2004, 2007, 2009). According to this research, between 1996 and 2003, in Britain on average only about a thousand complaints per year were submitted regarding discrimination due to pregnancy. In fact, later studies suggested that half of the pregnant employees in Britain experienced discrimination while pregnant, and de facto it was found that each year 30,000 women in Britain suffer a reduction in wages, are dismissed, or resign due to discriminatory behaviour toward them during pregnancy.

Causes of inequitable treatment by employers is difficult to pinpoint, however, researchers believe that the main grounds are difficulties in employer-employee communications, lack of awareness by the employer regarding the financial cost of unjust dismissals, and ignorance among mid-level management and in small companies of the laws protecting against dismissal during pregnancy (Young and Morrell 2005; Leighton and Evans 2004).

Another study, which addressed dismissals during pregnancy in Ireland, examined 54 cases brought before the labour courts and the Commission for Equality between 1998 and 2008. These bodies refer cases of discrimination due to pregnancy for voluntary, expedited mediation behind closed doors. Research presents the final outcomes of court decisions but critiques the inability to examine institutional behaviour in the hearings (Russell and Banks 2011a).

Comparative, independent studies carried out in Britain (Pagonis 2002; James 2004, 2009) on women whose dismissals came up in court in different years examined close to 600 women and found that female employees from all economic backgrounds and occupations experienced dismissal in pregnancy. Another study performed among 1,368 female employees found that in more than 20% of the cases, dismissal notices were given only days, and sometimes hours after the pregnancy was announced (James 2009). Other studies noted that young women with less seniority were more likely to be dismissed during pregnancy than older women with seniority in the workplace (James 2011). In more comprehensive studies, which examined female employees across Europe, findings showed that those who were on the margins of the labour market were more likely to experience gender discrimination. Young women, lesbians, the physically challenged, temporary workers, immigrant workers, women belonging to ethnic minorities, or those employed by a human resources agency all underwent more discrimination based on gender, resulting in illegal dismissals during pregnancy (EOC 2005; Leighton and Evans 2004).

It is rare for employers to report that a female employee has been dismissed due to gender discrimination or directly because of her pregnancy. In studies carried out among British employees who suffered from discrimination during pregnancy, findings demonstrated that during pregnancy only 13% undertook formal action such as bringing the case before the courts, submitting a complaint to the human rights division, turning to the union, or to an lawyer. Just 34% of the women went to the employer or to their direct manager, and the rest (53%) took no action at all or shared their experience with colleagues, friends, or family (Adams et al. 2005).

The attempt to estimate the financial cost of dismissing pregnant employees exists in a very limited sense in the research literature. There are estimates which focus on the employer and on the production costs of the business, as well as costs involved in training, and those of dismissals involving legal suits (Tahmincioglu 2007). Studies exist addressing the price paid by the female employee that argue that beyond the direct financial damage of loss of income, the dismissal delays the employee's promotion, her productivity, and the continuity of her career trajectory. This finding particularly characterises white, educated women in white-collar jobs. In the short and medium term (3–6 years), the productivity of the women dismissed dropped from 5 to 10%. In contrast with the expected assumption that productivity would be harmed by the period of unemployment, researchers discovered that it was the experience itself of dismissal during pregnancy which affected output. This finding was explained by the argument that after giving birth and dismissal, there was a drop in the rate of personal capital acquisition, which also manifested in the acquisition of financial capital (Del Bono et al. 2012; Rake 2000). In this context, researchers of the theory of personal capital claim that the temporary distance from the labour market reproduces gender wage gaps whose long-term consequences are notable at retirement when these women are forced to exist in financial straits (Duncan and Prus 1992; Mincer and Ofek 1982). According to the theory of personal capital, the lack of employment continuity interrupts the training path, which affects fertility and salary accordingly. Employees whose period of employment is halted are seen by employers as less committed to their job, and their ability to be considered for desired positions is damaged (Gronau 1998; Stafford and Sundström 1996).

In a survey written by the Israeli Knesset's Centre for Research, the budgetary significance of a change to the Women's Labour Law was examined. It emerged that an employer who seeks to dismiss an employee returning from maternity leave will be forced to continue employing her for 30 days in addition to the 45 days following her return from maternity leave. Data was examined from female civil servants aged 29–31, whose average salary in 2005 was about 7,400 NIS, and whose monthly wage reached 8,900 NIS. The estimated budgeted annual cost for the employer (the state)—determined by the assumption that each year close to 300 women in the civil service would be dismissed following their return to work following maternity leave— is 2,670,000 NIS for each employee (Alzwehr 2005).

The review of available advanced research—in particular regarding the phenomenon of dismissal during pregnancy, for all its causes and results—focuses on countries whose court system is responsible for examining these dismissals after they have happened. In these studies, the researchers address the lack of ability to closely study the conduct of the legal profession and its clients, leading to less research emphasis being placed upon the interventional mechanisms and their functioning. Differences between the European and Israeli legislation in this field are liable to influence the degree of involvement by women in dismissal proceedings, given that in Israel there is a process which bypasses the courts and examines the dismissal request before it occurs. The formal Israeli procedure does not require action on the women's part. Therefore, the current research has focused on responses to the following question: how in fact does the state's protection mechanism, whose purpose is to examine requests submitted by employers for dismissal during pregnancy, function? Despite the fact that, by law, in Israel women do not need to be active in order to protect their positions, is there not nevertheless some need for action? In addition, in cases where women took action, how did this affect the state's decision? Likewise, the behaviour of Israeli employers was examined with regard to the system, their attitude to the interventional law, how the clients' backgrounds influenced the interaction with the state as well as the long- and short-term repercussions of the state's decision vis-à-vis the employment profiles of the women dismissed.

The central goal of this book is therefore to examine the research claims based on theories of the state and law in action—according to which the discrepancies between legislation and its implementation are influenced both by an interpretation of the law according to varying organisational interests, and by the interaction between policy-makers and clients.

Chapter 2

Empirical Background, Research Subject—Evolution of the Law

Dismissal during pregnancy is one phenomenon in a broad group of law infringements in the field of gender equality in the labour market. In the Israeli research discourse, a fairly wide debate exists concerning legislation on the subject.[29] Research focuses on various aspects of the legislation, including comparisons of Israeli legislation with that of other countries, and the status of women in diverse occupations. A number of the studies take a critical look at legislation from the early days of the state and contradict

---

29 Fogel-Bijoy 1999; Raddai et al. 1995; Doron 1992, 1994; Frenkel, Hacker and Broida 2011; Rimlet 2010; Barak-Erez 2010; Yizreeli 2000; Sevirsky 1999.

the claim that the social policies regarding women were intended to lead to gender equality. They argue that the importance ascribed to dealing with demographic problems, such as infant and maternal mortality among those who lived in temporary refugee camps, was what stood behind the state's willingness to institute a generous programme for working mothers.[30]

The existing research argues the importance of laws designed to prevent gender-based discrimination, to reduce inequality among men and women, and to avoid harming the status of women during pregnancy and birth (Davidov 2009; Mundlak 2009). Even so, the study emphasises that "policy implementation" in fact requires separate investigation (Doron 1994; Eisenstadt and Gal 2001). As previously stated, this book will attempt to fill — insofar as is possible — some of this void, and to examine the discrepancy between the law and its implementation, as well as the logic and the motivation behind the mechanism entrusted with executing the Women's Labour Law to prevent dismissals during pregnancy. Therefore, the core of this background chapter is the history of the law and the creation of an interventional welfare system, the influencing structures involved, and their roles. The chapter's central argument revolves around the idea that the changes in the state's view of dismissals during pregnancy, which have

---

30 Berkovic 2003; Fogel-Bijoy 2003; Ajzenstadt and Gal 2001; Doron 1994; Mundlak 2009; Ajzenstadt and Gal 2001.

occurred over the years, are anchored in the socioeconomic paradigmatic shift as well as in the power of the unions. Therefore first we will attempt to characterise the Israeli labour market.

Inequality in the Israeli Labour Market

The research discourse surrounding working women in Israel tends to deal with discrepancies regarding the participation of men and women in the labour market, the causes of these divergences, and the entrance and exit patterns of women in general and mothers in particular within the labour market.[31]

Over the years, the rate of participation of mothers of one or two children in the workplace has increased, from around 30% at the end of the 1960s to close to 80% at the start of the 21st century. The Israeli labour market is characterised by growing numbers of working mothers (Nadiv 2005).

Among researchers focusing on gender inequality in the Israeli labour market, an argument emerges according to which women who work part-time do not always choose to do so. Findings showed that women worked an average of close to 36 hours weekly, as opposed to men,

---

31 Fogel-Bijoy 2003; Berkovic 2001; Doron 1994; Ajzenstadt and Gal 2001; Bernstein 1992; Mandel and Shalev 2009.

who work 46 hours weekly (Fogel-Bijoy 2003; Shteyer 2006). In this context, an explanation may be found for the discrepancies between men and women regarding working hours. The answer may focus on two aspects: the needs of employers and the demands of the labour market on one hand (Albrecht, Björklund and Vorman 2003), and employees' characteristics and supply within the labour market on the other. The inherent discrimination is manifested in the few opportunities available for the promotion of women, in the predetermined concentration into "women's professions" — care or service professions — and in occupations with flexible work hours.[32]

In studies which followed women who broke the glass ceiling on their paths to management positions, findings indicated that in the past decade there has been a significant rise in the number of women in managerial posts. Despite this, statistics show that the number is still smaller than that of men. The magnifying glass used to examine women is more uncompromising, and women feel a strong need to prove themselves. The central reason for the growing amount of women in more senior positions is that there has been a significant increase in the number of women with graduate degrees in financial and technical fields — an increase which at times outstrips the number of men

---

32 Petersen and Meyersson 1999; Bygren and Kumlin 2005; Kramer and Lambert 2001.

holding comparable degrees (Wirth 2002). Nonetheless, in 2014, there were still notable discrepancies between women and men in Israel.

Despite the fact that women are more highly educated than men, they earn less. A report by the Israeli Central Bureau of Statistics, published in 2014, found that in 2012 the average education of female employees stood at 14.2 years, in contrast with only 13.8 years in the case of male employees. In the same year, 65% of the candidates for matriculation exams were young women, 52% of those who fulfilled the criteria for university entrance and 57% of university students were women. However, notwithstanding the higher rate of education, in 2012 the discrepancy in the average wage for men and women was 33.9%; the median salary for women that year was 5,489 NIS, their average salary was 7,244 NIS, and the average hourly rate earned by women was 46.8 NIS. In comparison, the median salary for men was 7,744 NIS, the average salary was 10,953 NIS, and the average hourly rate was 55.1 NIS. Subsequently, women formed 67.3% of all employees in the bottom 10% and only 23.3% of the highest 10%. Furthermore, over a third of female employees in the economy earned up to the minimum monthly wage of 4,300 NIS in 2012, in contrast with 17% of men. Research carried out by the National Insurance Institute's Research and Planning Division in 2014 discovered a discrepancy of 13%-17% in the hourly wages of men and women in similar jobs and with similar abilities in 2010-2011.

One of the main reasons for the salary inconsistencies among women and men is the different number of working hours. In 2013, among female salaried employees, 66.7% worked full-time, compared to 86.6% of men. Meanwhile, 14.8% of the women who reported working part-time noted that they would have preferred to work full-time but were unable to find a full-time position. The same was true for only 11.9% of the men. Among employed women, 91.3% were employees, as opposed to 83.8% of the men. A further notable aspect of the employment of women that influences their salary is employment through human resources agencies. In 2013, it was found that women made up 50% of the total employed through human resources agencies while the percentage they formed of employees in general stood at only 48.7%. The rate of women at the managerial peak of the larger companies remained mostly unchanged in recent years though the presence of women in management stood at 25%, and in directorial positions, two women were found for every 10 men. The number of female managers reached 30.8%. In division according to occupation, 95.6 thousand women worked in high tech, amounting to 36.6% of all employees in the field.

A report published by the Israeli Bureau of Statistics on the occasion of World Women's Day in 2014 showed that in 2012, 41% of women were employed in the same six "traditionally women's" occupations that are characterised by low salaries, as in the past two decades: nursing, teaching, secretarial work, sales, administration, and cleaning (March 2014). The study also pointed out that the discrepancies are diminishing with time. In 1990, the average salary for men was 43% higher than for women. By 2012, as stated, this had been reduced to only 34% (IBS, March 2014). Many women choose to leave the employment cycle at various points in their lives and thus return to it in a position inferior to men's. In 2013, 58.2% of working-age women (15–61) were employed, in contrast with 69.4% of working-age men (15–66). The difference is especially striking in the Arab sector, where according to IBS data from 2011, only 22% of the women were a part of the labour market, and 40% of female university graduates were unemployed.

The decrease in salary discrepancies among men and women is in keeping with the drop in the birth rate in recent years. Notwithstanding this, in relation to western countries, Israel is still considered a country with a high birth rate and a notable gap between men's and women's wages. IBS statistics indicate that 166,130 women gave birth in 2012. The average number of children a woman in Israel may expect to give birth to in her lifetime is 3.05, a statistic that is higher than the OECD average of 1.7 children. Accordingly, one could say that the likelihood that women employed in Israel will experience dismissal during pregnancy is higher than those of women in OECD countries. In this context, we will examine the structure of the Israeli labour market.

Double Duality

In order to understand the history of the labour market in Israel, it is crucial to address the term "duality" in two, complementary contexts. The first relates to the duality in the Israeli labour market, and the second to the dual attitude toward women employed in Israel.

The "dual labour market" theory was developed in the 1970s and 1980s, in the United States. This research discourse focused principally on issues of poverty and discrimination. Findings showed that there was a secondary sector within the labour market, characterised by a high rate of unemployment, high turnover, and unstable, temporary jobs. This sector is noted for positions which do not require professionalism, and it offers flexibility in the market, supplying employees who can be hired and fired as required at low cost. This stratum of employees have "non-standard employment arrangements," which do not offer benefits such as pension plans, full employees' rights, opportunities for promotion, a modicum of employment security, or mutual commitment between the employer and the employee.[33]

From 1967 and through the mid-1990s, we can divide the Israeli labour market into two main sectors, both large but differing in their power and influence. The first, main sector is the bureaucratic sector, which identified with the

---

33   Gordon 1972; Saint-Paul 1996; Grinberg 1991.

Labour Union labour federation and the Labour party, both of which were headed by veteran Ashkenazim (Jews of European background). This sector included employees who enjoyed membership of a professional union, steady employment, work stability, benefits, and the protection of the state against any threat to their job. The second was the private sector, where some employees belonged to the first group while others—including Palestinians and Jews of Middle Eastern origin (Mizrachim), who were at the bottom of the social hierarchy—suffered employment instability and insufficient working conditions.

The two sectors maintained contact but were separate status-wise. The first sector, known also as the "main sector," was satisfied with the existence of the secondary sector, given that it performed cheap service work. The main sector could compete within its own sub-fields while relying on the services or products acquired from the secondary sector.[34] The main distinction between the two was in the conditions of employment.

In the first decades following the founding of the state, women held a marginal role in the labour market. They were cheap labourers, untrained, of limited authority, and, for the most part, worked a shorter working day. They were only needed in marginal areas of the labour market, where men did not offer their services. Nonetheless,

34 Rosenhek 1999; Farjun 1983.

there were many women in the main labour sector—
employed primarily in government institutions and in
the public service as teachers, kindergarten teachers, and
nurses—who were protected by employee organisations.
Women were perceived as "secondary earners," within
an institutionalised paternalistic ideology based on
maintaining social order and not damaging the place of
women as carers (Bernstein 1992). During this period,
women were also split into two main ethnic groups: those
of Middle Eastern origin, who were less educated, had
more children, and were less present in the labour market
(33.9%), and Ashkenazi women, whose involvement in
the labour force was higher (49%).[35] This gap narrowed
significantly after the 1980s (Kraus 2002).

From 1994 on, as the Labour Union's power waned,
the status-based duality of the labour market was blurred.
Despite this, beginning in the 2000s, the division in the
labour force again has shown signs of duality. On the
one hand, there are employees with permanence and
seniority in their organisations, particularly in the public
sector—those who are protected and have social benefits
and generous pensions. On the other hand, there is a
secondary sector, characterised by employment through
an external source, or through human resources, who
employ primarily women (60%) (Binyamin 2003; Nadiv

---

35 Data on the second generation in the labour market from the
    mid-1970s.

2005). This employment pattern emerged following the rise of neoliberalism in the country, which legitimises the right of market powers to compete with one another within the capitalist economic viewpoint. This economic environment encourages flexible and temporary employment arrangements in hiring, according to the needs of the organisation—preventing the accumulation of seniority and social benefits (Toshav-Eichner 2009; Davidov 2009). There are, nonetheless, researchers who claim that the labour market, including labour law, has undergone significant changes since the beginning of the current century. A decrease in the power of professional unions, along with the fact that employers have taken advantage of this, requires the state to develop special protection for employees. The changes have occurred primarily in two areas: intervention in the agenda of employers and regulation regarding discriminatory dismissals, such as during pregnancy (Mundlak 2008; 2009).

The expedited development of globalisation and a rise in neoliberal economic pressures accelerated changes in the world of employment and led to increasing processes of legalisation. The courts reconsidered the repercussions arising from intervention in the employers' agendas, and thus the employment stability decreased among some employees, forcing the courts to expedite a response to the changing reality (Mundlak 2009; Davidov 2009).

There are researchers who claim that the status of Israeli women in the labour force of the 2000s has remained just as it was in the first decades after the founding of the state, and that women are still secondary earners, "In Israel, there is love for motherhood but not for mothers" (Fogel-Bijoy 2003). Within this context, it can be said that the duality in the labour market affected the dual attitude toward the employment of women, who are seen as fulfilling the traditional role of contributing to the demographic balance while maintaining a secondary status in the labour force (even if de facto they belong to the main sector). This attitude has existed since the early days of the state, despite the accelerated entry of women into the labour market, a significant upswing in their education in relation to men, and their integration in high-tech[36] and management professions. Therefore, the duality is manifested in the ambivalent relationship that on the one hand encourages women, while on the other maintains their inferior position in the labour market.

Against this background of a dual labour market alongside the dual concept of the contribution of mothers to society and to their work, the paternalistic view of women as secondary earners, increasing business competition, and a neoliberal market, women in Israel are likely to find themselves increasingly threatened by dismissal during pregnancy. This is due to the complex reality that leads

---

36 Fogel-Bijoy 2003; Berkovic 2001; Bernstein 1992.

some employers to believe that the diminished contribution of pregnant and post-natal workers may damage the financial strength of their organisation.

The Law and Its Implementation

The Family Policy aimed at protecting the positions of pregnant women in Israel is located in Section 9a of the Women's Labour Law of 1954, "An employer shall not dismiss an employee who is pregnant and has not yet left on her maternity leave without the permission of the Minister for Labour and Welfare, and the Minister shall not permit dismissal if it is, in his opinion, linked to the pregnancy, and this in the case that the employee has worked for the employer or in the same place of work for a minimum of six months."

The Women's Labour Law was passed in 1954 as part of the first wave of legislation aimed at granting women special rights. In the first decades of the state, the purpose of the law was to protect the place of women in the labour market and then later to prevent gender inequality. The law protects women during the periods that their physiological state is not the same as that of other employees.[37] Within the framework of the Women's Labour Law, which was amended and updated over the years, the State of Israel

---

37 Fogel-Bijoy 1999; Radday et al 1995; Doron 1994; Yizreeli 2000; Sevirsky 1999.

granted a series of employment protections to female employees—from fertility treatments through pregnancy and maternity leave to breastfeeding and parenting. The goal of these protections is to make it easier for the female employee to integrate her family life with her participation in the labour force. It is worth mentioning that protection of pregnant women within the Women's Labour Law was not a result of any aspiration to increase equal opportunities but rather stemmed from the desire to ensure high birth rates without relinquishing the fruitfulness of the contribution of mothers to the labour force in Israel (Berkovitz 2001).

In most western countries, beginning in the 1960s, laws were passed safeguarding the jobs of pregnant women. As in most countries, this protection occurred through parental rights, or MJR (Maternity Job Rights),[38] which also include security during pregnancy, though the difference lies in the type of protection. This policy, which characterises many western countries, is translated in the case of Israel into a specific bureaucratic system whose task is to examine dismissals during pregnancy, and to permit or prevent them. Israeli law is considered relatively advanced in comparison with other countries, in that it places the responsibility of preventing dismissals squarely upon the shoulders of the state and removes the responsibility to act from the pregnant women, who

---

38 MJR is the term for parental protection laws and for rights granted to parents during pregnancy and following birth.

sometimes do not possess sufficient resources to do so. Nevertheless, the state itself offers the legal possibility of dismissal during pregnancy, not as a result of pregnancy. Furthermore, the regulation requires a pregnant woman to deal with interventionary investigative mechanisms, and she is also forced to remain in a workplace where she is not wanted (if her dismissal was not authorised). These characteristics are unique in comparison with most welfare states, which protect female employees through legislation alone, with no interventional regulations. According to the law in these countries, an employee dismissed illegally during pregnancy is permitted to appeal to the courts in order to deal with her employer. There are countries such as Germany, Luxembourg, Greece, and Portugal who carry out pre-trial inquiry proceedings against the employer concerning the legality of the dismissal during pregnancy, however, none of these steps offer a hearing for the employee and the employer with the purpose of allowing the employee to return to her place of work (Gornik and Meyers 2003; Gornick 1999).

The system employed by the Ministry of Industry, Trade, and Labour (currently the Ministry of the Economy), whose purpose is to protect the jobs of pregnant women, is a regulation that deals with both enforcement and suggestions for amendment of legislation. At the same time, the state mechanism is intended to aid all employers and citizens in an equal manner, with no fee required to be paid and no need to appeal the courts or hire a lawyer. The first action by the system was taken by the Ministry of Labour and Welfare, in the area of preventing dismissal of pregnant women in 1951, with the legislation of the Law for Organised Supervision of Labour. This law was enforced by the Section for the Supervision of Labour, and its powers of enforcement included, among others, ensuring security at work as well as the Women's Labour Law. Within this framework, the section initiated the regulation for inquiries into requests for permission to dismiss during pregnancy (Toshav-Eichner 2003, 2006). According to the law, the minister of labour is meant to decide, though in fact the decision is made by an appointee. In the mid-1980s, a committee was formed to examine each case individually. Within this context, the employer and the employee are questioned separately, and after a few months, the decision is made whether to allow the employee's dismissal or to refuse it and return her to her position. The committee is headed by an inspector, and the investigative material is given to the deciding appointee. As of 2009, the authority to make the decision was also granted to the appointee's agents.

The implementation of the law was manifested in the interventionary regulation whose purpose was to examine the request to dismiss a pregnant employee, and to decide whether the request was linked to the pregnancy or whether there were other influencing factors to consider such as performance at work, closing the business, or cutbacks in personnel. From the day the legislation was passed until 2003, the regulatory system belonged to the

Ministry of Labour and Welfare, and with the structural changes involved in merging the Labour Ministry with the Ministry of Industry and Trade, the regulation was rezoned to the authority of the new ministry—the Ministry of Industry, Trade, and Labour. Up until 2006, all requests from employers to seek permission to dismiss an employee, as well as complaints from employees dismissed without authorisation during pregnancy were shifted to the appointee for Women's Labour Law in the labour law supervisory section at the ministry. In 2006, the section's responsibilities for planning and enforcement were split up. Requests by employers were dealt with by the planning sector, while employers who had broken the law and were considered criminals—and whom had had complaints concerning illegal dismissals brought against them—were investigated through the enforcement section, who were given legal authority including the ability to punish with up to a year's imprisonment and a fine of over 130,000 NIS for employers who broke the Women's Labour Law. Within the framework of the law, the employer is requested to attend to a hearing with a warning, while an appointment is made with the female employee to give her testimony at a location close to her home.

A further law, enacted in June 2012, is the Law for the Increase of Enforcement of Labour Law,[39] which sets

---

39 Website for the Ministry of Industry, Trade, and Labour www.moital.gov.il.

an immediate fine of 35,000 NIS or higher for those who infringe upon the Women's Labour Law. Within this framework, this infringement is considered a managerial crime wherein the employer is not sent to trial for it. The law was drafted by the legislature, the Ministry of Industry, Trade, and Labour, and representatives of the employers in the market, in an attempt to increase deterrence for employers seeking dismissals during pregnancy. Following the 2013 elections, Naftali Bennett, head of the Jewish Home party was appointed Minister of Industry, Trade, and Labour after his party won 12 seats in the Knesset. The name of the ministry was again changed, this time to the Ministry of the Economy and Religions, and its authority was further expanded from that given to the Ministry of Industry, Trade, and Labour under Ehud Olmert only 10 years previously. Most of the research focused on the Ministry of Industry, Trade, and Labour, and therefore, that is the title used in this study.

From 2008, close to 1,500 requests for dismissals were submitted to the resolution section. In times of economic crisis, such as the one that occurred in 2008, an increase was noted in the number of requests—there were close to 2,300 dismissal requests made, of which about half were authorised.

In 2011, 348 applications were made to the enforcement section concerning dismissals of pregnant women. Out of these, 278 were made for the purpose of receiving information on the subject, 70 were classified as complaints in which there was suspicion of infringement upon the Women's Labour Law, investigations were opened for 35 of them, and a further 35 complaints await consideration. During the same year, 16 indictments were made on charges of breaking the Women's Labour Law.

If a connection between the request for dismissal and pregnancy is found, including for women who are protected for social reasons, the employees are meant to return to work at the organisation which sought to dismiss them. Some of them actually return and some of them reach a financial arrangement with the employer. The employees whose dismissals were authorised are expelled from the labour market and are able to realise their legal rights to unemployment payment, on condition that they fulfil the qualifying period criteria according to the National Insurance Institute.

Accordingly, other laws relevant to our subject are the Unemployment Laws[40] of 1996, according to which a woman's right to unemployment payments require a probationary period of age, seniority, and job range. The probationary period changes constantly and an employee with insufficient seniority will receive a percentage of the unemployment benefits based on the percentage she has accrued up until her dismissal. This period is decided

---

40 National Insurance Institute website September 13, 2013.

by measurements determined by the National Insurance Institute, and it is identical for all unemployed people of 18 years of age or over, who have paid their social security payments to the National Insurance Institute, as required by the law.

Apart from the Women's Labour Law, there are laws and regulations whose purpose is to protect the dismissed employees. For example, the Equal Opportunities Law of 1988, Section 2a, forbids the employer from discriminating against employees or those seeking employment based on their gender, sexual tendencies, marital status, pregnancy, fertility treatments (including IVF treatments), their being parents, their age, religion, nationality, country of origin, opinions, political inclination, or reserves service. Furthermore, Section 2 (1a) states that an employer shall not discriminate against contract workers employed by them, or job candidates sent to them with regard to break times or conditions in the workplace. This law complements the Women's Labour Law, which does not protect the female employee in the first half-year of her employment and addresses relations between the employer and the employee during the period of employment and up until the decision is given. There are female employees who worry that the employer will harass them, and thus the Equal Opportunity Law's Section 6a instructs that "an employer shall not harm an employee based on a complaint, or suit by the employee related to this law, or because they aided another employee with regard to a complaint or suit based on this law." Women who are discriminated against based on pregnancy are permitted to sue the employer in the Labour Court according to Section 9 (2a) while the responsibility of proof is on the employer if the employee has proven that nothing in their behaviour or actions gave cause for dismissal. According to Section 10a, the Labour Court has unique powers to consider civil suits based on the infringement of this law, and may according to Section 1a, award damages as they see fit, even if no monetary damage has been caused.

Nonetheless, the enforcement process shows a much more complex picture, which can be explained using Bourdieu's theory of fields. As stated above, according to the theory of a society composed of a series of fields, the field is a social space in which numerous candidates, struggle for the fruits offered to them in the field, participate. Not every candidate will attain the reward, and the ability to do so is what determines the ranking. The fields are not static. They have a dynamic history based on struggles, with the constant struggle forming the engine of the field. In keeping with this, it is possible to explain the implementation of Section 9a of the Women's Labour Law according to the sub-fields which it is composed of. The struggle occurs between the woman and the employer, with each of these parties fighting to attain their material goal. At the core is the system where the operators have the power to decide to whom to grant the prizes available in the field. There are further players in the field who affect the actions of the system.

Intra-state Assistant

Presentation of the assistance framework composed of further influencing factors from within the state is crucial to understanding the field of research, given that this is what directs its actions and determines its limits.

In the background, one finds labour courts, who have it within their power to appeal the decisions by the system protecting against dismissals and thus diminish the system's power of control. The labour court is not the central influencing factor; however, its presence influences the decisions reached, given that the state's clients are allowed to petition them in order to attack the decision made by the policy mechanism, and thus the labour market affects the actions of the system that is located in the sub-field of labour relations. By the same token, courts are inclined to rule in favour of the employer while in the absence of a lawsuit, more often they rule in favour of the employee.

In the Israeli legal structure, the labour courts are a unique system that emerged from the Labour Courts' Law of 1969. The system is an independent arena of judgment, specialising in ruling within the legal fields of labour and social security (national insurance, national health care, and others). There are five local labour courts, whose jurisdictions run parallel to those of the district courts as well as the national courts, which in turn provide a field for the appeal of rulings by district courts. In specific matters, the national courts are the first instance. In the field of labour law, the National Labour Court is the highest division, and no appeal of its rulings exists. Nonetheless, one may appeal to the Supreme Court to appeal the ruling from a national court, on condition that there was a clear and obvious mistake in the ruling, or there is a public matter requiring an in-depth hearing.

The panel of judges in a labour court is unique to these courts. Apart from a professional judge (a lawyer), there are also judges who have been recommended for their positions by workers' and employers' organisations. Employee and employer representatives are not required to have completed higher education though they must have extensive experience in the labour field. In most civil proceedings, the district court is composed of three justices—three professional judges, an employees' representative, and an employers' representative. Women or employers who are interested in challenging the decision by the representative responsible for the Women's Labour Law are permitted to appeal to the labour courts, who are able to make a different decision than the state clerk. In court, the employee is able to sue for monetary damages, and the system is meant to instruct the employer as to whether they are to return the employee to her position or not. In this sense, both parties provide their clients with material resources, whether by monetary recompense or through the defence of the female employee's job. As regards the employer, the outcome of the proceedings before either party may save the material expense of paying a salary to an unwanted employee.

It is worth mentioning that the interventionary mechanism, which acts as a quasi-legal body, is strengthened by claims of the limited powers of courts to create social change. Researchers and officers of the law (Gabizon 2009; Rosenberg 2008) have claimed that the courts function under pressure and cannot achieve significant results. Rulings by the courts cannot lead to real social change, and at best they reflect a cumulative result stemming from other political, economic, and social processes. Three limitations prevent the court from creating social transformation. First, the accepted belief is that it is the task of the law to maintain the status quo and not innovate. Second, the legal system functions within a political-legislative system, utterly lacking in independence. The third limitation lies in the fact that the court has no jurisdiction to establish or consolidate comprehensive policy regarding social reform, and certainly does not have the ability to implement or finance it. There are those (Rosenberg 2008) who argue that the court can compensate for its shortcomings, such as with the creation of quasi-legal enforcement and implementation mechanisms, through investigating requests for dismissals during pregnancy.

Women who have been employed for more than six months have the right, as stated, to the protection of the system run by the Ministry of Industry, Trade, and Labour, however, there are women who are unable to use the system. There may be several reasons for this. First, their, or the employer's lack of familiarity with the law, and second, their unwillingness to confront the employer who may threaten them that turning to the ministry will, as far as they are concerned, lead to hostile relations. In these cases, the employer gives the employee a letter of dismissal, in order for the latter to receive unemployment benefits, without turning to the mechanisms within the ministry. These women go straight to the National Insurance Institute, and through the Employment Services, they receive unemployment payments based on their rights, with no intervening process and with certain leniencies.[41] As for the significance of going straight to the National Insurance Institute, without having made use of the laws with the ministry's regulatory function—this can be examined from several angles. On the economic front, the employee's petition to realise their right to unemployment payments during pregnancy negatively influences their ability to collect it following maternity leave, if they receive the state's protection and are dismissed following the period of protection. From the criminal/legal point of view, the attempt to make use of the system whose purpose is to dispense monetary resources alone is tantamount to giving a discount to the criminal employer and to ignoring the law which demands the submission of a request for permission in all cases of dismissal of a pregnant employee. From an organisational/employment standpoint, the avoidance of

---

41 It is worth noting that there are women who are not eligible for benefits and are therefore forced—sometimes against their will—to seek help from an interventionary process.

seeking help from the state is liable to cause the woman to exit the labour cycle for an extended period, given that many employers are loathe to employ the mother of a baby. From a personal/gender stance, within the framework of the interaction with the investigating inspector, the female employee may be able to make the case that she was dismissed for discriminatory reasons, which may enable her to maintain her status within the labour market.

Notwithstanding this, for women who are unable by law to turn to the state welfare system, there is a further influencing factor present in the field, the Commissioner for Equal Opportunity:

> There are women who were dismissed before they had completed six months of employment, and are unprotected by Section 9a of the Women's Labour Law. They are allowed to turn to the Commissioner for Equal Opportunity at the Ministry of Industry, Trade, and Labour. According to data received yearly, since the creation of the Commission in 2008, close to one-third of applications have been based on dismissals during pregnancy.
>
> (Interview with an investigator at the Commission, September 2012)

Before we continue with the discussion it is important to consider the population that has such limited social capital that the law offers it no protection and no true method of estimating the phenomenon from a research point of view.

In the State of Israel, at the bottom of the employment market ladder are labour immigrants. Neither the Women's Labour Law nor any of the laws we have mentioned thus far are relevant to them, and they are nonetheless employed in difficult physical labour even when pregnant. Apart from the immediate loss of income, the significance of dismissal for a woman in Israel with no status is that National Insurance will not cover their hospitalisation and delivery costs. These may reach 15,000 NIS for a birth without complications, becoming more expensive in the case of a complicated delivery requiring interventions. Furthermore, the woman is prevented from receiving the payment upon birth, which would help her support herself during her maternity leave. These facts take on the status of "expulsion protection," given that the authorities avoid granting these women or any asylum-seekers refugee status.[42] In Bourdieu's terms, these women are lacking in power and the ability to grasp the resources which the field could grant them, and therefore, they find themselves at the bottom of the field's hierarchy (Regev 2011).

Non-state Aid Factors: Women's Organisations, The Work Union, and Private Lawyers

Along with the formal, administrative process of state protection, there are other influencing bodies in the field, whose task is to empower clients in their struggle. One of

---

42 Workers' Hotline site 16.9.13.

these influencing bodies is women's organisations, which
have functioned as a significant player in the field as far
back as the mid-1980s when the phenomenon of dismissal
of pregnant women grew. Their presence is manifested
through representation in court of those dismissed during
pregnancy, through the consistent participation in the
Committee for the Advancement of Women in the Knesset
and in the response to requests by women through an
open telephone line on matters of work discrimination.
It is important to mention that the Na'amat organisation
also claims participation in public struggles to prevent
injury to women and for the advancement of their status in
society, in the economy, in places of decision-making, and
in the family, through organised information campaigns,
demonstrations, manifestos, and advertisements. Among
the information campaigns to recognise women's rights
and to create equal rights and opportunities for women,
some of the noteworthy ones that Na'amat has launched
in recent years include the campaign to encourage hiring
women and adapting the workplace for parents, the fight
for free education for young children, and the fight against
financial decrees. Furthermore, Na'amat was a partner
in drafting the legislation such as the Equal Rights for
Women Law, the Law for Equal Opportunity at Work, the
Law of Equal Pay for Male and Female Employees, and
the Women's Labour Law. In April 2007, Na'amat initiated
a treaty for the adaptation of workplaces for parents. The
binding and declarative treaty was signed by the Chairman

of the Labour Union, Ofer Eini, the Head of the Bureau for Coordination of Financial Organisations Shraga Brosh, the Chairman of the Labour Committee of the Bureau for Coordination of Financial Organisations Yair Rotlevi, and the Chairperson of Na'amat Lawyer Talya Livni. Within the framework of the treaty, the parties declared that they were interested in working toward the adaptation of the employment world in an egalitarian manner, which would facilitate work-life balance and family side by side, through respect for the rights of male and female employees and of the workplace. There are numerous declarations on the Na'amat website concerning the organisation's work, a historical review of feminism, partial information on gender inequality, and suggestions for dealing with it at the level of the state's budget. However, the subject of dismissals during pregnancy is barely mentioned.

Only a small percentage of women who request it receive legal representation by the organisations however, even those who do not receive representation are given instruction by the organisations regarding how to manage the state system. The legal advisors in these organisations report an increasing rise in complaints based on dismissals during pregnancy (protocol No. 160, February 14, 2005), and claim that "most women are completely unaware that they can complain or sue" (Lawyer Odelyah Levi-Ettinger, representative of the Lawyers' Association, participating in the enforcement project by the Women's Lobby). This claim concerning lack of awareness among women is held up in light of the 200 phone requests which reached the Women's Lobby following a daytime TV programme on the subject of dismissals in pregnancy, in which Lawyer Ziona Kenig, then-director of the Lobby's Legal Division, was interviewed (January 2005, Odetta Channel 2). In a similar context, a report by the Women's Lobby reveals that in 2005 nearly 100 women called the organisation's open line while in the year following over 280 women called; close to one-quarter of all the calls by women to the Lobby that year (Tamir and Nagar 2007).

Furthermore, meetings between the formal administrative channels of the state-provided protection given by the Ministry of Industry, Trade, and Labour and further protective channels provided by women's organisations often involve differences of opinion. For example, representatives of the women's organisations request a more liberal approach to examining cases that were closed in the ministry and claim that obstacles are placed in their path when they wish to examine the files (Lawyer Odelyah Levi-Ettinger, protocol No. 160, February 14, 2005). As stated, from the mid-1980s women's organisations began to assist in cases of dismissal during pregnancy — first against the court system and, once the hearings were institutionalised, also giving the women instructions before they faced the regulators. At first, assistance was given to women who approached the organisations — more educated women — however, at the end of the 1990s, the women's organisations began to offering legal defence for women with limited social and financial capital who lack the appropriate habitus to approach the government institutions in general and the legislation in particular. This is provided due to the encouragement of women by bodies such as the Women's Lobby, who seek to protect the rights of female wage labourers, as another act in the enforcement and entrenching of these rights in legislation. The approach is based on the idea that wage labour is a primary influencing factor in reducing dependence and inequality, and that remaining in the labour cycle means a chance to remain involved in society and to continue to develop social skills (Tamir and Nagar 2007).

Another influencing body is the Labour Union, who in recent years have made attempts to rehabilitate their status among workers and among employees in general. On the homepage of their website, it says:

> Hundreds of thousands of employees and pensioners who are assisted by the Labour Union, along with another hundred thousand who benefit from its activities, remain the last bastion of the value of equality and solidarity in Israel. In recent years, there has been a reduction in these values within Israeli society. We come across unending attempts to damage the status of employees and pensioners and to reduce the power of organised labour. The Labour Union's new path is manifested in the strengthening of the professional union, is free of foreign interests, and promotes labouring

without fear or bias, only for the good of the workers and pensioners. (Official website of the Worker's Labour Union, October 22, 2010)

The Labour Union claims that its information centre acts as a source of information for any woman dismissed during pregnancy, by providing an initial response to questions as well as guidance. They emphasise that the organisation's members receive legal representation if required. The following chapters of the book will examine the extent to which the assistance provided to these women by the Labour Union is effective for them.

Private lawyers must be added to our list of women's organisations and the Labour Union, in that both employers and female employees with financial capital and appropriate habitus seek help from them. The position of private lawyers has become more and more central in the past decade, in which legalisation has gained strength. In hiring the services of an lawyer for a fee, the employer and female employee receive personal instruction regarding how to behave in front of the committee chaired by the supervisor from the Ministry of Industry, Trade, and Labour. A lawyer may exchange correspondence with the organisation seeking dismissal as well as with the ministry, if necessary. Further, if the female employee or the employer is dissatisfied with the administrative process at the ministry or with its results, they may, as stated, appeal to the labour courts—a decision which is mostly carried out by private lawyers. In order to comprehend the value of employing a lawyer, we carried out an Internet search under the keywords "lawyer for dismissal during pregnancy." It turned out there are more than 80,000 pages. The following are some of the statements by these lawyers:

> I generally suggest a consultation prior to taking any steps in order to avoid making mistakes along the way. For example, a female employee who explains to her employer why he has broken the law by firing her during pregnancy will then have a difficult time finding evidence to support her claims. If the employer has submitted a request to the Ministry of Industry, Trade, and Labour for the dismissal of the employee, we can consult in order to examine which complaints may influence the Ministry's decision and keep the employee in her workplace, which are relevant, and what to emphasise during the hearing. At times, the employee thinks she has no case, and in consultation it turns out she has fairly good claims to argue before the Ministry. (Website of Lawyer Maya Tzechor, July 6, 2012)

> In these processes, it is a good idea for you to be represented both in drafting the written response and in preparing for questioning! … It is very important to know that in matters of the rights of pregnant women, there is a huge advantage to anyone using the services of a professional office familiar with the processes at the Ministry of Industry, Trade, and Labour, as well as with the specific processes in court. Not every labour lawyer

is familiar with the rights of pregnant women! Our office handles important suits by pregnant women against large companies in the market, government offices, and huge chains—we have experience in these sorts of cases. Do not hesitate to contact us and ensure your rights are respected! (Website of Lawyer Sharon Taitz, July 6, 2012)

After explaining all of her rights and the limitations faced by the employer to Michal, the colour returned to her cheeks, and she requested that we represent her in the case and work to stop the aggravating behaviour by her employer, who was trying to wear her down and get her to quit. We therefore sent a formal letter to the employer telling him to cease the bad behaviour and act according to the law. Michal's employer was shocked to receive our letter, and in conversations with our office, it was made clear to him what rights precisely Michal was entitled to, as well as emphasising that if these rights were not fully enforced, we would have no choice but to appeal to the courts. This resolved the situation. ... That same week we reached a compromise with the employer, according to which Michal would no longer be required to be present at work, and would continue to receive her salary, in exchange for agreeing not to sue her employer. Thus, Michal got her joie de vivre back, as she received an unexpected vacation, without losing her salary. (Website of Lawyer Chen Shtein, July 6, 2012).

It's notable that the lawyer in the first quotation emphasises that by employing her services, the female employee will avoid making mistakes, given that the assistance given includes point by point instruction on how to influence the decision by the Ministry. The second quote also demonstrates the pressure upon the employee to hire a lawyer who can assist in a significant way against the Ministry of Industry, Trade, and Labour, against the employer, and if needed against the courts. This pressure is especially clear in the final quote, which appears under the heading "Rights of the Pregnant Employee." Here, the lawyer specifies the letters sent to the employer who was harassing a pregnant employee and relates, as if by chance, the possibility of reaching a monetary settlement through the lawyer, without returning to work.

Using a lawyer promotes the success of those with the "necessary" financial capital and habitus. According to the theory, those with capital will succeed in maintaining their status and even improve it—as the lawyer stated, "[The employee] received an unexpected vacation without losing her salary." Accordingly, the status of women with lower status and lacking the appropriate capital will also be maintained.

It is worth noting that the many efforts made by the legislature to maintain the status of women in the labour market may be harmed by this sort of assistance, which ends with monetary compromise. We see here the alternative path carved by lawyers who bypass the process in the Ministry of Industry, Trade, and Labour, which is intended to be equal for all women.

This book will examine how socioeconomic capital and appropriate habitus assist with regard to access to the welfare system and with the ability to benefit from field resources. Furthermore, it will present the ways in which power relations are designed in the field and how influencing bodies such as lawyers, the Labour Union, and women's organisations aid in improving the power status of their clients.

In other words, this study will look at the complex actions of the state, in all its multiple, differing aspects— action that is largely dependent upon the specific combination of circumstances in which the woman facing dismissal finds herself: the defences available to her, her level of familiarity with the law, and the resources available to her that allow or prevent her use of the law to protect her interests and her position of employment.

Chapter 3

Research Method

This book is unique in that it simultaneously examines various aspects of the protection of pregnant women facing dismissal and the presentation of the state welfare system, both from the point of view of the influencing bodies and from that of the state's clients. The research addresses the active practices, the logic which guides these actions, and the subjective experience of the state's clerks and clients. The attempt to estimate the level of efficacy of any specific Family Policy in terms of its contribution to the equal integration of women and mothers in the labour market encounters serious, complex methodological problems. Comparative studies usually examine the statistical connection between the formal Family Policy employed by the state and the rate of employment of women in general and mothers in particular[43] in that country, the gender-based salary discrepancies in the same country (Mandel 2004), and promotion opportunities for women and the sectors in which they are employed. Nevertheless, these studies have difficulty isolating the direct influence of formal policy patterns enacted in the state from the influence of other cultural and socioeconomic variables that characterise it. Furthermore, the studies examining the formal policy and its consequences have a difficult time handling the discrepancies, which are known in the literature, between the formal policy pattern and its de facto implementation (Toshav-Eichner and Frenkel 2011).

I would like to jump ahead and state that the research that forms the basis of this book was carried out from 2000 to 2012 within the framework of the Research, Planning and Economy Administration at the Ministry of Industry, Trade, and Labour, where I was employed as an external researcher. There I discovered that researchers in academia and various functionaries, including representatives from women's organisations in Israel (Protocol 160, Knesset 2005), reported great difficulties in obtaining data from the Ministry of Industry, Trade, and Labour regarding the action of the Committee of Inquiries into Requests for Dismissal during Pregnancy. Furthermore, among the decision makers at the ministry, including the director of the legal division, there was great interest in

---

43 Mandel 2009; Mandel and Shalev 2009; Stier et al. 2001.

characterisation of the populations availing themselves of the policy regulation.

In this book, I am seeking to advance, even if in a limited manner, the understanding of the influence of Israeli policies for the defence of pregnant women faced with dismissal upon those women in need of this protection.[44] The book is based on a triangulation of information from five varying, complementary databases, which examine the actions of the state mechanism: (a) a survey conducted among 101 women who required the system's protection due to attempts to dismiss them during pregnancy, or immediately following their return to work after maternity leave; (b) data from Employment Services concerning pregnant women who sought unemployment payments during pregnancy—in order to present these statistics in context, we also analysed the results of the human resources survey carried out by the Central Statistics Bureau, in the decade between 1998 and 2008, that provides data about all workers in the labour market; (c) observations during hearings within the state framework; (d) interviews with the inspectors responsible for operating the welfare system, and interviews with employers who sought to dismiss women during pregnancy as well as with female employees whose employers sought to dismiss them;

---

44 As we will emphasise later, we are unable to estimate the level of influence of state organs concerning integration of women into the labour force.

(e) analysis of the state archival documents, newspaper articles, and Knesset protocols from the committees who addressed the subject of dismissals during pregnancy.

Each of the databases reveals a piece of the puzzle that is the firing of pregnant women in Israel and the attempt to prevent these dismissals. Through triangulation of data, we will attempt to offer a rich and profound vision of the issue in the Israeli context (Berg 1998). Data triangulation is based on the triangulation and verification of information from diverse sources during the process of investigation of a specific phenomenon. This method does not involve a simple combination of information sources but rather an attempt to find the correlations between them in order to strengthen the validity of the findings (Jick 1979). Triangulating the data and the information gathered from all the various sources permits a comprehensive, in-depth understanding of the system itself, as well as the consequent social significance of how it operates. Before we continue with a description of the study's findings, below is a description of the data collection and analysis in each of the study's four focuses.

A Survey among Women Who Needed the Dismissal Protection System

The survey was carried out through telephone interviews, and it was intended to characterise the research population and examine the range of assistance of the women and their employers who turned to the regulation for aid. The survey included 101 women who had requests submitted to the Ministry of Industry, Trade, and Labour for their dismissal during pregnancy in 2002. Of these, 51 were women who were protected from dismissal by the state and their cases were heard within the interventionary welfare system while 50 did not receive this protection.[45] In order to measure the repercussions of the dismissals, the survey was carried out four years after dismissal, in 2006–2007 (October 2006 to August 2007).[46]

---

45 In order to fulfil the quota of one hundred complete surveys, it was decided ahead of time in defining the sampling to interview more women in each layer. In the final examination, 51 surveys were found which had been completed among the group of women who received state protection. It should be noted that the comparison between the groups was carried out based on percentages, which cancels the discrepancy between 50 and 51.

46 The survey was performed by the Teldor Company, and the sampling under the supervision of Prof. Zvi Gilula of the Department of Statistics at the Hebrew University, as part of the workshop which provides statistical consulting services for researchers. The questionnaire was developed with other researchers from the Bureau of Planning, Research, and Economics at the Ministry of Industry, Trade, and Labour, and was headed by the Chief of Research Benny Fefferman and researchers from the bureau with a background in economics, sociology, statistics and gender.

The survey questionnaire was constructed according to the employment status of the female employee and, in fact, included three questionnaires with an average of 120 questions. Questionnaire A was aimed at women who were employed at the time of the survey, four years following the request for dismissal, at the organisation from which the request had been submitted. Questionnaire B was directed at women who were employed on the day of the interview at another organisation, and Questionnaire C was intended for women who were not working on the day of the interview.

In all three questionnaires, the interviewees were asked to note their seniority prior to the dismissal date, their occupation, position on the salary scale, work days, work hours, method of employment (through a human resources bureau, salaried employee, self-employed), salary, subordinates—all at the organisation that requested their dismissal, and when appropriate, in comparison with the organisation in which they were later employed. There were also questions about the level of satisfaction from their work on the day of the interview in comparison with the employment from which the request was made to dismiss them. Interviewees were later requested to respond to questions concerning the dismissal process and whether they acted to prevent the dismissal, and regarding the attitude of the inspector, and of the organisation and its members during the dismissal period. In the final section of the questionnaire they were asked to answer questions concerning the organisation and its size, as well as the sociodemographic cross-section to which they belong, including age, years in the country, marital status, education, income, and similar questions about their partners.

The participants were, as mentioned, women whose employer requested their dismissal in 2002, four years prior to the survey, so the data received was relevant not only to the dismissal process and hearing but also to the success of the women in reintegrating into the labour market, and the manner in which they interpreted the influence of the dismissal process or its prevention upon their financial and emotional welfare. The survey contained many statistics about the women's socioeconomic and demographic characteristics, their actions vis-à-vis the dismissal process and subsequent hearing, as well as their employment and family status at the time of the research.

The profile of the population of women participating in the survey was characterised by an average age of 33.7; most of them were born in Israel; 4% were single mothers, and the rest married. Close to a third of them belonged to the public sector and the rest to the private sector. The average number of years of the participants' education was slightly more than 14, and the salary level was between 5,000 and 7,000 NIS. One percent of the participants belonged to the Arab sector, close to one-third (31%) were secular Jews and the rest were traditional (45%), religious (16%), or ultra-Orthodox Jews (8%).

In order to carry out the survey, the sample population of those dismissed during pregnancy was divided into strata, according to statistics from the National Statistics Bureau. In order to do this, the women were selected from various regions in the country, and an optimal sampling of the strata was performed, with each region considered a stratum. Stratum sampling is carried out through dividing the population into sub-populations. Each sub-population is known as a stratum, and a sampling is taken from each. The sampling is randomly selected, and a sampling selected from one sub-population is not dependent upon that taken from another population. It is worth noting that no proportional sampling was carried out because the likelihood of pregnancy is not equal in all cities. In Jerusalem, for example, there are more pregnancies due to the relatively large religious population. There was, therefore, a need to know the variable being researched splits depending on differences in the population.

Survey Variables and Estimates

In order to examine whether an employee with many personal benefits will improve her chances *to receive assistance from the state*, a number of multivariable logistical regressions were carried out to consider the statistical link between the independent variables which affected the two dependent variables—"receiving assistance from the state" (refusal by the employer) and "return to the labour market" .The first dependent variable is labelled refusal (by the employer) because of the state's refusal to approve the request for dismissal. The independent variables selected are variables of direct personal benefits, such as education, seniority, and action to prevent dismissals, which may be influenced by the ability of the female employee to act (agency). This action may be composed, among other things, of an application to women's organisations. In addition, indirect variables were selected, such as using the services of an lawyer (lawyer), which is generally reserved for women with financial capital. Another independent variable is the organisation's size (org size), because as was mentioned earlier, women who belong to a smaller organisation, as well as younger women, have a greater chance of being dismissed during pregnancy. Accordingly, an age variable (age) was chosen as well. In addition, the choice of the working partner (partner) variable was made based on the assumption that women whose partners were not working would have more limited financial capital.

The second dependent variable we will examine is the return to the labour market, in order to study the long-term influence of women's action vis-à-vis state institutions. The assumption is that women who received protection, even if they were dismissed when the protective umbrella failed to safeguard their status, will quickly return to the labour market due to the empowerment they experienced. Encoding the variable was in keeping with the type of questionnaire filled in by the employee, based on her employment status on the day of the interview, four years after the request for dismissal. Of all the women participating in the survey, 15% were employed on the day of the interview at the organisation which had sought to dismiss them (questionnaire A). The remaining women worked elsewhere (45%, questionnaire B) or had remained outside of the labour market (40%, questionnaire C). The independent variables examined in relation to this variable were: protected, academic, working partner, age, seniority—as detailed in the chart below, which presents all of the variables, the encoding, and research function for the choice of variable.

Chart: type of variable, method of measurement and research function

Type of Variable	Variable	Method of Measure-ment	Research Function
Dependent Variables:	Was the woman protected? *(refusal by the employer)*	Yes (1) No (2)	The variable was chosen in order to examine who the women are who receive aid from the state.
	Return to the labour market following dismissal (labour market)	Yes (B) No (C)	The variable was chosen in order to examine how the opportunity to return to the labour market following dismissal is affected by the women's personal capital characteristics. The variable characterising the type of questionnaire completed by the female employee in accordance with her employment situation on the day of the interview, four years after the request for dismissal. This variable applies only to questionnaires B and C. Of all women participating in the survey, 15% were working on the day of the interview by the organisation seeking to dismiss them (questionnaire A) and were thus not included in the regression. The remaining women were employed in other places (45%, questionnaire B) or were left outside of the labour market (40%, questionnaire C).

	Working partner (partner)	Yes (1) No (2)	An employee who bears responsibility for supporting her family in cases where her partner is unemployed will tend to make more of an effort than others to return to the labour force, irrespective of the amount of protection she received from the state in her struggle to prevent dismissal during pregnancy.
	Was the woman protected? (refusal by the employer)	Yes (1) No (2)	The variable was chosen in order to examine how the state's protection affected chances to remain within the labour market.
	Organisation size (org. size)	Consistent variable	The variable was chosen in order to examine the idea that the characteristics of the organisation seeking dismissal, such as its size, are likely to influence the state's agreement to approve dismissal.
	Lawyer's assistance (lawyer)	Yes (1) No (2)	The variable was chosen because it was likely to affect the women›s chance of receiving protection from the state.
	Assistance from women's groups	Yes (1) No (2)	The variable was chosen because the knowledge provided by the women's organisations could improve the woman's chances of receiving the state's protection.

Independent Variables:	Actively attempted to prevent dismissal (action)	Yes (1) No (2)	Chosen in order to estimate the link between active actions and the prevention of dismissal, among other characteristics of the woman. The variable estimates the woman's response to the question to what degree she was active in preventing her dismissal herself. This question does not necessarily reflect the level of activity that in fact occurred, but rather the sense of subjective control which the woman has regarding her fate or her desire for this sort of control.
Personal Capital Variables: **State Protection:**	University education (education)	Yes (1) No (2)	This variable was chosen because according to the theories, education is meant to influence one's chances of receiving aid from the state, as well as improving the chance of returning to the labour market.
Organisational Variables:	(age)	Consistent variable	The age variable was chosen in order to examine how age affects one's chances to return to the labour market.
Assistance Variables: Influencing bodies beyond the Formal Field	Seniority at dismissing organisation (seniority)	Consistent variable	The variable was chosen based on the assumption that a woman with significant seniority in an organisation would be better protected by the state, with the understanding that the pregnancy was the cause of her dismissal. If this were not so, she could have been dismissed during the years she worked prior to becoming pregnant.

Survey data >>2006

Results will be discussed in detail, in their relevant context, in upcoming chapters. Data processing was carried out using SPSS, and further findings were analysed using theoretical statistics.

The survey findings aid the understanding of the state's actions as well as the implementation of the Women's Labour Law from the point of view of the state's clients, as well as in comprehending the repercussions of the state's actions on the future employment of women who faced state regulations. An analysis of the characteristics of clients of the system for the protection of women's jobs would provide an answer to the question of who makes use of this system and in what way, if the woman employed further state or non-governmental influencing bodies, how she acted to prevent her dismissal, and how this aided in protecting her status in the labour market, both short and long-term. It is worth noting that the findings rely on facts reported and are not first-hand, which could damage their credibility. Nonetheless, one may assume that objective facts, such as organisation size, employer's sector and gender, are highly reliable. Furthermore, these findings act as a further dimension for observation. It is true that they are different cases; however, understanding the state's action and daily interaction could be clarified by a blend of all methods of observations, the interviews, and the survey.

Employment Services Report

In the first chapter I argued that within the theoretical discourse surrounding the issue of interface between society and the law, it is common to claim that the ability to seek assistance from the law is not to be taken for granted. A close examination of the state's actions and of the law thus required an initial study as well of the characteristics of those women who succeeded in receiving assistance from the state regulation, vis-à-vis all women who were dismissed during pregnancy. For this purpose, we employed a special database that was constructed in cooperation with the Employment Services and with IBM, facilitating the characterisation of the population of women dismissed during their pregnancies, from a sociodemographic stance. The data collected locates women aged 18–50 who were permitted to appear at the employment bureau monthly—a favour granted by Employment Services only to pregnant women. It was thus simple to isolate them statistically. It should be emphasised that the data file included only women who were dismissed during pregnancy and who were entitled to unemployment payments—a right given to those who fulfilled the qualification criteria. The qualification period changes from time to time and requires unemployment insurance payments for a minimum of 360 days, out of 540 days prior to the unemployment (people who receive a daily rather than a monthly, salary are required to pay only 300 days). The 360 days need not be consecutive (Employment Services data, 2012).

Combining the two databases (from the Ministry of Industry, Trade, and Labour and from Employment Services) makes it possible to locate a significant amount of the women who were eligible for protection under the law for the prevention of dismissal of pregnant women and yet were dismissed during their pregnancies. Although it cannot be assumed that all of the women dismissed in fact submitted requests for unemployment benefits, the manner in which childbirth allowances are calculated encourages women in Israel to request unemployment allowance if they are dismissed during pregnancy. The discrepancies between the number of women who chose to use their unemployment benefits from the National Insurance Institute and those who received assistance within the framework of the Ministry of Industry, Trade, and Labour permits an effective estimate of the range of coverage by the interventionary system. The Employment Services' database helps to characterise those dismissed during pregnancy as a whole, in terms of education, area of residence, age, years lived in Israel, marital status, and sector. These characteristics were compared with those of women whose cases were heard through the ministry's committees in order to receive an initial estimate about the differences in ability to access the state system. Because one must assume that most women whose dismissal was authorised are included in those eligible for social security allowances from the National Insurance Institute, the discrepancy between the two groups points to the characteristics of those who did not seek state assistance in preventing their dismissal or, on the contrary, those for whom the state did not initiate assistance in this matter.

Connecting the various data files from Employment Services according to identification numbers is performed in-house at Employment Services and the files are delivered only after identifying details (name and identification number) are deleted, so that there is no danger of violating the privacy of those receiving benefits. This database was analysed using comparative theoretical statistics tools with regard to women who acted in relation to the regulation. It should be noted that this file will include all those women eligible for unemployment allowance, and it does not include those women who reached a financial settlement with the employer and did not turn to Employment Services. Notwithstanding, the application for unemployment benefits is more likely to better—if still not optimally—estimate the general phenomenon of dismissal during pregnancy.

This study demonstrates the amount of assistance available through the welfare system of the Ministry of Industry, Trade, and Labour, as opposed to that available through other state sources. Within, there are signs of discrepancies between the law and its implementation, and non-uniform patterns of operation among different state institutions. For the first time, data belonging to the state is presented here concerning the number of women actively dismissed during their pregnancies, despite this step not being taken in coordination with the process set out in the legislation. Some of these women did not act in conjunction with the Ministry as dictated by the law. As stated, the data was processed by the Employment Services (with the help of IBM), and it relates to all of the women who benefited from an unemployment allowance during their pregnancies between 1998 and 2007. Data from Employment Services includes sociodemographic characteristics of these women, however, the data lacks information concerning the procedures carried out (or not) in order to prevent the dismissals, or regarding agreements reached between the women and their employers. Just as with submissions to the system for the prevention of dismissals at the Ministry of Industry, Trade, and Labour, applications to Employment Services require the female employee (or those around her) to actively participate, which depends on her knowledge of her rights and of the application process. In both the case of the ministry and of Employment Services, the weakest employees in the labour market—temporary and unofficial workers, with no salary receipts or employment consecutiveness— will not receive assistance. Despite the fact that the data received from Employment Services greatly improve our ability to estimate the size of the phenomenon of dismissal of pregnant women, there remains a need to suggest a comprehensive, absolute number of the rate of women dismissed during their pregnancies.

Analysis of Central Bureau of Statistics Human Resources Survey Data

The systematic collection of data was possible due to the unique nature of Israeli policy on the dismissal of pregnant and post-natal women, and its concentration within a limited number of state institutions. Joining two databases (from Employment Services and from the Ministry for Industry, Trade and Labour) made it possible to locate a large number of the women who employed state institutions in their attempts to prevent dismissal or in an attempt to benefit from assistance within the social network available through Employment Services. Notwithstanding, at the time the data was collected, it emerged that the size of the overall phenomenon is equal to the requests to the ministry. It was further noted that the number of the women dismissed was much greater than the sum of requests to the ministry and, in fact, even larger than the amount of requests to the National Insurance Institute. We, therefore, sought an estimate of the number of women actually dismissed during their pregnancies and to that end examined data from human resources surveys, which give an estimate of the phenomenon in its broadest sense, more clearly reflecting the actual situation. Among others, we based our work on the analysis of a human resources survey from 2002, in order to compare it with the year in which our survey was carried out.

Human resources surveys are carried out by the

Central Bureau of Statistics four times yearly. It is true that the surveys do not contain the direct question, "Were you dismissed while pregnant?" however, cross-referencing the question, "Were you dismissed during the past year?" with the data on new mothers and women who gave birth during the past year acts as an estimate for the range of the phenomenon.[47] The survey includes questions on education, number of children, age, and so forth, as well as questions on the woman's employment status on the day of the survey and in the months and years prior.

Given that the number of new mothers was compared with the number of women overall in the labour market, the estimate supplies the measure of the law as a deterrent. There are, however, limitations to the database; the data is an estimate alone. Furthermore, it is likely that the phenomenon is wider than that which appears in the survey, given that there are women who may hide their dismissal during pregnancy for various reasons.

The qualitative data collected through the survey and the analysis of the other databases created and analysed for the purposes of the current research teach us a lot about the women who use the various state mechanisms, and those who are unable to access assistance from the system. Nonetheless, an examination of the law in action demands more than merely consideration of the results

47 Prof. Hanna Stier employed a similar method in her research (Stier 1998).

and instead requires an in-depth look at the legal process, both from the point of view of the interaction between the various influencing bodies and from the standpoint of the experience, whether empowering or weakening, as felt by those going through the process i.e. those citizens whose fate is decided thereby. An understanding of the process, and not only in terms of its outcome but also of the interaction that occurs within it and the subjective experience of each participant, sheds further light on the process and on the deviations that may emerge within it.

Observations

Researchers of law in action often complain about the fact that they are prevented from observing legal proceedings, in particular when they do not take place in open court before the public but rather in bureaucratic tribunals, such as those of the state's system for the prevention of dismissal during pregnancy. The opportunity afforded me within the framework of this study, to observe hearings and speak with the participants immediately following the hearings, led to a deeper understanding of the process and its significance.

As a rule, observation facilitates focus on the person, in action, within the explanation they themselves give the actions and on the process more than on its outcome (Dushnik and Tzabar Ben Yehoshua 2001; Tzabar Ben Yehoshua 1990). The task of the researcher is to find meaning or to explain a phenomenon in terms that people use to describe them (Denzin and Lincoln 2000; Adler and Adler 1994).

By means of the observations, the issues at the core of the theory of law in action were examined, including the claim by researchers in the field that despite the fact that the legal arena, along with other policy arenas, is meant to be characterised by rationale, there remains an influence by external influencing bodies and varying values, irregularities, and dealing with different people day to day. The claim is that there are people who may lead legal influencing bodies to irrational behaviour, and there still remains influence from prejudices (Ewick and Silbey 1998; Kritzer and Silbey 2003).

The methodological framework for examining the research claims is based on observations carried out during the study of women and employers in the committees examining requests for dismissal. The procedure of the hearings was studied, through emphasis on the attitude of the supervisor toward the employers and the women, on resources available to them during the investigation, and on the verbal and non-verbal interaction which occurred during the hearings.

Through the observations, the interaction was also noted between the state and its clients, through tracking the manner in which the written legislation was translated into de facto action during the hearing. The observations took place during 2005–2010, and close to a hundred hearings were observed and were nearly evenly divided among investigations of employers and of women. Each hearing lasted close to 30 minutes on average, except for hearings by the Ministry of Education, which were shorter.

Due to the limitations of the observation method, which focuses on the procedure more than on its outcome (Dushnik and Tzabar Ben Yehoshua 2001; Tzabar Ben Yehoshua 1990), it was impossible to know beforehand which hearings would result in dismissals and when the case would reach an agreement. Nonetheless, through observation, it was possible to analyse the behaviour of the system when the possibility of compromise is offered at a hearing.

The observation method was chosen for the inherent advantages for this research subject, such as the observable behaviour, and non-verbal information such as body language, moments of silence, and tears. The observation had its drawbacks nonetheless. First, due to the researcher being the tool through which data was collected, a problem with validity emerged, there was a limited ability to focus, a restricted field of vision, which unknowingly led to filtering of the viewed material, therefore, the researcher's conclusions stemmed from subjective interpretation, and it was often difficult to compare observations. Second, the location of the researcher in the field was liable to influence those present at the hearings (Weber 1949; Denzin 1994).

Thanks to the observations, we followed the stages of the welfare mechanism in an attempt to comprehend the rationale behind the state's action in deciding whether to maintain the woman's status within the labour market or to permit the organisation to dismiss her. Despite the fact that the intention behind the observation was to create distance between the viewer and the interaction, one could assume of course that the very fact of the researcher's participation in the hearing influenced the supervisor and the clients, and therefore, a better definition of this type of observation would be "participatory observation." Participatory observation is quite similar to observation, however, the researcher here becomes, if only marginally, part of the group being studied. Thus, the viewer can describe the experience in the first person and still form part of the interaction described. However, the description in a participatory observation must fulfil the criteria of an observation: to neither add nor remove from the description of what occurs but only describe things as they are, including the interaction between the researcher, the environment, and members of the group among themselves. For the sake of anonymity participants in the observations that will be presented in this book, their names and organisational identities have been hidden.

Interviews

Within the context of the study, periodical conversations and interviews were held and took place between 2005 and

2014, with relevant political influencing bodies: supervisory appointees for the Women's Labour Law, employers, lawyers in the legal bureau, employees, decision-makers in government ministries who are directly linked to the process of dismissal during pregnancy, clerks at the National Insurance Institute, at the Ministry of Education, and at Employment Services, and lawyers at the labour courts. The interviews lasted on average between half an hour and two hours, and the conversations following hearings took about 10 minutes.

During the period of the study, three supervisory appointees were replaced. Five interviews were held with the first, as well as continuing interviews once she was appointed director in chief, responsible for Women's Labour Law and the Licensing and Resolution Bureau. Her replacement participated in two interviews, and the third appointee, who was an inspector with the Bureau, participated in 15 interviews.

Half of the interviews with the inspectors, the appointees, and National Insurance Institute representatives took about two hours, and so did interviews with half of the employers, including the interview with the representative from the Ministry of Education. Interviews with representatives of the Legal Bureau took close to an hour, and the same occurred with representatives of Employment Services. Telephone conversations took place with 20 pregnant women who had initiated steps, with each conversation lasting an average of a half an hour, as well as one conversation with the partner of a woman who had been dismissed. The interview was semi-structured in that apart from the questions, time was also left to address other items related to the interviewees. The interviewees' responses were written out by hand in copybooks, and later, during processing, the relevant quotations from the interviews were inserted.

Altogether, 127 interviews were carried out; 54 of them were held with policy-makers and designers, as well as with state clients, including women and employers. Most of the interviews with the inspectors were held following observations of the hearings. The observations were used to examine whether and to what degree the inspectors carried out the inquiry based on their experience, their instructions, opinions, and their relationships with the background from which the women and employers came. Furthermore, note was taken whether their opinion of granting permission for dismissal of pregnant employees was influenced by their own background and from their worldviews.

During the initial stage of the field work—the "initial contact stage"—open, in-depth interviews were held with relevant influencing bodies The advantage of these interviews lies in the fact that they permit a context within which both the interviewer and the interviewee are separated from everyday reality (Mishler 1986). This is an opportunity for the interviewee to consider their behaviour, to create central categories, and comprehend the significance of the phenomenon being studied.[48] Apart from data collection, the purpose of these interviews was to examine the matter from the point of view of the interviewees, through an attempt to consider the "state in action" theory and understand insofar as possible the sometimes different views and interests that create a lack of order, discrepancies, and lack of cooperation that may damage the state's attempt to protect citizens from inequality. Furthermore, within the "state in action" context, the interviews' contribution is significant in understanding the logic behind patterns of action and comprehending the consequences that may lead to a discrepancy between the language of the law and its de facto implementation.

In-depth interviews are as one of the more common and obvious ways in which it is possible to understand the interviewee. At the core of the in-depth interview is the desire to understand the interviewee's experience and the significance they give it. The interview allows access to cultural contexts of various behaviours and provides an opportunity to comprehend their significance. Drafting the questions and analysing the responses is therefore not a simple task. Precision is crucial in order to estimate the nature of the experience, and it is important to always

---

48 The interview was conducted over two hours in February 2008.

recall that there may be a lack of clarity due to incorrect interpretation of the interviewee's comments. In addition, the limits of the method lie in the level of preparedness of responses given by the subjects and in their level of desire to describe reality as they would have it, or as, in their opinion, they are expected to respond, due to social forethought (Williams and Anderson 1994).

Archive Documents, Protocols from Knesset Committees, and Newspaper Clippings

In order to comprehend the history of the state's actions regarding the Women's Labour Law, to study which changes occurred in the law, and the logic of the state's actions through the years, including the socioeconomic background influence, we employed original documents that characterise the period. Findings also included relevant archival material, from the day on which the law was tabled at the Labour Committee in 1952 and up to 1979 (legal immunity applies to documents issued over the past 30 years, and I was, therefore, unable to access them). The archive documents detail the debates concerning amendments to the Law, the internal policy communications with employers and female employees, and debates in the Knesset. Furthermore, the documents included correspondence that pointed to the process of regulation between the inspectors from the Ministry of Labour and the employers who sought to dismiss pregnant women, responses from the Labour Union, and letters to women informing them of the results of the process.

Archival documents were analysed using the constructivist paradigm (Tzabar Ben Yehoshua 2001), which does not seek causal explanations for phenomena but rather tries to find processes of significance creation in the world of those being studied. In order to characterise influencing bodies' experience of reality and their world of experience within the field in the most reflective manner, lacking potential informants,[49] the documents were analysed critically and reflexively.

Despite this, in the case of some of the aforementioned documents, a partial picture emerged, such as in the case of correspondence between the ministries, which in the end did not document the letter received by the employee. Further, given that the archive contains multi-system knowledge, it is likely that there are relevant documents under a different keyword than Women's Labour Law. In addition, because the Archive Law does not permit exposure of documents written as of the late 1970s, a need has been created to expand the knowledge of the partial picture, which may be seen when examining the archival material. The complementary methodology is located in a separate database, in newspaper clippings. To this end, 200 news items were scanned from the daily newspaper *Yedioth*

---

49 The estimated age of clerks hired in the 1960s in the Ministry of Labour is close to one hundred.

Ahronoth, which was published even prior to the founding of the State of Israel, using the keywords "dismissals during pregnancy" and "women's labour laws."

Another source of completing the picture lay in protocols from Knesset committees. Within the context of hearings at the Committee for the Advancement of the Status of Women, the Women's Labour Law was debated an average of twice a year beginning in 2000. This was the arena in which employers, state, and legislative representatives encountered one another, with this field acting as a stage in which the logic of the state's formal actions was exposed. Relevant quotations from the committees were entered contextually into the study.

Study Limitations

It should be noted again that we are dealing with a distinct case of the state's treatment of women whose employer has requested to dismiss them during pregnancy, and thus the conclusions, claims, and assumptions focus on this population. Due to ethical issues of interviewee confidentiality, names of participants observed or interviewed during the research were not mentioned. The survey is limited to a population of women dismissed in 2002, and it is likely that socioeconomic events influenced the attempt to dismiss them. We attempted to neutralise this limitation by performing the survey four years later, in order to examine the employment continuity of the women from the date of their dismissal. Findings emerging from the study first characterise women whose cases were heard through the state system, and the results fit this population alone. The study was limited in its ability to characterise women dismissed during pregnancy as a whole, given that some of them did not undergo any institutional experience. Regarding the limitations of using archival materials, there was previous mention of the partial picture that these may give at times, for example when one document is lacking in order to see the complete picture.

Given that the study dealt primarily with the state's activities and understanding the discrepancies between the written law and its de facto implementation, it should be emphasised that during the years of data collection, analysis, and writing, there were occasionally changes in process and in the law. Thus, the research does not end at the point in time when the writing was completed. In other words, this has been a continuing process in which we tried to address the entire field, however, due to its complexity it is likely that some of the changes were not included in this book.

Using so many varied databases implies several advantages and disadvantages. On the one hand, the wealth of sources allowed us to paint a broad, diverse picture of the various characteristics of the process as they are presented by the numerous influencing bodies participating: the many state institutions, the employers, and the women. On the other hand, some of the databases are only partial, and it is difficult to examine them in-depth and present the multiple links between them. Therefore, the study's findings presented later in this book reflect only part of the rich diversity of facts that exist.

Chapter 4

Development of Policy for the Protection of Pregnant Employees: Between Paternalism, Feminism, and Neoliberalism

In order to comprehend the creation of gaps between the written law and its de facto implementation, it is crucial to understand the developmental background. We will, therefore, focus on the chronology of "family welfare" development in Israel. This chapter reveals the ways in which the system for the protection of pregnant employees has functioned since its inception, by tracking the development of the law and the intention of the legislature throughout, while comparing patterns of policy implementation and its de facto outcomes.

125

In the background chapter, we described the sub-field in which the various forces, linked to the system for preventing dismissals in pregnancy, act. In the current chapter, I wish to examine the claim that the changes initiated over the years regarding the state's attitude to dismissals in pregnancy are anchored in a socioeconomic paradigm shift and in the weakening powers of organised labour. This claim will continue to be considered in light of Bourdieu's theory of fields. As mentioned earlier, Bourdieu views society as a collection of fields (Bourdieu 2005a). The social, political, and economic fields influenced the manner in which the labour market field was operated, and within it the sub-field of labour relations.[50] In this field, one finds a preventative mechanism, which acts under the pressures of influencing bodies, each with their own varied logic of action, and the greater the ideological distance becomes between them, the deeper the power struggles in the field. If, for example, we formulate the argument at the core of the chapter, we can address the developmental process of the system for the prevention of dismissals during pregnancy as a part of the labour relations field, wherein the conflictive space of the clashing, power-wielding bodies has increased over the years.

---

50 Given that Bourdieu approaches each sub-field as a space that functions according to its own rules and norms, I will treat the labour relations sub-field located in the labour market field as a separate field in which the system functions.

Bourdieu ascribes great importance to the history of the field and claims that it defines the means and limitations of what is possible. As a result, what occurs in the field is never a direct reflection of the external pressures or demands but rather a symbolic expression—a sort of light refraction caused by the internal logic of the field itself. History, which is affected both by the field's structure and the influencing body's habitus, is the same prism that locates itself between the external world and the field, diffusing all of the external events (economic, political, or social crisis) through the prism's reflection. Bourdieu explains that what creates otherness in a period is not necessarily a shared culture but a shared "problematic," which is no more than a collection of stances related to the marked collection of stances within the field (Bourdieu 2005a).

With this in mind, the current chapter focuses on the historical gaze of a series of positions, or "problematics," and stances of influencing factors in the labour relations and regulations field, as well as on an examination of the opposing forces in the field—the profit-and-loss logic generally inherent in the labour market as well as the gender-based thought logic that appears in activity by women's organisations. Further, complementary theoretical aspects of the "field theory," according to which this logic was examined, belong to the "state in action" theory.

Two Periods of the Family State

In studies that address the subject of gender in Israel, it is common to divide the protection of pregnant women into a number of periods.[51] The existing research focuses less on comprehending the changes in policy implementation, translation of the Women's Labour Law into state action, or studying the homogeneity inherent in this. Given that we seek to fill this space, we will divide the 60 years during which the law was enforced into two main periods. The first, which covered the first 30 years since the legislation came in, 1954–1984, will be labelled "The Paternalistic Homogeneity Period."[52] The period is characterised by paternalistic protection which left no space for women's voices to be heard in their own defence, and by homogeneity among the various influencing bodies working with the state in its dealings with the issue. The second period, which began in 1985 and continues until today, will be called the "Fragmented Period." This period reflects a growing neoliberalism and the attempt to promote gender-based human rights and prevent discrimination. It is a period in which a conflict exists between discourses; a schism that leads to polarisation of the fragmentary nature of the state's actions. This period is characterised by the privatisation of labour relations, a decrease in union power, tempering of the labour market, a rise in liberal feminism, and the

51 Shalev 1999, Safran 2006; Ajzenstadt and Gal 2001.
52 For Paternalism see footnote no. 1, above.

spread of gender inequality. Further, the voices of women began to be heard during this period within the framework of the hearings held by the prevention mechanisms.

On the basis of analysis and processing of archival material, protocols from Knesset sessions, newspaper clippings, and interviews with regulation influencing bodies, we will closely trace the development of the Family Policy intended to prevent the dismissal of women during pregnancy and after giving birth in Israel, and examine the intended and unintended results of this development. Findings point to an increasing fragmentation in the state's actions, as well as to the influence of neoliberalism, the centrality of professional ideologies and institutional interests intertwined with the policy implementation, which affect the level of success of the policy in achieving its goals.

The First Period: State Regulation in the Era of "Paternalistic" Homogeneity

Researchers examining the social changes that have occurred in the State of Israel concur that in the early days of the state, most events took place in a single political, social, and economic arena, and that labour relations were arranged for the most part in a manner organised through the Labour Union labour federation, although even during this period there was a secondary labour market of vulnerable workers.[53] At this stage, the Israeli women's organisations dealt mainly with handling the specific needs of women by establishing day care and promoting protective legislation, while strengthening the ties of women to political parties and unions with which their movements were associated. Throughout this period, the participation of women, and mothers in particular, slowly increased in the labour force. The trend occurred principally due to the increase in education among the women, modernisation, and a decrease in fertility, as well as a trend to financially contribute to the family unit (Ajzenstadt and Gal 2001).

The Logic of Labour Relations in the Labour Market

Israel is an immigrant state that blends a traditional population with a modern one. The state was characterised from the start by a low level of working women, but also by a strong ideology of protection and an attempt to integrate middle-class women into the labour force (Fogel-Bijoy 2003). Over the years, the increased entry of women into the labour market created special requirements that led to changes in legislation and its enforcement. During the decades following the founding of the state, social, political and economic developments began that influenced the

---

53 Shalev 1999, Safran 2006; Ajzenstadt and Gal 2001; Yuval-Davis 1997.

Family Policy regarding women and characterised the pattern of their integration into the Israeli labour force (Berkovitch 1999). In this section, using the field theory (Bourdieu 2005a), I will consider how the place of female employees in the field emerges.

As stated, up until 1954, the Women's Labour Law in Israel forbade the dismissal of pregnant women and granted the Minister of Labour (who was responsible for enforcement of the law) the jurisdiction to cancel such dismissals. Due to the lack of data concerning the implementation of the law in the years following its legislation, and given that the state clerks who worked on the implementation at the time retired years ago, we used the Ministry of Labour archives in order to investigate the creation of the law and the manner of its implementation at the outset. In the archive, we discovered several dozen documents dealing with amendments to Article 9a of the Women's Labour Law, which deals with protection from dismissal during pregnancy, and among them correspondence concerning how to protect women, on the one hand, while, on the other hand, not penalising the employer. Further, a small number of files were found that gave information on the de facto implementation of the law, and about the treatment of cases involving protection from dismissal during pregnancy. Among these were documents from the Ministry of Labour, letters from employers at government influencing bodies, or letters from government ministries that employed unionised female employees. It is important to note that no documents were found from small, employers without unions. The absence of these documents highlights the duality of the labour market and the hierarchy of the primary and secondary labour markets described in earlier chapters of this book.[54]

Given the lack of conflicting data from the clerks at the Ministry of Labour employed there from the mid-1970s on (interviews 2007, 2008, 2010), and based on the low number of women in the labour market in the early decades following the founding of the state, it is implied that throughout the initial period, the implementation of the law in Article 9a was limited and rare in relation to the legislation's indication (from archival material from 1954–1978). From the material located there nevertheless emerges an interesting picture regarding the way the system functioned and the women who benefited from its protection.

Institutional Homogeneity: The Development of Paternalistic Regulation in the Labour Market

In the first decades following the founding of the state, women had a marginal place in the labour force. They were cheap, untrained labour, with limited authority, and they generally worked a short work day (Bernstein 1992). Reinforcement of the perception of the paternalistic state's

54   Rosenhek 1999; Farjun 1983; Shalev 1996.

role in the specific context of protection from dismissal during pregnancy is seen in the absence of the dismissed employee's voice. The debate concerning her case took place among the various state clerks and occasionally with the employer. The process played out with no committee to examine the employee's claims against the employer's.

A letter from November 1964 written by S. Winkler, the labour supervisor for the Jerusalem region who was responsible for implementation of the law, demonstrates both the process and the state's attitude to the female employee. It appears from the letter that along with the request to seek what she deserves by turning to her employer, it is suggested to this woman, who is benefiting from the state's protection, consult the relevant clerks close to her home in order to receive what is her right. The letter is addressed to Mrs. A from Kiryat Yovel in Jerusalem:

> RE: Women's Labour Law of 1954, Subject: Your letter of October 11, 1964: "Given that the minister of labour did not grant permission for your dismissal, the dismissal does not hold and the place of work is responsible for payment of wages. Please contact the labour relations desk in our ministry, as that is the department which deals with wage protection laws. You must demand the payment due to you plus the agreed percentages from the time of the withheld wages. Please contact our office, Room 317.

(Regional supervisor's archive, Jerusalem, November 1964)

This letter, copies of which were sent to the legal advisor for the Ministry of Labour, to the Centre for Independent Education, and to the supervisor for regulations and services from the Ministry of Education and Culture in Jerusalem, shows that the decision concerning protection of the woman was made without involving her at all in the process, which became common only in the mid-1980s. The woman only received instructions to act upon. Furthermore, copies sent to government organisations imply cooperation and cohesive and accepted processes among the state bodies. The employee's instruction to demand her rightful wages is characteristic of workers employed in the primary labour market, which was unionised and offered rights and benefits. It is impossible to learn from the letter whether the employee was meant to return to her position, as was common in later stages of the law's implementation.

At this stage of policy development, all inter-ministry actions took place with full coordination with a further influencing body, the Labour Union. Below is an excerpt from a letter by the legal advisor of the State Service Commissionership, Mr. Zvi Bar-Niv, to Mr. Y. Shaari of the Workers' Association (Vaad HaPoel) regarding the Women's Labour Law and the obligatory leave prior to giving birth:

I received a copy of your letter regarding the matter of the minister of labour's State Service Commissioner. Kindly inform me if the Labour Union has defined their stance with regard to the regulations suggested previously. (March 12, 1961, Labour file, archive)

Testimonies were found in the archives from the Ministry of Labour regarding a small number of events in which employers requested legal authorisation for the dismissal of women during pregnancy or after giving birth. Nonetheless, the behaviour in each of these few cases reflected, as stated earlier, homogeneity, consensus, cooperation, and coordination among the legislative and implementing bodies.

The document below was written by the government legal counsel to the State Service Commissionership, concerning protection for temporary employees and a comparison of their working conditions with those of permanent employees. This correspondence was carried out within the context of doubts on the part of the government legal counsel regarding the rights of non-union workers who were employed in temporary positions.

In the meantime, it seems to me that we should continue to act according to the letter of the law as determined by the Supreme Court, and not terminate the employment of *a pregnant woman working for the state*, even if she is a temporary employee, without authorisation for this from the minister of labour. It is preferable to be as stringent as possible with ourselves and not to deny working women the rights that the legislature perhaps intended to grant them.

(November 10, 1959, Labour file, archive)

This letter demonstrates the protection received by women employed by the state. One may cautiously speculate that similar protection was not available to non-union employees.

A letter from January 23, 1965, from M. Glick, the inspector to the supervisor, is further testimony, highlighting the fact that cases handled by the state were those of female employees who belonged to the primary labour market. This case also emphasises how decisions were made based on institutional homogeneity, as we see from the letter:

> Given that an argument began following the request from the employee regarding termination of employment, with regard to the manner of treatment and interpretation of the law (post-amendment), I present the problem to you and request your opinion on the matter. A worker was employed for a pre-determined period, according to a *special contract at a government office*.[55] The

55 Author's emphasis.

contract was extended three times, and in effect, the employee continued to work continuously for three and a half years. The extended contract will expire on May 15, 1965, when the employee will be in her eighth month of pregnancy. The question is whether, in your opinion, a specific ministry has the legal duty to submit a request for authorisation of dismissal of the aforementioned employee, who has been "temporary" for three and a half years (though this was based on a special contract), and this taking into account that in the contract itself it states that an employee is no longer considered "temporary" after six months of employment. Further, this should not be seen as dismissal but rather as termination of employment relations. Given that the problem will be current in the near future, I would ask for your opinion as soon as possible.

(Labour file, archival document, January 23, 1965)

This example once again demonstrates the decision-making process that took place with no input from the employee.

Despite the few cases found, one can assume that regardless of the inter-institutional correspondence, the regulation functioned in few cases alone, and in a one-sided manner. These cases involved female employees of government offices who benefited from relatively organised working conditions. The voices of women who worked in the secondary sector were not heard at all, and we are unable to evaluate the phenomenon of dismissal during pregnancy for this population. Nevertheless, women working for the primary sector were also denied the right to a hearing, as we discovered in later stages of the research. These examples demonstrate the limited power of women in the labour market field of "temporary" workers, employed in fact for years with temporary status. The research, which focused on the development of the Israeli labour market, found that in the public and unionised sectors dismissals were generally avoided, and an attempt by an employer to dismiss generally led to a fight with the professional union. Non-union employees in the private sector were, for the most part, temporary or immigrant workers, who presumably had limited knowledge of the language and the law, thus, their requests for protection from dismissal were extremely rare, and no signs of them appeared in the archive files.[56]

In these contexts, it is interesting to discover how the field theory (Bourdieu 2005a) is manifested. It appears that the marginality of the female worker's location within the labour market field is symmetrical to her low place in the hierarchy established by the state mechanism. Thus, in effect, the lack of authority granted to women in the labour market is reflected in the lack of voice. It could be said that these inferior places fed into one another and shaped the low position of women in the field.

---

56 Farjun 1983, Shalev, 1996, Rosenhek 1999.

Labour Relations Field: The Logic of Action in Drafting the Law

In the early days of the state, there were numerous debates surrounding the lack of participation by women, and, in particular, mothers, in the labour market. Members of Knesset were at a loss for ideas as to how to encourage women to enter the job market, and in the first two decades, the discussions focused on the lack of workers.[57] Therefore, the Knesset legislated laws that would assist women and mothers in particular, in entering the market.[58] However, the legislation protecting women proved a double-edged sword, because it limited their chances of employment and did not allow them to set personal priorities, plus it dictated social stereotypes (Berkovitch 1999). On the day the vote took place in the Knesset for the Women's Labour Law (Sevislovsky 1954), there was a unanimous vote to send it to the Labour Committee. Despite the fact that the minister of labour, Golda Meir, praised the members of Knesset for their enlightened debate, there were those who claimed that working hours for women should be lowered in order

---

57 State archive documents, Prime Minister's Office and the Ministry of Labour, December 21, 1960, a letter from Y. Hausman, Labour Division Director at the Association of Industry Owners in Israel, concerning the lack of manpower in industry.

58 Sevirsky 1999; Yizre'eli 2000; Fogel-Bijoy 1999; Radday et al. 1995 "What are the Rights of the Working Woman?" Yedioth Ahronoth July 30, 1952; Berkovitch 1999.

to allow them to make time for their families, protect them during pregnancy, and increase their earnings during this period. Even then, there were those who claimed that "special privileges" would put off employers, due to the extra financial burden involved when hiring women.[59]

In its early days, the Women's Labour Law was intended to provide protection from dismissal during pregnancy to all female employees from the day they started work. However, a decade from the day of legislation, it was decided to make some amendments to the law.[60] The first limited the ability to dismiss both temporary and occasional workers and added a condition, that the law must protect the employee as long as she has been employed for a minimum of six months at the place of employment, with the claim that labour relations are consolidated only following said probationary period, and it would be unacceptable for the employee to become pregnant and thus a burden to the employer who had not even decided if he wanted to keep her on. This condition partially limits the special protection understood from the law. It is important to mention that this instruction does not exist in any other western country, where pregnant women are protected from dismissal without conditions surrounding the length of their employment. Reinforcement for this development

59 Yedioth Ahronoth December 30, 1952.
60 Labour law texts at the Legal Department of the Ministry of Labour.

may be found in a letter from Labour Minister Yigal Allon, who presented the government with a bill reminiscent of the Women's Labour Law (amendment), in which he suggested, in Article 3, "It should be clarified that the prohibition from dismissing an employee while pregnant, unless there has been permission given by the minister of labour, should also apply to temporary or occasional employees if they have worked for the same employer for more than six months." With regard to this amendment, a response came from Y. Schwartzbaum, the law's supervisor from the Ministry of Labour:

> I am not certain whether this amendment will solve all of the problems. What is the legal standing of a woman who has worked in for less than six months, was dismissed for a number of days or even a few weeks and returned to work, and now they want to fire her for being pregnant after she "recently" worked for less than six months, although in fact the two periods together surpass the six (or even 11) months? Perhaps it is prudent to add to the amendment, 'within a 12-month period, prior to the day of dismissal or the day the request for dismissal was submitted.' Also, what is the fate of a woman who was hired for a specific period from the start, or to fulfil a specific function ahead of time, and who then continues working for more than six months? Do the usual excuses of "I'm not dismissing her," or "the contract is up" still hold?

> (Archive file, January 1963)

It is interesting to note how even at this stage, the state was careful not to harm the employers more than necessary, and despite the minimal experience in dealing with complaints, an amendment to the law was decided upon (Amendment 1963), in order to ensure that the employer would not be forced to grant permanence to the employee.

Interpretation of the law in a similar spirit can be seen in the words of a senior clerk from the Ministry of Labour, "We established a clear criterion and always act according to it. *If there is a connection*[61] to the pregnancy, we deny permission and if there is no link, we grant it. That way there are no complaints about discrimination, arbitrariness, nepotism, etc." (A. Meibam, March 1963).

This exchange of letters is especially important for our debate, as we can see in it the seeds of interpretation of the law and of the supervisor's discretion on determining whether there is a link between the request for dismissal and the pregnancy. These are the seeds of logic that guide the state's actions in its attempt to interpret the law. This is meant to be routine language, but it is interesting to analyse words such as "we established," "clear criterion," and "always," and see how homogeneity and cooperation emerge. These are words that indicate a unified, coordinated, inarguable action; they are words that express consensus and a clear stance in the field of actors responsible for enforcing the law before the legislature.

---

61 Author's emphasis.

The above cases teach us about the manner in which the employers' power was established in relation to the women in the field, with the state's encouragement. Bourdieu claimed that not every actor in the field could receive compensation. Thus, for example, in 1964 the Women's Labour Law was amended to grant permission for dismissal during pregnancy beginning in the woman's sixth month of employment, with the argument that work relations are not properly established in the initial months of employment, and the female employee would be protected by the Women's Labour Law only after a six-month probationary period (Toshav-Eichner 2003). This amendment limited the protection for women as initially intended by the legislator, however, the employers fought for the state's support for the creation of a probationary period within the field (Regev 2011). It is important to note that the fields are not static, and they have a dynamic history full of struggles. These struggles do not fragment the field—in fact, Bourdieu says that the battle is always the "engine of the field" (Bourdieu 2005b). These power struggles are not always worded in terms of a clear and obvious struggle, and in many cases, they are beneath the surface. They locate the actors in the field in hierarchically understood "positions." We have shown that the struggle between women and their employers is not blatant, but is manifested through state bodies, which tend not to over-harm employers. I will now address this in more detail.

The Logic of the Gender Approach: Over-protection of Pregnant Employees

Let us examine how this approach formed the state's relation with the issue of dismissal during pregnancy, and how this relationship increased the inequality toward pregnant employees while strengthening gender-based discrimination. In the context of avoiding harm to employers, manifested in the gender-based approach typical of the period, one could examine the "urgent" proposal by Ms. Ruth Satner, legal counsel for the Ministry of Education:

> My ministry believes that at this time, the following article ought to be inserted into the law's amendment, "Female employees who are dismissed by an employer unaware of the pregnancy must inform the employer of the pregnancy, within two weeks of receiving notice of dismissal. If they have not done so, the dismissal stands and no sanctions will be taken against the employer." The cause is obvious—we hear of the event when it is too late, and this matter leads to *complications and numerous problems*.[62]

(Archive documents, Labour file, February 20, 1961)

This position, which takes the employer into account yet sees the lack of information concerning the employee's

---

62 Author's emphasis.

pregnancy as an "event" that breaches the work routine, emerges from the following as well:

> I believe that the existing version of the Women's Labour Law, Article 9b, criminalises employers who dismiss women without being aware of their pregnancy. In my opinion, this should be corrected, and the criminal act ought to begin only once the employer has been informed of the pregnancy and has not withdrawn the dismissal until receiving permission, if this is forthcoming.
>
> (Y. Schwartzbaum, legal supervisor for the Ministry of Labour, Labour file, archive, September 9, 1963)

In these documents, we again discover the state's position of favouring the employer. Furthermore, we are witnesses to the state's approach concerning the employee's pregnancy as well as "complications and numerous problems" that arise in the workplace as a result of lack of knowledge of the employee's pregnancy. One could even cautiously assume that they contain the seeds of the approach that considers the employee's pregnancy to be a burden to the employer. This is a gender-based discriminatory approach, and is expressed even more clearly in the document below, with regard to education workers such as physical education teachers, who, according to a senior clerk in the Ministry of Education,

> ...are incapable of continuing with their work after the fourth month of pregnancy, though they

nonetheless continue, without properly carrying out their duties. Discussions should be held regarding the extension of maternity leave from 12 weeks to 24 weeks prior to the estimated delivery date. This arrangement would make it easier to convince the physical education teachers to take their leave without pay at the start of their fifth month of pregnancy.

(Y. Sarid, Ministry of Education, to the acting State's Service Commissionaire, Labour file, archive, July 19, 1961)

This quotation demonstrates the paternalistic "over-protection" approach. The position seeks to take the employer into consideration, on the one hand, while on the other it sees the pregnant employee as a body to be over-protected from injury during the pregnancy rather than a woman who ought to be consulted and have her opinion considered concerning her condition, in order to ensure her right to equality. These approaches further limit the power of women in the field. It should be noted that copies of this letter were sent to the legal counsel at the Ministry of Labour, to the addressee as well as to the head physician at the Ministry of Health. This is further proof of the paternalistic attitude to pregnant women, and to the cooperation, the homogeneity, and the coordination among ministries on the matter. We further learn of the attempt to synchronise positions, which is a further expression of the homogeneity within the field, during the paternalistic period.

Action by Women's Organisations

In keeping with the approach described above, the women's organisations Wizo and Na'amat, who at the time assisted in strengthening the infrastructure of the new state and saw in the advancement of the status of women an important value for building a just society in Israel, took action. The main business of these organisations focused on expanding the network of daycare centres, acknowledging the independent membership of the wives of Histadrut members, connecting women with courses and institutions for professional training, and assisting female immigrants and their children. Only in 1975, with the advent of the liberal-feminist discourse and following personnel changes, did Na'amat's management begin to develop an approach to women during pregnancy and after giving birth, when the Council of Women Workers submitted a report to the public committee for the improvement of conditions and service to these women (Safran 2006). These changes were seen in 1976, when for the first time in Israel, a committee headed by Ora Namir formed to examine the status of women. She presented the government with a detailed report containing 241 proposals for fixing the reality of gender-based discrimination in Israel. In 1975, the women's groups Wizo and the Women Workers' Committee increased their support for the actual enforcement of the Equal Rights for Women Law of 1951, whose intention was the prevention of discrimination against women. In an article describing the activities of the women's organisations, the argument was made that "the law will act as a revolution in Israeli society, which is currently defined as patriarchal, given that women are dependent on their husbands" (Geller 1975). Thus only toward the mid-1970s, as the liberal-feminist discourse began to awaken, did the debate begin surrounding the core aspects of the Equal Rights for Women Law of 1951, and simultaneously, awareness of the rights of female workers increased. Below is the letter from Zohar Karty, the Director of the Unit for Employment of Women at the Ministry of Labour, to Mrs. Levinfish, the CEO of the Committee for the Status of Women at Wizo Tel Aviv:

> I tried to find a way to assist Wizo in setting up information centres for women. I consider this matter to be of the utmost importance, given that at the moment there is no address to guide or instruct the working woman about her rights or duties in the legislation or regarding other problems, such as professional counselling, social security, income tax, etc. For this, well done on your initiative and on your willingness to act on this matter. The Ministry of Labour is willing to offer you any guidance, instruction, or information required by the counselling centres. In addition, we will be pleased to provide you with a sum of money up to 500 Israeli liras for the current budget year for advertising and other promotional activities. As you must be aware, government instructions are to cut 50% of all promotional budgets for government

ministries, thus, we are unable to offer a larger budget. We would be grateful if the matter can be taken up by Wizo.

(Labour file, archive document, May 5, 1972)

The letter exemplifies how women were denied knowledge about their rights as workers, and points to the start of the state's awareness of the inaccessibility of information to women about the law. Further, the letter reflects the spirit of the period in which the various institutions had only begun to discuss the problem and its repercussions. From this, we note the minimal presence of women in the labour market in the first decades following the founding of the state. Of particular interest is the fact that no state organ was established with the purpose of guiding working women. This is the spirit of the paternalistic approach, which sees women as a weaker factor that must be cared for—an approach which explains to some degree the inferior position of women in the field.

To summarise, in this initial period that we examined, the attitude to women was arguably one of patriarchal protection of a weaker population with special needs that needed to be forcibly integrated into the labour force while protecting it from harm (primarily physical and health-related harm). The emphasis at this stage was manifested through integration, but not necessarily while providing equal opportunities regarding salaries or promotions. It is worth emphasising that the protection was granted solely to strong women in the primary sector and given the lack of documentation addressing this we understand that weak women (in particular Mizrachi and Arab women) did not benefit at all from the protective umbrella. Given the lack of mechanisms that would allow them to sue, these women were utterly exposed to dismissal with no authorisation whatsoever. During this period, the position of women in the labour relations field was established, defining them as people who were voiceless and completely unaware of their rights. In the spirit of the field theory, we could claim that a symmetrically similar position also characterised the inferior status of women in the labour market within the labour relations field. We further identified the manner in which the powers in the field were established as well as the power of employers who were strengthened by the state, and we demonstrated that in the absence of the female employee's voice, and given the absence of women's organisations in the field, the dynamics of the labour relations field was shaped through cooperation and coordination, not through struggle. In the following section, we will examine how the changes that ensued influenced a renewed placement of powers within the field.

The Second Period: State Regulation between Conflicting Discourses

With the decline of the first period, the neoliberal period began in the mid-1980s, and it continues to the time of writing. The second period is characterised by the advent of conflicting discourses; the winds of a liberal feminism on the one hand, and the spirit of globalisation and neoliberalism, based primarily in the United States and Britain, on the other.

Researchers who studied the period are in agreement that the globalisation of Israel's economy led to a reorganisation of the labour market and of the norms as well as work and management patterns that characterised it in the past, before it was exposed to a global economy. From a society that sought full employment, a living wage, the existence of a social safety net, and stability in labour relations, Israel has become a society that worships individualism, free enterprise, competition, flexibility in employment, and the mobility of capital and manpower.[63]

In studies examining the neo liberalisation period in Israel, there is much criticism aimed at the state, which is increasingly weakened in comparison with market powers (Maman and Rosenhek 2009; Harvey 2005). In the early 1980s, an increase began in the rates of women's participation in the labour market (an increase that continued up until 2014). At the same time, Israel initiated a western privatisation policy, characterised by

---

63 Ram 1999; Gotwin 2000; Sevirsky and Connor-Attias 2001; Bareli 2002; Avnimelech and Tamir 2002; Frenkel, Hacker and Broide 2011; Nosek 2002; Rosenhek 2002; Fogel-Bijoy 2005; Shalev 1999; Shafir and Peled 1998; Radaï 2002.

an upswing in the power of capitalism, the strengthening of market powers, the entry of international concerns, the establishment of privately owned factories, an increased competitiveness stemming from the need to maintain profitable, and efficient organisations, along with a weakening of the power of the professional unions and their ability to protect their workers. On the political front, too, there was a revolution that allowed a less centralised economic direction than that which had existed under the Mapai (Labour) rule.

The labour market during this period witnessed an increase in the rate of participation by women in the labour force, stemming, among others, from the weakened importance of physical strength in the new world of work. There was a shift from heavy industry to an economy based on knowledge and technology (Toshav-Eichner 2009). All of these led to a decrease in the power of the Histadrut and of the professional unions, and to the rise of flexible arrangements and "unusual" deals through contractors. In exchange, and particularly with the rise in preference for business considerations over human-social ones, this led to an increase in the rate of dismissals during pregnancy as noted during this period. Clerks employed during this period claim, "During the economic slump of 1985, we received hundreds of requests from employers for dismissal during pregnancy" (Interview with inspector, February 12, 2009).

The beginnings of this period go as early back as the late 1970s, however, the signs were significantly clearer from the mid-1980s. In contrast with the previous period, which was mostly characterised by economic growth and nearly full employment until the mid-1960s—particularly among men—the second period was notable for the lack of economic stability and waves of mass dismissals, even in organisations which had previously been considered symbols of stability. From the mid-1970s, economic inequality in Israel grew, and its levels during the second period were among the highest in the western world (Gottschalk and Smeeding 1997; Dahan 2001). The gender inequality grew during this period on the basis of decentralisation of labour relations. The various systems that had promised centralisation led to a drop in the rate of employee organisation. In 1981, 81% of all employees were members of workers' unions, as opposed to only 43% in 2000. The coverage rate of collective agreements was lowered, and there was a general decrease in workers' bargaining ability in all sectors, both public and private (Crystal et al 2006). Only in 2012, following the social justice protests that took place during the summer of 2011, was an attempt made to organise large unions by workers' unions, such as the new Histadrut and the Koach La'Ovdim—the Democratic Workers' Organisation. This kind of struggle succeeded, for example, after protests by the employees of one of the cellular phone companies. Despite this, of 3.2 million workers in Israel employed in 2012, the rate of unionised workers was only 25–26%, about half of what it had been a decade previously (Subar-Heiruti et al. 2013).

Given this, it appears that the lack of stability in the economic field that characterises the second period has automatically influenced the adjacent field, the labour market, and was manifested through the waves of mass dismissals. A group of women with the most limited power were the first to suffer. In this section, I would like to examine the influence of the rise of neoliberalism and the drop in the power of unions on the phenomenon of dismissal during pregnancy.

The Labour Market Field

Events during the second period prove that the state's actions are often characterised by a lack of coherence and are influenced by conflicting interests.[64] Alongside the growing discourse on gender equality during this period, there is a conflicting discourse about neoliberalism, whose basis lies in limiting the interference of the state in economic issues. As a rule, the labour market is defined by flexibility in labour relations, by complexity and uncertainty, at a global and more particularly at a local level. All this clearly affects the manner in which the state acts. We will now explain the nature of the conflict between the two discourses.

There are researchers who claim that the expression

---

64 Calavita 1992; O'Connor 1973; Rosenhek 1999.

of a shift from welfare to capitalist policy is the central explanation for the increase in inequality in manpower and the creation of gender inequality (Daharn 2006). These researchers note three main factors in the policy, which led to the expediting of change in the structure of the Israeli labour market field, and particularly affected women. The first factor is, *labour made cheaper* through hiring workers through manpower firms. In this framework, the worker has no tenure at the place of work, and social benefits are almost non-existent. Most of those employed through this irregular method of practice were women, and as their numbers rose steadily, there was a significant decrease in their power within the field. Another factor in the policy of lowering the cost of labour was the "import" of cheap, obedient manpower, with no social benefits or unions. This is the import of migrant labour (foreign workers), which began in 1993 and has since grown due to the pressures of the agricultural sector, the construction business, and other branches of industry. Women have made up a relatively small number of the migrant workers in Israel, however, from the point of view of the Women's Labour Law, there is absolutely no reference to this population.

The second factor, *delegitimisation of the labour market*, is linked to the first and is a process that is manifested in the deviation from laws, limitations, and mechanisms that protect workers and their rights in the national labour market (Frenkel, Hacker, and Breudeh 2011), as well as by the non-enforcement of laws concerning protection for female employees, such as the Minimum Wage Law and the Law for Equal Pay for Male and Female Employees.

The third factor is the *dismantling of the welfare state and the commercialisation of welfare services*. As a result of this process, those with the means are able to purchase services in the market (daycare centres, medical treatment, appropriate settings for children with special needs and more), while groups who are unable to afford these services find the responsibility shifted onto the family, and in fact, onto the women in the family. This further responsibility has added to the difficulties of women in getting out of the house and integrating into the workforce. Keeping in mind that the state and the welfare services are the largest employers of women, the dismantling of the welfare state has increased unemployment among middle-class women as well (Dahan 2006). Furthermore, the Histadrut did not prevent these developments. From the mid-1980s and in particular during the 1990s, international corporations stipulated their investments in Israel (as in other countries) upon the weakening of organised labour or even its disappearance, and this demand severely weakened the Histadrut's standing and its bargaining ability. Despite this weakness, within the framework of the collective agreements in the past three decades, those who rank highest in the field—mostly men—more or less maintained a solid position regarding their salaries and even increased them, while those ranking lower—workers that are most often women—were unable to maintain their salary levels (Sembol and Binyamin 2007; Fogel-Bijoy 2005).

Researchers examining the period claim that the three government elements, along with the weakness of the Histadrut, created a no-brakes policy, and as a result, with the advent of neoliberalism there was an increase in gender inequality in the labour market.[65] Accordingly, this study also found that from the mid-1980s and during the 1990s, public discourse began to address the inherent gender discrimination in the labour market. One could point, for example, to the much-covered public debate concerning employers who due to the economic slump find legal loopholes and manage to dismiss temporary employees during pregnancy or immediately upon their return from maternity leave (Berenzon 1984).

An example of the public debate taking place in the context of dismissals during pregnancy in this period is an article published in the early 1990s. A medical journal warned doctors not to hire female physicians as "They get pregnant and prefer to raise children."[66] Several years later, another article was published, reflecting the changes in the spirit of the period, with regards both to the start of a public discourse surrounding equality and changes which had occurred in the labour market. The article appeared with the headline "An Amendment to a Chauvinist Law," and contained a critique of the "chauvinist" spirit of the previous article:

---

65 Fogel-Bijoy 2003; Dahan 2006; Crystal et al. 2006; Argaman-Barnea 1985; Eshet 1990.

66 Yedioth Ahronoth, "7 Days" supplement, May 29, 1992.

The main intent of the Women's Labour Law was to protect the health of women. The legislator assumed that economic trouble would endanger the women and their fetuses and that they needed to be protected from themselves and not only from employers seeking to take advantage of them. This chauvinist calculation has led to great injustice against women. Almost a limitation for them has become, over time, an excuse for discrimination against them ... such as the prohibition to work overtime. ... The legislator who drafted this article envisioned a woman labourer standing 12 hours a day. ... Member of Knesset Efi Oshaya envisions an average academic in a responsible position. She will not go home before completing her work, but because of her pregnancy, she is working for free. In order to find a balance between the labourer who must rest and the attorney who needs to be prepared to appear in court, the law proposes that a female employee is allowed to work overtime and that the employer is not allowed to demand it of her.

("An Amendment to a Chauvinist Law," Enosh, Yedioth Ahronoth, June 6, 1997)

From the early 1980s, with the accelerated entry of women into the labour market, studies focused on the attempt to resolve the physiological questions: Could employment during pregnancy physically harm the employee or the foetus? Is pregnancy a disease? How could tiredness, for example, harm productivity? (Saurel and Williams

1980; Kaminski 1986). The article also mentions research literature from the second wave, which began in the 1990s and mainly dealt with aspects of legislation and institutionalisation, the blend of work and family, and the level at which organisations supported women during pregnancy and after giving birth (Grover and Crooker 1995; Calloway 1995). Consequently, awareness of legal aspects of the influence of pregnancy on work reached a higher level, manifested legally as well as in the level of public awareness. The entry of women into the labour market field, alongside the possibility of experiencing dismissal during pregnancy, became a weighty issue within public discourse—unlike during the first period, in which the phenomenon was marginal and not exposed in the media. Supposedly, there was an improvement in the status of women from a public point of view, and we have witnessed the awareness of their status and growing power. The question remains, however, whether the actions of the preventative mechanism will be affected.

The Labour Relations Field—Legal Logic, the Beginning of Fragmentation

Researchers studying the current Israeli legislation regarding the protection of women's jobs in general and those of pregnant women in particular, are of the opinion that the law in Israel is advanced and enlightened in relation to western countries (Mundlak 2009). Although until 1998 the law was almost unchanged from its original legislation in 1954, by the end of the 20th century we had witnessed a significant rise in public awareness surrounding dismissals in pregnancy, and numerous amendments were introduced—some proposed by members of Knesset and some by the state or by women's groups. Along with this, there were uncertainties and long debates, in particular within the Committee for the Advancement of the Status of Women. This committee was formed in 1992, but it only began to work most significantly in 1998, when the Authority for the Advancement of the Status of Women was founded in law in the Prime Minister's Office. In 2014, the name of the committee was changed to The Committee for the Advancement of Women and Gender Equality.

In general, one could say that at the start of this period, the Knesset dealt with economic matters and debates with the religious parties and their demands from the secular parties. Female members of Knesset initially saw their role as representatives reflective of their parties, and less as representatives of a political-gender agenda (Ilberg 1983). Nonetheless, in the spirit of neoliberalism and the economic crisis, in the late 1980s, the RATZ party began to promote rights issues, including equal opportunities. The 12th Knesset legislated two fundamental laws dealing with human rights: the Free Enterprise Law and the Respect for Man and Freedom Law—legislated after it became clear that the Knesset was unable to pass a fundamental law addressing all aspects of human rights. Within the context of the Women's Labour Law, an amendment was introduced in which dismissal was prohibited during maternity leave, as were notices of dismissal to the employee during this period, or during the extended period following. This instruction held equally for temporary or occasional workers. Employers who did not intend to renew contracts for pregnant employees were obliged by law to request permission for dismissal.[67] It was precisely during this period that the hearings began at the Ministry of Labour.

It could be argued that the neoliberal hiring arrangements, the periods of economic slumps, and the rise in active involvement by the state in matters of dismissal during pregnancy all contributed to the growing response by the women's organisations. These groups acted as a parallel path to that of the state, and represented women in court, cracking the homogeneity of the state's actions by placing indirect pressure on the existence of an actively preventative policy for the prevention of dismissals. In this context, it is important to pay close attention to the beginning of the apparently internal conflict in the state's behaviour, given that part of the neoliberal ideology includes the withdrawal of the state from involvement in employers' agendas, and during this period we instead note a deepening of the state's actions in the area of protection from dismissal during pregnancy, an issue which we will now address.

67 Women's Labour Law, Amendment #9, Article 1324, July 26, 1990.

From the end of the 20th century and at the start of the 21st, Knesset committees regularly addressed issues relating to the Women's Labour Law. Among the committee discussions, there is a clear and significant influence noted that due to the family welfare policy changes undertaken by the European Union, along with an apparent desire to ensure that beyond the contribution of Israeli women to the good of the nation through increased birthrates, their continued integration in the labour force will also be safeguarded, and they will benefit from broad protection insofar as is possible (Frenkel, Hacker, and Broide 2011). From 2000, constant changes were made to the law, and in the Committee for the Advancement of Women, numerous discussions ensued on this matter. The constant debates of the Committee regarding issues surrounding women in the labour market point to the need to promote gender equality in the employment context. In 2004, apparently due to the liberal policy that granted permits against the wishes of the legislature, the law was amended in a manner that limited the decision-making power of the regulative system and prevented the retroactive granting of permits for dismissal, except in cases of bankruptcy or mass firing,[68] as emerged from the words of the committee chair, Yael Dayan:

> Today we are revisiting the subject because of the accumulation of issues occurring against regulation

---

68 Committee for the Advancement of the Status of Women May 24, 2000.

or for which there is a problem enforcing the existing regulations. I believe that there are fewer comments regarding the regulations themselves than there are for their implementation. Insofar as I recall, at the session in which we addressed the subject, problems were mentioned relating to the retroactivity of dismissals.

The legislators, members of Knesset who entered the labour relations field, understood that dealing with these aspects of the law could increase their power. For example, Gideon Sa'ar, who was chair of the committee in 2006–2008, was appointed minister of education one year later. During his years as chairman, numerous debates took place within the committee concerning Section 9a, and eight amendments were added—including the 1998 amendment expanding the period of protection prohibiting dismissal during the 45 days following the end of maternity leave. This significant amendment acted as a "step up" in expanding the umbrella of protection for women,[69] and on the basis of this, the protection was extended for a further 15 days in 2007.

A salient example of the human rights gender discourse is the in-depth debate surrounding the issue of dismissal during pregnancy initiated by the Knesset, in which the

---

69 Knesset protocol, comments by the Chair of the Committee for the Advancement of Women, Gideon Sa'ar January 31, 2007.

right to speak was given to a variety of actors relevant to the field, ranging from the chairperson of the Committee for the Advancement of Women, through workers' representatives, representatives from the Ministry of Industry, Commerce, and Labour, and women's organisations, and including both employees and employers. The legislature's position was manifested through a series of amendments to the law, such as Section 9a of the Women's Labour Law (2008), in which the defence of pregnant women from dismissal was extended to the period following the employee's return from maternity leave[70] (at first for 45 days and later for 60 days). The amendment was debated in the Committee for the Advancement of the Status of Women chaired by the Chairman, Gideon Sa'ar:

> There are several ways to look at the issue of dismissal during pregnancy, and the view we employed wishes to encourage the re-integration of women in the labour market, because this, in the end, is the principle which we wish to protect. ... If we examine the labour market from a broad view and wish to encourage the return of women to the labour market ... the amendment to the Women's Labour Law seeks to extend the period of protection from dismissal from 45 to 60 days in order to make the proceeds of the period less worthwhile for the employer and thus strengthen the aim of the

---

70 Amendment 2007.

law, which is, as stated, to safeguard the female employees' workplaces.

(Protocol No. 37 of the meeting of the Committee for the Advancement of the Status of Women, January 31, 2007)

This quotation is proof of the spirit of the discourse surrounding gender-based human rights, in order to safeguard the place of the female employee in the labour market. In expanding the protection to 60 days, Gideon Sa'ar argued that the employer would be forced in a sense to pay the employee for a longer period, thus granting the employee the time to prove that despite her motherhood, her availability to the employer was not harmed. In spite of the above, the spirit of neoliberalism remains present, given that it is a case of pressure to integrate people into the labour force and a reduction of benefits, which could indicate other interests of the legislators In this context, we will again return at the end of the chapter to examine how fragmentation is notable in the spirit of the legislature as well. Nonetheless, it is worth emphasising that there is no conflict here between human rights and the neoliberal approach, as leaving women within the workforce is seen as one method of avoiding the need for benefits.

Later protocols from the Knesset Committee for the Status of Women, which promoted change in the legislation, note a sense of despair—even if not blatant—among members of Knesset, due to the apparent cooperation between employers and the regulatory system, which reduces the protection set out in law as well as the efforts of the legislators to halt this cooperation. MK Tzipi Hotovely, the chair of the Committee for the Advancement of the Status of Women said:

> The discussion today was, in fact, a debate following a debate which the committee held a month ago, regarding the extremely worrying data on the rise in the number of pregnant women being dismissed. In effect, the conclusions drawn from the discussion are that the process through which the employer finds it easy to dismiss pregnant women requires some sort of addressing. … The debate will be opened by the Ministry of Industry, Commerce, and Employment. A representative of the Ministry of Industry, Commerce, and Employment will present a survey of the regulations through which women in the various stages of pregnancy may be dismissed, and from there we will attempt to locate where the problem for which we have reached this reality, in which more and more pregnant women are unprotected in their workplaces during pregnancy, lies.
>
> (Protocol No. 36 from the session of the Committee for the Advancement of the Status of Women, February 16, 2010)

Hotovely's comments express subtle criticism of the Ministry of Industry, Commerce, and Employment, who are responsible for protecting women from dismissal, although in fact, as she states, "more and more women are unprotected during pregnancy."

Presumably, given that the labour laws and the norms within the institutionalised labour market in Israel limited the employer's ability to dismiss workers—which is unrelated to whether they are parents in the main labour market—this over-protection was not seen as actually damaging to the rights of the employer. Only with the rise of the neoliberal discourse, emphasising the rights of the employer to hire and fire workers as they see fit and depending on their needs, did the protection of pregnant women and those who have given birth become blatant "extra rights." In this context, researchers claim that in the past decade the law raised the issue of the dismissal of pregnant women to peak conflict between the neoliberal and the human rights discourses (Frenkel, Hackre and Broide 2011). According to their argument, "This issue severely limits what is considered one of the cornerstones of organisations in our time, in other words the employer's claim to the right to hire and fire as they wish and in accordance with the organisational flexibility resulting from this right, is considered necessary to assure the organisation's profitability."

As we have demonstrated, the conflict between the two discourses is manifested primarily in the gap created between the aims of the legislature—with the intent to protect pregnant women from dismissal—and the actual protective mechanisms that are not making the best use of the possibilities granted by the legislature. I now wish to present the ways in which the mechanism for prevention of dismissal of women during pregnancy was created.

The System in Action

In 1985, a committee was formed to examine each case of dismissal of women during pregnancy. In this framework, the investigation is carried out through separate hearings for the employer and employee, and after a number of months the decision is made whether to authorise the employee's dismissal or to refuse it and return her to her job. The committee is headed by a supervisor, and the investigative material is then sent to a senior supervisor, who makes the decision. In 2011, jurisdiction to decide was authorised by the supervisor who testifies at the hearings, too. During these years, a regulation was inserted, according to which the employer is questioned and his or her version of the situation is sent to the employee before the hearing, in order to allow the employee to respond. Investigations were carried out by supervisors in three centres: Jerusalem, Tel Aviv, and Haifa. Since 2011, investigations have taken place only in Tel Aviv.

In the early 1990s a structural, internal shift occurred in the Ministry of Labour, which stemmed from personal, political causes. Thus, in order to grant authority and personal power to the political cronies of the decision-makers, the regulatory authority was split between two functionaries: "The Section for Labour Supervision" and "The Section for Oversight of Labour Laws," which, among other things, enforces the Women's Labour Law and the Sabbath Labour Law. Criticism emerged more than once about the fact that "in the Ministry of Labour manpower resources are mostly channeled into dealing with the Sabbath Labour Law, claiming that this is the law which brings money into the state's coffers, unlike the 'Women's Labour Law,' whose enforcement is not profitable" (interviews with functionaries who operated the system during two different periods: February 2009 and February 2008).

During this period, women began appealing directly to the courts, allowing the employees themselves deeper participation in the process, and the ability to represent their cases in an institutional arena. The Ministry of Labour (for whom a court decision was seen as infringing upon their right to decide as set out in law) was forced to change their patterns of action and to create a more organised process of enforcement, which had space for the point of view of the dismissed woman. Thus, according to one of the first supervisors who carried out the hearing procedures at the Ministry of Labour:

> When we first began to work with the law in the mid-1980s, we began to form committees and hold

hearings for employers and employees. We did not really know how to interpret the Women's Labour Law, and we therefore granted many authorisations. Only later did we understand that the "at the discretion of the minister" section could have been interpreted in several ways, so we researched more and employed more consideration as the law states, and we granted somewhat fewer authorisations. ... As a rule, during periods of inflation and economic slumps there were more requests ... and many more permits granted. Later the women's organisations were established as well and really pushed us not to make it simple for the employers.

(February 2009, Interview with a supervisor)

The quotation is a great example of the manner in which the state's actions are greatly influenced and shaped by two of the processes that took place during this period. First, is the process that took place within the field of institutional state action, the institutionalisation of the regulatory process of granting an opportunity to the parties to make their arguments heard at a hearing. Although it is important to note that control of the regulatory process was in the hands of the independent Ministry of Labour, whose clerks generally maintained the traditional, paternalistic method of protecting employees and saw enforcement of the Labour laws as a source of institutional and professional power. Furthermore, another issue arises from this quote regarding the entry of women's organisations into the field, and the effect of their pressure vis-à-vis the way authorisations were granted. As chairperson of Na'amat Chedva Almog stated: "Ministry of Labour supervisors are not examining the complaints in depth but rather hand out dismissal permits generously" (Enosh 1999). Her words reflect criticism about the ease with which the Ministry of Labour permits dismissal during pregnancy. This quotation may be seen as "correspondence" with the words of the supervisor who is influenced by the pressure brought to bear by the women's organisations regarding the pattern of issuing authorisations.

The second process necessary for understanding the way in which the state's actions are performed forms the basis for the fragmentation and sees in the field theory the economic and political atmosphere of the state's actions, and the increasing pressure by the employers and their supporters within the neoliberal economic policy is notable also in the actions of the regulators. Numerous permits were granted due to the fact that the article about "the discretion of the senior supervisor" was not yet broadly implemented. This was shown in the newspaper interview with the senior supervisor for the Women's Labour Law, Rafi Kachlon, who made headlines due to the period in which "the Ministry of Labour approved 70% of the requests to dismiss pregnant women":

> Most of the requests for dismissals are submitted
> based on closing businesses, downsizing, or

reorganisation. In these cases, I am not authorised to prohibit the dismissals, and the Ministry of Labour has no tools to prevent them. ... The law does not require employers of pregnant women sent from manpower companies to continue employing them.

(Enosh, *Yedioth Ahronoth*, May 16, 1999)

The quote demonstrates the inflexible approach to granting permits, which characterises this entire period. Only in later years would these same claims by employers lead to a detailed investigation by the senior supervisor, and discretion was employed in cases linked to pregnancy as well.

Two further structural changes significantly influenced the actions of the system. The first was manifested in the integration of the Ministry of Labour in 2003 within another government ministry, the Ministry of Industry and Commerce, and the subjugation of the regulatory mechanisms to the government ministry responsible for the advancement of employers' interests. Some claim that the expansion of the Ministry of Labour's authority to the Ministry of Industry, Commerce, and Employment was borne out of political consideration for the desire to expand the responsibility of the new minister, Ehud Olmert, which is similar to the expansion that occurred a decade later for the Minister Naftali Bennet, who received broad electoral support (interviews with clerks during the years of research). The second shift was manifested in the creation of institutional distinction between mechanisms of resolution and enforcement in 2006, which created a structural separation between the mechanism responsible for granting permits for dismissing women during pregnancy and the mechanism responsible for locating employers who were breaking the law and bringing them to justice.

The first structural shift clearly reflects the neoliberal spirit in Israel during the second period. While the state structure that promoted change combined the Ministry of Labour with the Ministry of Welfare and made them responsible for the welfare of employees and the promotion of legislation protecting the workers from unfair employment, the new Ministry was named the Ministry of Industry, Commerce, and Employment, a title indicating the state's encouragement for employers to help them increase the rate of employment, without any link to the type of work offered, or its conditions (interviews with clerks during the years of research).

The conflicts within the state's actions have a structural explanation. State regulation whose function is to protect the positions of pregnant women is, in fact, a welfare mechanism that interferes in the employers' prerogative. Its purpose is to prevent a loss of income during the period when it would be very difficult for a female worker to find alternative sources of income. One could, therefore, assume that the natural place of regulation would be in the

Ministry of Labour, however, the structural change created in 2003 contradicts this assumption. Placing the protective mechanism within the jurisdiction of the Ministry of Industry, Commerce, and Employment—instead of within the Ministry of Labour (whose job it is to care for the welfare of employees) as had been the case prior to the change—created structural conflicts with regard to the purpose of the mechanism, whether at the level of the interests of the decision makers, or with regard to the public reputation they wished to create. Locating the welfare regulation within a ministry with economic orientation is liable to damage the aim of the legislature to promote gender equality and keep women within the labour cycle.

In the research discourse that examines the state's actions, it is common to argue that institutional changes have a developmental nature characterised by a tapestry of changes throughout a long period of time, and that these are opposing processes with, on the one hand, a desire to maintain stability and on the other a wish to change (Campbell 2004; Thelen 2004). Reinforcement of this complex picture emerges from the interviews with supervisors. These supervisors are responsible for carrying out hearings for employers and employees concerning the pressures brought to bear on them in the institutional environment. Thus, one supervisor explained:

> On one hand we have the employers' organisations and on the other the women's organisations. The former claim that it is difficult to obtain permission,

and the latter claim it is simple ... and I find myself between a rock and a hard place. My manoeuvres within the resolution system are more difficult because unlike in the past we are dealing with employers who turn to us legally, and they are represented by lawyers and come prepared, so it is much more difficult to refuse their requests.

(Interview with supervisor, February 2008)

The internal conflict that the supervisors experience raises the question of who the public before whom it is important to maintain a reputation is (O'Connor 1973). The employers are represented by the Ministry of Industry and Commerce, but the employees are represented by the Ministry of Employment. According to the supervisor who worked for the Ministry of Labour prior to the amalgamation, the shift in the public's perception that the ministry is meant to serve changed the nature of her work and the type of pressure she experienced. The welfare approach that characterised the clerks of the Ministry of Labour got caught within the new ministry, in a neoliberal discourse that prefers protecting employers, and the clerks, whose target audience is composed mostly of industrialists who demand the flexibilisation of the labour force and the autonomy to choose regarding dismissal of their employees often felt helpless.

The structural shift thus created an inner dissonance among the clerks:

Since the change, I am utterly confused. I want to be empathetic to the female employee, but I know that the ministry represents the employers as well. I know that this employer is in financial straits and that the employee was not just fired illegally—she really is in trouble.

(Supervisor in the Enforcement Bureau, Interview, February 2008).

These dilemmas create irregularities and feelings of conflicting loyalties among the regulatory workers, and they often affect the public reputation, both among female employees and among their employers. Given the lack of organised processes of change, these structural shifts have created a conflict in the institutional thinking patterns of several supervisors as well as in their enacting of the regulation:

The choice is made to identify with the E of employment, rather than with the IC of Industry of Commerce. (Supervisor at the Enforcement Bureau, Interview, October 2007)

Although the system changes in amalgamating the ministries occurred years ago, the laws that in the past were under the auspices of the Ministry of Industry and Commerce have yet to be transferred to the authority of the Enforcement Bureau (which in the past belonged to the Ministry of Labour).

(Supervisor at the Enforcement Bureau, Interview, October 2007)

Reinforcement for these arguments appeared in 2011, nearly a decade after the ministry amalgamation, when the Ministry of Industry, Commerce, and Employment was branded with the slogan "The Ministry of Industry, Commerce, and Employment: a strong economy for you." Thus, in effect, those at the helm of the ministry stressed the expansion of neoliberal ideology, which gives centre stage to the interests of employers and their autonomy, while abandoning any thought of the employees. Various interviews with supervisors from the Ministry of Industry, Commerce, and Employment raise a similar sense of frustration surrounding the subjugation of the issue in which they are forced to deal with irrelevant political caprices:

> Every minister arrives with his own ideas; one is more socially-minded, one more economically. The point of the economic slogan of a strong economy for you, in which it is unclear who this "for you" is, may be fine for industrialists and merchants, but the employment service is also ours, just as the dismissal of pregnant women is ours, and profession training is ours—is the strong economy for them? … They have utterly abandoned this part of the work in this campaign, and from the start, they are more interested in money and budgets from industry. There was no real amalgamation and we have completely different committees and aims. … The Ministry of Industry, Commerce, and Employment is just a political inflation of

jurisdictions for ministers, without much logic in putting us together. The Ministry of Industry and Commerce was linked to Tourism in the past and was split because of political considerations. Labour will no doubt also be split away from the Ministry of Industry and Commerce. ... Who knows what will happen in the next elections and who they will want in order to expand the ministry.

(Conclusions of interviews with former clerks from the Ministry of Labour in all regions of the Ministry of Industry, Commerce, and Employment— Jerusalem, the Centre, South, and North, December 2011)

Statements like this illustrate the attitudes of the clerks working in the ministry to the structural shifts that occurred with no planning or preparation for the employees, from political and not necessarily practical considerations. The employees were not prepared for the changes, and the system did not ensure that the new organisation was well balanced. Without these processes, the change was, as stated, only cosmetic. Externally, the organisation appears different, but this is only a "face-lift," with no actual inner parallel (Schein 2003; Lewin 1936). This argument is consistent with the views of employees in 2011, eight years after the change, and becomes stronger in light of the expansion of the authority in the Ministry of Industry, Commerce, and Employment and its name change in 2013 to the Ministry of the Economy and Religious Affairs.

The above approach is consistent with claims by researchers of the state in action, according to whom various interests stemming from opposing political views may create irregular state action.[71] The lack of clarity regarding the system's purposes and the public for whom the public reputation must be maintained created irregularities in the state action. As argued earlier, institutional changes carry a developmental pattern characterised by the accumulation of minor changes over a long period of time. In this sense, processes of stability and change are intertwined, and the process of stability is also characterised by conflict (Thelen 2004; Campbell 2004). The conflict surrounding the institutional arrangement does not reach its conclusion at the end of the institutionalisation because it influences the magnitude and the division of resources (Thelen 1999). Structural changes which were carried out due to political considerations, and not through coherent thought about the good of the public at large for whom it is important to maintain fairness, created conflicts and institutional pressure on those who enacted regulation and damaged the aims of the policy system that acts as the executing arm of the legislature, whose interest is the protection of women. I will mention here that the ministry is responsible for industry, commerce, and employment. It could, therefore, be said, in Bourdieu's language, that by reducing the power of managers who deal with employment and employees,

---

71 Berkovitch 2001, Rosenhek 1999; Gyenes 1988; Panagiotis 2010; Werum and Winders 2001.

the state at once expanded the field powers of branches dealing with industry and commerce, and this in effect weakened the power of the employees. These changes came about under the influence of neoliberalism. The change was manifested through the split that occurred in 2006 between enforcement and resolution jurisdictions within the framework of organisational reform. The significance of the change was the separation of law enforcement agencies. Thus criminal jurisdiction—the investigation that takes place against employers who have not applied as per the law for authorisation for dismissal—was transferred to clerks in the Enforcement Bureau, who are responsible for enforcing the law with regard to preventing the dismissal of pregnant women. The authority to deal with employers' requests remained, as in the past, with the Resolution Bureau. This structural change also led to dilemmas and a lack of clarity.

> In several cases, the transfer of critical information between the two enforcement mechanisms was avoided. If they do not send us the material on time, there is dragging of feet, and not long ago a case collapsed because of the statute of limitations, the employee in effect fell through the cracks and was dismissed illegally, and those who were meant to help her did not.

> (Interview with the Senior Supervisor for Women's Labour Law, Resolution Bureau, February 2008).

Following the split between the resolution and enforcement mechanisms, employers who sought to dismiss pregnant employees legally turned directly to the Resolution Bureau, while every week the Enforcement Bureau received complaints from women who were illegally dismissed.[72] The bureau sends a registered letter to the employer requesting a return to the previous situation[73] while the Resolution Bureau receives over a thousand requests per year from employers who applied for permission to legally dismiss a pregnant employee.

As was seen from arguments by supervisors in both bureaus, the driving orientation of their actions is different. While supervisors think in terms of welfare, which is a logic derived from their continuing socialisation in the Ministry of Labour that gives priority to the needs of the dismissed (an approach rooted in the first period), the Enforcement Bureau is characterised by the legal orientation of law enforcement, which lacks the moral element of protection for the weaker population. Thus, from the point of view of the enforcement system, dismissal of pregnant workers is only one link in the chain of many breaches of the law. Statements of this sort concerning the approach of enforcement workers may be heard in the Resolution Bureau:

---

72 In these cases a criminal investigation is undertaken, which can lead to a fine of up to NIS 134,000 or a year's imprisonment.

73 In 2010 this branch handled 250 complaints from employees who were illegally dismissed while pregnant.

Given that enforcement in this case in more complex
and collection of fines at that end is more ethical
and limited, the enforcement researchers prefer to
deal with other legal questions and do not make an
effort to enforce the Women's Labour Law. In other
words, I'm saying, they prefer the laws in which
there is money in the fines, rather than protecting
weak women.

(Interview with the Supervisor from the Resolution
Bureau, February 2008)

If so, according to the quote, in enforcement they are
interested in money, while the supervisors in resolution are
interested in protecting women. It is interesting to see how
even at the beginning of the period, blame was ascribed
to those responsible for enforcing the laws involving fines
with the hope of maximising profit—a behaviour in line
with the spirit of neoliberalism.

Apart from the differences exposed following the split—
between the neoliberal approach which views everything
through an economic filter and that of the paternalistic
resolution whose role is to protect the weak—the structural
shift led to continuing complications and a lack of
coordination in the state's actions. Within the framework
of the separation of powers, there is occasionally a double
bureaucratic process of two hearings before the ministry
clerks in both bureaus—enforcement and resolution.[74]

---

74 The problem of double hearings arose in a session of the
Committee for the Advancement of Women, February 2010.

An example of the complications caused by the separation may be seen in the case of Y, whom I was told of by two separate supervisors from two bureaus:

From the Resolution Supervisor	From the Enforcement Supervisor
"After she applied to enforcement, the employer's complaint reached us. We believed the employee's version that the dismissal was due to pregnancy, however, the length of time it took to work through the Enforcement Bureau led to the Statute of Limitations[75] for the file and made the assistance available within the framework of the resolution system irrelevant and useless. I feel bad that the employee lost her right to our protection. If it hadn't been for all of the unnecessary bureaucracy, she at least could have received a salary until the pregnancy and a part after the birth." (Interview with a supervisor of the Resolution Bureau, May 2007)	"The employer dismissed her without permission, and she applied to the Enforcement Bureau. In order not to get dragged into criminal matters, the employer later also applied to the Resolution Bureau to receive authorisation for dismissal. In retrospect, due to the lack of manpower in the legal department of the enforcement system, the case dragged on for a long time." (Interview with the supervisor of the Enforcement Bureau, May 2007)

It is noteworthy that until 2008 each complaint sent to the Enforcement Bureau carried a statute of limitations of one year. Following that date, the statute of limitations

---

75 In an enforcement process, the statute of limitations comes in after one year. In "resolution" there is no such issue because it is an administrative process.

was extended to five years, after an amendment to the law regarding the severity of the breach of the Women's Labour Law.[76] Applications to the Resolution Bureau carry no statute of limitations, as they are considered an administrative process whose results may be appealed for up to 45 days following the decision.[77] These statements embody the way the state actions are designed as well as discrepancies between the spirit of the law and its de facto implementation. Meanwhile, the supervisors testify to the fact that the state's actions, in fact, complicate matters, and as a direct result of this harm is caused to the clients.

A qualitative analysis of the various words used by the supervisors reflects differing approaches to the state's actions and its role. The supervisor in enforcement presents an instrumentally administrative approach: "the employer dismissed," "presented an application," "the file dragged on", while the approach presented by the enforcement clerk is more humane, sensitive, welfare-linked, and makes use of expressions such as "we believed the employee," "I feel bad that she lost," and so forth. The manifestation of the discrepancies in approach creates an atmosphere of lack of both communication and cooperation between two bureaus who both answer to a single government ministry. Thus, supervisors in the two bureaus complain

---

76 Telephone conversation with supervisor, September 2013.

77 Telephone conversation with senior supervisor, September 2013.

about one another that "they are driven by considerations of power and prestige, and their actions conflict with the spirit of the ministry. The conflict between bureaus has reached a state of disconnect, and therefore they did not send us information" (Interview with the supervisor of the Resolution Bureau, May 2007), or, as one supervisor from enforcement summed it up, "It's a case of watch my back, and I'll watch yours" (October 2007). The supervisor was referring to the lack of cooperation and transfer of information among bureaus.

Furthermore, in later interviews that I carried out with enforcement clerks who had been with the ministry for two years, I was told:

> The law is bad for employers. Israel is the only country that has this sort of law. The employer is stuck with an employee just because his lawyer did not include an article about employees for fixed periods. … A temporary worker, who became pregnant while replacing another employee on maternity leave. … The law protected her despite the fact that in fact they should have dismissed her. With this sort of law, it is no wonder that employers think twice before employing women.

(Interview, February 2014)

This sort of statement reflects the increasing influence of neoliberal ideology, which also fits the stance of the then-Minister of the Economy Naftali Bennet, who said, "We will clean out every regulation" (Globes Conference, January 14). True to his word, in the first year of his appointment, 80% of petitions for dismissal were granted. Within this context, it could be said that the supervisors (SLB, Street-Level Bureaucrats, located in direct contact with clients) in the Enforcement Bureau are driven by the neoliberal spirit. This spirit emerged from the minister's bureau and trickled "down from above" to the way of thinking and action patterns in the field.

If so, it could be said that the structural, in-office shift created a double bureaucracy and complications in the performance of two similar hearings for clients—pregnant women and their employers. This fits the theory of the "state in action" that was presented in the theoretical section of the book, according to which a lack of internal cooperation in the ministry, stemming from differing institutional interests and different approaches, has created irregularities in the language of the law and thus a complicated implementation that directly harms those whom the law is meant to be protecting. Furthermore, it is clear that welfare logic alongside conflicting neoliberal logic developed within the habitus of the bureaucrats, and from there the active strategies emerged. The use of the logic of action is done within the context of power relations and interests of groups who choose from among all the approaches available to them, according to their interests and to the limitations of actors in the field. I now wish to examine the source of the welfare logic that shaped the actions of the Enforcement Bureau supervisors, and to move from a description of the structural shift to an analysis of its influence and the characteristics of the second period upon the results of the regulatory actions.

The Logic of Regulatory Action—'Patriarchal Inertia'

Within the regulatory framework, numerous hearings were held for employees and employers in four centres around the country. From 1998 on, the process was performed by female supervisors, only one of whom had been given legal training. The hearing lasted on average 20–30 minutes, however, there are cases in which the hearings were much shorter. The employee was not permitted to bring anyone into the hearing apart from a lawyer who was not permitted to intervene meanwhile the employer was permitted to attend with a companion as well as a lawyer who was allowed to intervene when required. The difference in these instructions stems from the nature of the testimony. The employee gives her version, and the employer is examined under a caution. During the hearing, the supervisor questions the employee concerning her personal, family, and socioeconomic situation. Furthermore, the employee is asked about the circumstances of her dismissal and the nature of her work in general and during pregnancy in particular. The employer is called for investigation after receiving a letter in which the senior supervisor explains, "The purpose of the law is to provide the pregnant employee with special protection from harm during the period in which her *status is inferior*[78] to that of other male or female employees, and during which she would find it difficult to find alternative employment if dismissed" (formal letter sent to employers, quoted on December 10, 2009).

In the investigation of the employer, the burden of proof, that there is no connection between their request for dismissal and the pregnancy, is upon them. At times, the committee does not have the evidence to decide whether to authorise the dismissal or to reject the application. In this case, they request the women and/or the employer to provide further evidence, such as productivity reports for the employee. As of 2010, it was decided that a ruling had to be made within 30 days of the date of the investigation. In fact, the system rarely meets this target.

Findings from this study reveal that the regulatory system's action patterns are not uniform, and the results of the process are often reliant upon the discretion of the bureaucrats and the logic they employ within the framework of the hearing in each and every case. On the one hand, it was noted that the logic of action of the more senior supervisors in the Resolution Bureau was influenced by what I call "patriarchal inertia," while, on the other, the logic of action among the relatively new supervisors in the Enforcement Bureau was driven by the logic of economic efficiency. The expression "patriarchal

78 Author's emphasis.

inertia" was created on the basis that the source of change in the labour market lies in social, political, and economic changes and these all affected the prevailing gender approach, which in turn influenced the regulatory actions. As the approaches became more and more distant ideologically, the power struggles in the field intensified. Thus "patriarchal inertia" is defined as an inherent approach based upon traditional-cultural logic, which sees the state's role as follows; women must be protected because they are incapable of protecting themselves due to their "inferior status in relation to other employees."[79] This approach does not conduct dialogue with women but relies on the policy-makers and decision-makers— men/clerks—in matters of the best interests of women. The approach stems from "the power of inertia" of the historically unequal treatment that women experienced in Israel (and all over the world), which determines that the role of the woman is a caregiver for the family cell, and thus her place in the labour market is seen as secondary.

At the core of the expression "patriarchal inertia" lies the assumption that even if the spirit of the times changes, the action strategies will continue to be taken from the norms and values found in the habitus of the supervisors. These are manifested within a framework of thought that guides the actions of policy implementers, even though the policy-makers already employ another mode of thought.

---

79 A quote from the letter by the senior supervisor to employers.

These cultural frameworks create a different interpretation of the law, which leads to conflicts among the legislature and the enforcing organs. Thus, irregularities deepen, and the attempt to protect pregnant women from dismissal is harmed. Translation of the law into regulatory practice through a hearing at the Ministry of Industry, Commerce, and Employment takes place according to criteria that were established in the 1980s and since then have not undergone any significant changes. Thus, for example, in each of close to one hundred observations, the employees were asked to respond to questions concerning their partners' employment, about whether they would receive unemployment benefits if they were dismissed, and whether their families had financial obligations such as a mortgage or rent. When asked about the connection between the questions and the state's decision whether to protect or to permit dismissal, the supervisor operating the system answered, "The Women's Labour Law has always belonged to a group of social laws. We are not here to protect only the woman but rather the entire family. If their economic situation is not good, we take it into account" (Interview, June 2008).

The set structure of the questions demonstrates the social nature of the system, however, at the same time, it reflects the dependency of the woman on the family and thus denies the defamilisation approach. In this way the rule of domestication and "patriarchal inertia" of the system becomes entrenched. "If I see that there is a case in which someone is very unfortunate, even without a connection to the pregnancy, if she is the breadwinner, I try to protect her as no one else will do it" (Interview, June 2012). Despite the changes, it is clear that some logic remains from earlier periods and with these changes are the problems inherent in them. Examples of the second logic of action will be presented below when we examine the fragmentation in the state's action.

Employment Services

In keeping with the winds blowing from the labour ministries, bringing with them a large number of permits for dismissal during pregnancy, in the mid-1980s we also discover that a further player in the field—the Employment Services—did not make it easier for the dismissed employees, despite the fact that no employment solutions were found for them. In this context, it appears that the start of the second period continued the institutional consensus regarding the state's actions, which also characterised the first period. Women who were dismissed during their pregnancy were told by the Employment Services that there was no work for them, however, they still had to appear thrice weekly in order to receive their unemployment benefits.

> When I told them at the Labour Bureau that I was expecting, they said they had no work to give

me, only unemployment benefits of 160,000 Old Shekels. In order to receive this money I need to drag myself there three times weekly by bus, and show up knowing for sure that I would not be given employment. I think this entire situation borders on the absurd. It's as if this country is against increasing the birthrate.

(Nitzan, November 13, 1985, *Yedioth Ahronoth*)

However, despite the fact that the traditional, paternalistic approach of protecting employees through the state clerks remained unchanged at the beginning of the period, changes occurred in its actions over time. The change is manifested in special exceptions for pregnant women attending the Employment Bureau. They were not required to produce the permit for their dismissal. According to clerks in the service, "It was an unwritten rule whose purpose was to help the women and make it easier for them, given that the employers they could be sent to would not hire them in any case while they were pregnant, and it was a shame to bother them in their condition" (Interview with clerk, December 2007). This reflects a pattern of action that became entrenched in the middle of the second period, incorporating the cultural changes that occurred within the logic of action of the clerks responsible for employee welfare, within a neoliberal economic reality. This logic may be explained in the spirit of "patriarchal inertia," which is based on the premise that the action strategies of Employment Services' clerks are a cultural result that represents the changing values in society.

Thus, on the background of withdrawal of welfare policy, a welfare action strategy was created. This change could be explained based on the claims of researchers, according to which the political climate in Israel at the beginning of the 21st century is characterised by "withdrawal," or shrinking, by withdrawing and the weakening of the welfare state (Dahan 2006). This policy is put into action by the government ministries, including the Exchequer and the Ministry of Industry, Commerce, and Employment. The latter led programmes[80] whose aim was to encourage integration within the labour market through maximum reduction of income security payments. Employment Services also fell under the auspices of the Ministry of Industry, Commerce, and Employment, however, they undertook different action and employed a distinct normative system. The conflicting logical results between the two bodies who share a field—under the wings of the Ministry of Industry, Commerce, and Employment—will be addressed toward the end of the chapter.

The Logic of Promoting Gender-Based Equality-Action by Women's Organisations

Along with the sweep of neoliberalism into the political-economic discourse in Israel, from the 1980s a clear increase appeared in the influence of liberal feminism, which

---

80 Such as "MeHaLev" (From Secure Income to Secure Employment), Wisconsin and "Employment Lights."

came from the United States and affected both legislation in the Knesset, such as the Law for Equal Opportunity Employment (1988), and the manner of thinking and operation of some of the women's groups in Israel. This trend led the women's organisations to represent women dismissed during pregnancy in court, an act which somewhat raised the rights of pregnant women in the labour force in the public eye and forced the Ministry of labour to act more decisively to enforce the existing law.[81] During this period, the matter of dismissals during pregnancy was tabled, focusing on criticism of the ease with which the permits were granted. This protest emerged in the media, who demonstrated public interest in the phenomenon of dismissals during pregnancy,[82] and in the

---

81 Nitzan 1985, Enosh 1997; Berenzon 1984; Elah 1989.

82 The search was done in the newspaper archives under the keywords "dismissals in pregnancy" and "women's labour law," from the 1950s until 2012. Examples of headlines: "A Matter of Discrimination: a Guide for Employers to Employment and Dismissal during Pregnancy" (Dobrovitzky 2008); "Thousands of Pregnant Women Fired without Permission" (Kotz-Bar 2002); "Without Law and Order, the Annual Report on Citizens' Rights Paints a Morbid Picture" (Tzimuki and Paz 2004); "They Earn 22% Less than Men — A Draft to Expand Protective Instructions for Women Against Harm from Employers during Pregnancy" (Lior Gad and Shivi Chaim 2005; "Can I be Dismissed Even Though I'm Pregnant and They Prove There is No Work in the Company; Questions and Answers Regarding Dismissals during Pregnancy in

proposals for amendments to the legislation that were put forth primarily by women's organisations, action which in itself received quite a bit of media coverage.

Complaints by female employees reached the women's organisations even before they arrived at the Ministry of Labour (Elah 1989; Nitzan 1985), and one could assume that the women's organisations sometimes acted as an alternative route to the Ministry of Labour's mechanism. Two central processes seem to form the pattern of action for the women's groups in the Labour relations field, which deals with protection of pregnant employees. On the one hand the American influence, both in the feminist agenda and regarding women's rights in general, and in terms of the most efficient path to protecting women, led

---

Cooperation with "Employee Hotline" (no name 2002); "Questions and Answers with Employee Hotline, Can and Employee be Dismissed during Pregnancy (no name 2007); "There is a Pass — No Thoughts about a Plan for Protective Laws for the Employment of Pregnant Women: (Barak Beni 2002); "A Kick in the Soft Parts — 66% of the Complaints That Reach the Women's Lobby Hotline Are from Pregnant Women Who Have Been Dismissed" (Regev and Feingold 2007); "A Pregnant Officer Was Dismissed from the IDF As Well" (Regev 2004); "Pregnant Woman Dismissed after 5.5 Months of Employment and Will Receive Compensation" (Regev 2006); "A Bad Year for Working Women, Following the Women's Lobby Report That Indicates Downturn for Working Women in Israel, Discrimination of Mothers Based on Pregnancy" (Regev 2007).

the courts and the state's institutions to a deciding arena in the field of their rights. On the other hand, the most important women's group, Na'amat, whose power until 1985 stemmed from being a member of the general workers' union (the National Worker's Organisation), could no longer rely on the corporate relations framework among the employees, the unions, and the state who guaranteed the workers' rights, and they too entered the field of labour relations (Zilber 1997; Berenzon 1984).

The legal bureau started by Na'amat in 1985, the year considered a turning point in the political and economic rule in Israel (Shalev 1999) and the beginning of the neoliberal era was immediately flooded by numerous complaints from pregnant women who feared dismissal or who had been illegally dismissed. According to Na'amat figures, 17% of all the applications for help in the year the bureau was founded were from pregnant employees who had been dismissed (Argaman-Barnea 1985). The suits against employers in these cases contributed to the general workers' union in the struggle to maintain power against the employers—who were getting stronger—and within the framework to maintain their position as an organisation that protects pregnant employees. Furthermore, in the same year, Na'amat initiated an amendment to the Women's Labour Law, expanding the protection from dismissal to include a period following the return from maternity leave (Amendment 1985).

Following a wave of mass dismissals during pregnancy that were covered by the media,[83] and after a number of court decisions that reflected the success of legal defence provided by Na'amat's lawyers, the movement's chairperson, Ms. Masha Lubelsky, was quoted as saying: "Na'amat promises to launch further suits in cases of discrimination against female employees and to warn employers that this sort of dismissal will not be quietly ignored" (Argaman-Barnea 1985). From this sort of statement, one learns of the increasing pressure brought to bear on the non-state player, the alternative channel for women's protection, who challenged the actions of the formal players in the field for not doing enough to prevent gender-based inequality. During this period, 100 out of the 600 women who turned to WIZO were dismissed during pregnancy (Nitzan 1985). At the same time, Na'amat clearly came out against the employers, claiming that they were taking advantage of the economic slump in order to get rid of manpower and, in particular, pregnant women or those who had recently given birth. Furthermore, in 1985 Na'amat proposed a law according to which it would be impossible to dismiss an employee immediately following maternity leave. The activity by Na'amat in this area, in fact, led to an amendment in the law, expanding the state's protection to include a period following maternity leave.

---

83 Kotz- Bar 2002; Lior and Shivi 2005; Regev 2004, 2006, 2007; Tzimuki and Paz 2004; Barak 2002; Regev and Feingold 2007.

Along with the winds of feminism blowing from the United States, a women's lobby was founded, which was an independent and non-affiliated body that worked to promote women through legislation, lobbied the Knesset and raised public awareness based on liberal feminist principles of the creation of a successful, achieving woman, similar to men. One of their first acts was to examine, in the mirror of reality, those recommendations submitted 10 years earlier in the report on the status of women in Israel. They concluded that only a few of the recommendations had been implemented and that the status of women in Israel still required improvement (Argaman-Barnea 1985). [84]It was therefore found that women's groups at the start of the neoliberal period were a supportive, alternative, or complementary channel[85] to the state regulation whose purpose was to protect pregnant employees. Thus, we see in this period the beginning of the fragmentation in the state's actions and the first cracks in the state homogeneity, which will be discussed later.

Women's groups often argued against the state, claiming it acted with no greater, organised plan, and that the legislation was carried out with no proper regulations but with patches and corrections based on the Women's Labour Law. They claimed that the women required

84 "Women Go Home," Yedioth Ahronoth, October 27, 1985.
85 For example in cases when an lawyer from the women's groups represented female employees in court.

protection, such as exists in the law for employees who leave for reserve duty. This regulation functions[86] according to the Law of Released Soldiers Return to Work (1949), within whose framework the Employment Committees According to Law 41a were established. Within this context, there are clear regulations in which a committee is struck, which then instructs the employer to respond to claims of prejudicial dismissal within 10 days. The committee is composed of four members: the chair, who is able to act as court judge; union representatives; and legal and professional people, who carefully weigh each request for dismissal. The compensation paid for illegal dismissals is up to five times the salary, and in each case, the employee does not return to the place of work that sought her dismissal. These employees are represented pro bono by lawyers. The difference in the higher position in the field held by men who serve in the reserves as opposed to the lower status of women dismissed during pregnancy is clear from the make-up of the committee, in their jurisdiction and in the instructions and clear assistance granted within this framework. These distinctions are a clear demonstration of the inequality inherent in the state's behaviour toward dismissals in pregnancy as opposed to dismissals during reserve duty. Accordingly, the claims

---

86 According to Roni Ashkenazi of the Ministry of Defense, Chief of Employment and Career Army, at the Committee for the Advancement of the Status of Women February 16, 2010.

by women's organisations of patchwork legislation are analysed through the differences in the Women's Labour Law and the Law of Released Soldiers.

According to the protocols of the Knesset committees (February 16, 2010), it was found that the senior supervisors for the Women's Labour Law were required, more than once, to handle the complaints of women's organisations who were upset by the amount of time taken to reach decisions. In the words of Bracha Sa'ad, the new Histadrut representative and a member of the Status of Women Committee, "This is the time that the employer abuses the employee." In response, the senior supervisor said:

> I do not know what "abuses" means. We do our work, and it is the work of the complaint itself. Regarding the rest, we are unable to do anything. Our intention is to make the process more efficient. We are just starting out, and the way looks good, and I hope it is successful.

The clash between the demands of the employers' organisations and those of the women reveals something of the conflicts that characterise and form the field of action under discussion. In terms of the theory of "street-level bureaucracy" (Lipsky 1980), it could be said that the acts of the state clerks are in fact a result of intertwined pressures, which contribute to an understanding of the theory of policy implementation "from the bottom up," as manifested in the comments of the senior supervisor:

The union of employers claims that it is difficult to get permission, and the women's organisation claims it is simple to get permission. In fact, we find ourselves within a conflict of interests between the two organisations. We take into account all comments by the organisations in order to make the matter more efficient, and not because we agree with what they say. We listen carefully in order to make the process more efficient. When a request is received, the tendency is for the employer to minimise explanations, too, and to bring them up only when his version is accepted. This, in fact, means that the employee is not exposed from the start to all of the employer's claims. She thus arrives unprepared, and then the process is dragged out while we request responses from one party and then the other. In light of this, we decided that a case would be opened only when all of the claims and proof had been already submitted to the other party, both by the employer and the employee. In this situation, we receive all responses, and the parties arrive prepared unless they have something to add to their versions. We expect this to shorten the process and that the employee will be much better prepared to make her claims. We began this as a pilot even before the procedure was publicised, and are analysing the process. It looks good, and the employees are much more prepared. There was a pilot with the committee (as in the case of the reserve duty), but I did not find that it helped very much in reaching a decision. It helped somewhat to shorten the time because the file was ready.

(Protocols of the Knesset Committees, February 16, 2010)

The senior supervisor's comments fit the definition by policy researchers mentioned in part in the theoretical section of the book. According to this, a change in policy is liable to emerge as a result of internal and external pressures (Howlett and Cashore 2009; Howlett 2009), and street-level bureaucrats carry significant weight in the de facto implementation of policy (Lipsky 1980). The pressures brought to bear by women's organisations and by the employers were addressed by the senior supervisor, who says that "we listen carefully in order to make the process more efficient." This response is appropriate for the approach known as "management by groping along," a model which functions in many cases of implementation of new policy (Goffen-Sarig 2004), and is based on learning through doing, or a quick translation of ideas into action as well as the introduction of change when needed.

The senior supervisor continues, "We began this as a pilot even before the procedure was publicised." We therefore see that the implementation process was not systematic but rather dynamic, and it addressed issues that arose through trial and error. This case exemplifies the influence of women's organisations upon the acts of the SLB clerks and on the de facto implementation of policy.

Furthermore, we understand from the senior supervisor's comments that the spirit of the reserve duty model is seen as a comparable process to the work of the prevention mechanism. This spirit creates conflict (even if latent) among resources in the field that do not belong to the system whose aim is to prevent dismissals in relation to a system meant to avoid dismissals during reserve duty.

Women's organisations and members of Knesset generally see eye to eye in the matter of dismissal during pregnancy. In the second period, women's organisations played a respectable role in their involvement in the matter, in influencing the legislation and the administrative process. This involvement can be seen in the significant representation in each of the Knesset committees that deal with the Women's Labour Law. Thus, for example, in the annual report that took place on March 12, 2012 in the matter of the Women's Labour Law—dismissals of pregnant employees/fertility treatments—close to half of those invited to the debate in the Committee for the Advancement of the Status of Women were representatives of WIZO, Na'amat, and the Women's Lobby.

We can learn about the level of involvement of women's organisations in the issue from comments by MK Orit Zuaretz. Her comments were made against the backdrop of a discussion that took place by the Committee for the Advancement of the Status of Women, dealing with the question of why an employer was permitted to attend accompanied by a lawyer or any other person, while a woman employee could not:

> The one who generally attends with the victim is not usually a lawyer but a companion from one of the organisations. If there is a need, we make sure there is a representative from one of the organisations to accompany them. We are changing this situation also in cases of victims of prostitution, who arrive with volunteers to submit a complaint. There is no reason that women should not come with the companion of their choosing, whether they feel safer when their partner accompanies them, or their friend. I believe that this is an issue which needs to be addressed.
>
> (Protocol 135, Committee for the Advancement of the Status of Women, March 12, 2012)

It is interesting to see how Zuaretz, a member of Knesset, emphasises the cooperation between members of Knesset and the women's organisations with the word "we." In other words, the legislature and the women's organisations together "will make sure there is a representative from one of the women's organisations to accompany them." The discrepancies between the manner in which the supervisors interpret the law and do not permit companions into the hearings, and the approach of the legislature and the women's organisations, are just an example of the conflict that can emerge at the level of the state clerk who is responsible for implementing the law. Using

Bourdieu's language, one could say that the influence of neoliberalism increased the struggle within the field due to the exertion of economic and political power, which affected the power struggles within the labour relations field. Thus, for example, the entry of women's groups into the field influenced the regulator and managed to create improvement in the status of women, if only because they were given the opportunity to make their voices heard. If so, we will find that along with the historical shifts—the rise of neoliberalism and the decrease in union power—there is an increase in the conflictual space of the organs that exert opposing power. Here Bourdieu's argument that what creates the otherness of a period is not necessarily a shared culture but a shared "problematic" emerges, and the system change is a result of the struggle—a change that would not occur in a homogeneous period. The results of these struggles will now be examined.

Fragmentation in the State's Actions As a Result of Power Struggles in the Field

Researchers studying conflicts in the state's actions are in agreement for the most part that the various interests that stem from opposing political approaches are liable to create fragmented state action. [87]As mentioned, the pressure from women's organisations and from the courts

---

87 Berkovitch 2001; Rosenhek 1999; Werum and Winders 2001; Glenn et al. 1988; Panagiotis 2010.

led right at the start of the period to the beginning of formal and more organised procedures for caring for pregnant employees whose employers sought to dismiss them. These procedures continued to develop during recent decades, but alongside them, there was an expansion of the conflicts of interest that form the actions of the regulatory mechanisms originating from several structural shifts that had occurred in the Ministry of Industry, Commerce, and Employment.

The state's acts in the context of protecting the pregnant employees are a reflection of the events in the labour market. Therefore, we find a growing fragmentation in the attempts of the Ministry of Industry, Commerce, and Employment to protect pregnant employees. The fragmentation stems from structural shifts, from changes in approaches to roles and from the various interests, and a new view of the public reputation of regulation and state bodies who are involved in it. I would now like to present three of the fragmentations which were located in the state's action.

First Fragmentation: To Weaken the Weak—The Case of Human Resource Employees

The level of fragmentation of the state's action is highly influenced by discrepancies among the events in the legal field and their translation into regulatory implementation. Despite this, the following case reveals that the discourse struggles that characterised the labour market field also affected the uniformity in the spirit of the legislature.

As stated, it is common to argue that in Israel there is a relatively advanced law in the area of the protection of pregnant employees. As far back as the early days of the state, encouragement was given to the entry of women into the labour market, along with the legislation of laws whose intention was to protect women in the labour force and ensure places of work for pregnant women in order to permit them to return following maternity leave.[88] Initially, the Israeli legislation was characterised by paternalistic thought, which emphasised the protection of women. However, in recent years, in keeping with shifts in the western world, the state also sought to adopt a similar legislative approach, aimed at promoting gender-based equal opportunity in the work world in the spirit of gender-based human rights discourse.

From the frequent debates in the Knesset[89] attempts are made to create an equation that will create protection for women during pregnancy and after giving birth, while fulfilling the linkage to the feminist legislative approach, which promotes the meritocratic ethos—as opposed to the previous legislation, which "protected" women or mothers of children, yet in fact discriminated against them. Thus, for example, the case mentioned in

---

88 Fogel-Bijoy 1999; Raddai et al 1995; Doron 1992, 1994; Yizre'eli 2000; Sevirsky 1999.

89 See, for example the protocol from February 2010, February 2008, January 2007.

this chapter, discusses where in late 2007 an amendment was made to the Women's Labour Law, and according to the amendment it would no longer be possible to pay the salary of an employee who gave birth while she was still at home, because the employer wanted to dismiss her at the end of the maternity leave in any case (adding 45 days of notice). The protective period was thus extended to 60 days, with the condition of returning to the labour market. By extending the length of protection for women after giving birth, the legislature sought to encourage women to return to the labour market and thus return them to financial independence. We see here how the legislating apparatus tried to halt the "protective" approach, which had been preserved from the previous period, and to introduce new rules in which the pregnancy and post-partum periods were time-constrained. Furthermore, despite the relatively advanced legislation and despite the clear intent by the legislature to promote gender-based equality and prevent the dismissal of pregnant women or women who had given birth, we find fragmentation here.

The source of the irregularities is in the conflicting legislation between the Women's Labour Law, Article 9a, which has been in existence since the first decades of the state, and Article 12a of the Law for Employment through Human Resource Contractors, which came into being in 2008. While the former instructs protecting all women from dismissal in pregnancy—as long as they have been employed for over six months—in the latter the Knesset legislated a conflicting law (Human Resource Contractors Law, 1996) according to which the dismissal of women is permitted during pregnancy if they were temporarily employed through human resource contractors, and as long as their dismissal occurred during a period that is not longer than nine months from the date of their hiring.

The background to this law rests in the desire of the legislator to deal with the reality of flexible employment arrangements typical of the "new labour world" that functions according to the rules of the neoliberal game. Therefore, the law instructs the employer who hired the services of an employee through a human resources contractor to hire the employee as a regular employee, and at the end of the probationary period to grant them the same rights and benefits as other employees. During the initial nine months of employment, there is, therefore, a temporary employment contract between the employee and the employer. At the end of the period, the employer can, as stated, choose whether to recruit the employee, to return them to the human resource agency employing them, or to request a permit from the Ministry of Industry, Commerce, and Employment for an employment extension of up to six months. This is an apparently enlightened provision that fits the spirit of the period, although in practice it conflicts with the intention of the legislature in Article 9a to prevent dismissals during pregnancy, as we see in the comments of the senior supervisor for the Women's Labour Law:

In the past, I used to hold hearings for representatives of the human resource agencies, and I requested to see, on the lists, assignment possibilities for employees after they had been dismissed by the employer. At the time, the responsibility fell on the human resources agencies, but today it's simply discharged. *There is no doubt that the Human Resource Contractors Law contradicts the Women's Labour Law.*[90] I receive many submissions from women who were let go because of this article, and there is nothing I can do, their dismissals are legal as they were hired on a temporary basis. The moment an employer discovers that she is pregnant, it is rare that they will say that they are interested, after such a short period, in hiring this sort of employee. The hiring agencies have nothing to do with her while she is pregnant, and the worst is that these women fall through the cracks; they are not eligible for our protection under the Women's Labour Law, and they have not accumulated enough seniority to receive unemployment benefits from the National Insurance Institute.

(Interview with the Senior Supervisor for the Women's Labour Law, September 2012)

As to the question of how such a conflict is possible within the law, the senior supervisor replied, "The law is meant to protect women as well as employers. An employer should not feel that now he is 'stuck' with an employee

---

90 Author's emphasis.

who will not be at work more than she will be." In these comments we see, on the one hand, the approach that employing a pregnant woman is an obstacle or a burden to the employer, and on the other we see in them the results of the fragmentation, the absolute injury to women, and their being left in a situation that makes it difficult for them to earn a living or support a functioning economic unit.

On the other hand, we hear from an accountant who was employed through a human resources contractor, "In my opinion the human resource contractors should be removed from the labour market because they only look after their own interests. They have a give and no take approach. In my case the behaviour was humiliating and hurtful" (Survey, 2006).

In light of this, we could attempt to answer the question: How are the discrepancies created between the neoliberal approach and the gender-based rights discourse, and what is the cost of these discrepancies? The senior supervisor's comments highlight the depth of the fragmentation in the spirit of the legislature. From one point of view, the legislator's approach is characterised by an attempt to promote the gender-based equality discourse, with the intention of allowing the women to maintain her place of work, as in the instruction to return her to the place of work following maternity leave and thus reduce the gender-based inequality. From the other viewpoint, the legislation is characterised by a neoliberal approach that highlights the economic good of the employer and his interests, at the expense of the pregnant employee.

Indeed, according to the figures of the past decade, there has been a downward trend in the rate of employment of contract workers. In 2002 human resources employees made up 4.3% of all the employees in Israel—lower than the figure from 2000 when employees hired by contracting agencies formed 5.8% of the labour force, 65% of whom were women. It is worth noting that in keeping with this, it is significant that legislation concerning employment after nine months of work was in fact implemented by the employers. Over the years, there was a drop in the amount of those employed through human resources agencies, and in 2009 they formed only 3.5% of all employees, of whom 1.3% were women and 1.2% were mothers of children under the age of 4. From this, we see that among 18–64-year-old women, new mothers formed the majority of those employed by human resource contractors (Nadiv 2005; Pichtelberg-Bermetz and Harris 2011).

Nonetheless, in contrast to the downward trend in the rate of those employed by human resource contractors as seen from 2002 on, in 2002–2003, the year in which the survey participants were dismissed, 12% of all women for whom requests to dismiss had been filed were employed by human resource contractors. This figure is almost three times higher than the overall rate of those employed (both men and women) by human resource contractors during that period. According to the survey's findings, for over half of the women, not even a minimal effort was made to find alternative employment after the employer submitted the request for dismissal, as the law demands.

The relatively high rates of women employed through human resource contractors and dismissed during pregnancy strengthen the argument that employment through irregular means is considered "bad," unstable hiring that is mediated directly to the secondary labour market, which is temporary and discriminatory (Nadiv 2005). The high proportion of women dismissed during pregnancy who were employed by human resource contractors reflects a strong reality where the labour market is located within two conflicting discourses: the neoliberal discourse, which further weakens the powerless, and the gender-based human rights discourse, which attempts to minimise the gender discrepancies in the labour market. Furthermore, given that the legislature itself acts in a non-uniform manner in this matter, the fragmentation is strengthened both at the implementational level and at the ideological level, and it significantly damages the ability of the state to truly protect the pregnant employees.

The internal discrepancies in the spirit of the legislature, alongside the conflicts in the state's action, reduce the ability of the state to promote significant social change and reduce inequality.

The senior supervisor's comments hint that she herself accepts the premise that pregnant women are inferior employees, "An employer should not have to feel that he is now 'stuck' with an employee." This approach fits the patriarchal logic entrenched in the first period, and we are thus witnesses to the unchanging habitus of the players in the field. This assumption is particularly significant in understanding the logic at the basis of the state's actions through which the discrepancies are created between the legislation and enforcement.

The Second Fragmentation: Weakening the Weak—The Case of Dismissing Pregnant Teachers

Within the neoliberal logic of action, the state took upon itself many of the employment patterns that characterise the private sector, and with these the responsibility for maximum employment efficiency and flexibility as the largest employer in the market. This stands in opposition to the principle of tenure, which still applies to employees of the State of Israel. The attempts by state elements to allow flexibility of the civil labour force in the spirit of neoliberalism, through abolition of the principle of tenure (as is done in other sectors of the Israeli market) met with sharp responses from the civil service union—one of the strongest unions in the market—and was subsequently rejected. The combination of legal protection and the tenure of civil servants were intended to protect pregnant civil servants as best as possible, however, the inherent contradiction between the logic driving the state as a regulator and the logic driving it as an employer led to the opposite result, which in fact left the civil servants, the teachers, exposed to dismissals even more than other women.

The clearest example of the structural fragmentation emerged in the agreement signed in 2000 between then-Minister of Education Limor Livnat—responsible for the largest employer of women in the Israeli market—and the senior supervisor of the Women's Labour Law at the time, Lawyer Rivka Makover. This agreement almost automatically authorised the dismissals of non-permanent pregnant teachers, as submitted by the ministry. In keeping with this agreement, Article 29 of the memo from the senior section chief for human resources in education for 2002–2003 stated:

> In requests to authorise dismissals for pregnant employees, there is no obligation to mention the name of the teacher replaced by the teacher about whom the request has been submitted—instead, it shall mention that the ministry promises to place this teacher *if the requirements of the system and the hours available at the school permit this.*[91]
>
> (Ministry of Education website: www.education,gov.il, September 23, 2013)

---

91 Author's emphasis.

In an interview with one of the supervisors following the Makover-Livnat agreement of 2000, the supervisor stated:

> According to this agreement, the regulatory system will authorise the dismissals of pregnant, non-permanent, teachers in their first years of employment while promising to absorb them back into the ministry following their maternity leave. Needless to say that while the dismissal permits are granted automatically by us, there is no mechanism in place to oversee the second half of the agreement or the re-absorption of the teachers into employment. I know that there have been cases where teachers with less seniority entered positions before pregnant teachers returned from maternity leave, despite this being against the law. They [at the Ministry of Education] dismiss the teachers every time they get pregnant and then re-hire them so they won't earn seniority during the maternity leave period. They then place them in positions according to the seniority earned up to the pregnancy. If someone has less seniority than her, priority must be given to the teacher who has had a baby, but in fact, this does not always happen. The Ministry of Education is just like everybody else, although in my opinion it is a conveyor belt—I am always supposed to grant permission.

Question: Why is there an arrangement specifically for a profession which is clearly female?

Answer: The agreements made are supremely unfair. It is true, the female teachers, in this case, are harmed and it comes from within the interpretative framework of the Women's Labour Law, according to their discretion.

(From an interview with a supervisor at the Resolution Bureau, August 2005)

The need for this far-reaching cut involving the number of teachers' standards on the one hand and the difficulty in dismissing teachers with permanence on the other have turned the system for dismissal during pregnancy into an available, simple solution, which is in utter opposition to the logic displayed by the state in legislation. Unlike the minor attempt to dismiss teachers in the main labour market as in the first period, in the second period, no internal state debate ending in a consensus decision was attempted in order to halt this. Only a broad public protest by the teachers and their unions led, in the end, to an attempt to enforce the second part of the agreement and guarantee new absorption of teachers in the Ministry of Education. Against the background of massive teacher dismissals that occurred following the speaker's report, a wide public call of complaint arose regarding the dismissal of pregnant teachers. The criticism was echoed in the print media (Trabelsi-Haddad 2003), where the Ministry of Education[92] promised there would be no dismissals of pregnant teachers.

---

92 Yedioth Ahronoth , 19.4.2005.

In reality, however, the teachers continued to appear for hearings and numerous permits were granted for their dismissal[93] with no detailed hearings, as was common for other professions. Of close to one hundred observations carried out for this study, nearly 15% were for teachers. Each investigation lasted five minutes at the most— sometimes to the frustration of the supervisors themselves chairing the hearings. One supervisor explained, "This should not take longer than two minutes; we are only a rubber stamp here" (January 2006). Only following personnel changes in the role of senior supervisor for the law in 2006 and in the position of minister of education that same year (Yuli Tamir replaced Limor Livnat) was there apparently more care taken, and this followed ideological thought patterns that were different from those guiding the Makover-Livnat agreement in 2000. In this context, one could examine the theoretical argument that the conflict around the institutional arrangement does not end with the expiration of the institutional period because it influences the magnitude and division of resources. It is difficult to appeal during routine times, however, when a new window of opportunity opens up, the conflict will soon reappear (Thelen 1999). Thus, for example, it was noted that personnel changes such as Livnat's approach as opposed to Tamir's affected the attitude of the clerks responsible for enforcing the agreement in full. As a clerk

---

93 Observation at hearings, interviews with supervisors from 2005-2009.

in the Ministry of Education explained, "In Livnat's day, no one checked us. Now even their senior supervisor in the Ministry of Industry, Commerce, and Employment drives us crazy, and here, the Minister sees the return of the teachers as highly important, so we now take much more care with this" (Interview, May 2008). In reality, however, of the list of teachers who returned to work, it appears that this is only a tiny percentage of the number of teachers who were dismissed each year during Yuli Tamir's term. The clerk addressed this, "You should have seen the ease with which they used to let me dismiss people [during Livnat's term]. Today every one of the 10 names you see on the list is the result of a war with the minister and the Ministry of Industry, Commerce, and Employment."

It appears that the state action in this case, at least at a statement level, is influenced by the various ideologies and interests that have affected the attitude toward its nature. In reality, no significant change occurred in the behaviour toward the teachers, as one of the supervisors revealed in conversation during the period following the personnel changes, "Between us, what happens with the teachers is simply unfair. One of them just needs to launch a High Court suit, and they will massacre us" (April 2008).

In order to understand the breadth of the phenomenon of dismissed teachers, we can examine this diagram, which represents the scope of the cases referred by the Ministry of Education in 2002.

Permits according to cause of dismissals during pregnancy 2002

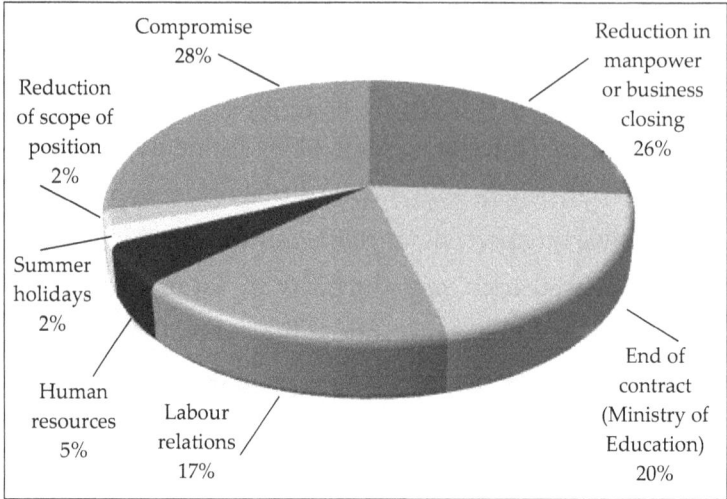

Compromise
28%

Reduction
of scope of
position
2%

Reduction in
manpower
or business
closing
26%

Summer
holidays
2%

Human
resources
5%

Labour
relations
17%

End of
contract
(Ministry of
Education)
20%

Ministry of Industry, Commerce, and Employment figures 2002 (Information Sheet for Dismissals During Pregnancy, Nirit Toshav-Eichner, Human Resources Planning Authority).

According to figures presented by the Ministry of Industry, Commerce, and Employment for dismissal of pregnant teachers, it emerged that more than a fifth of those dismissed during pregnancy in 2002 were teachers, demonstrating that the state is not providing them with the full legal support meant to protect their jobs in a manner equal to other women. In the years following 2002, figures continued to point to a similar picture: in 2007, 43% of all requests submitted by the Ministry of Education were for the dismissal of pregnant teachers; in 2008, 28%; and in 2009 close to 15.5% of submissions.

From 2011, the Enforcement Bureau omitted the formal figures concerning the number of teachers dismissed, claiming that they "were located under a separate plan" (Conversation with the senior supervisor, August 2012).

It appears that when the state's aims as an employer do not mesh with the regulation, it does not use the usual regulatory process with its employees. The state's action as an employer relies upon the neoliberal principles of flexible employment. In the state's coordinated approach to dismissals during pregnancy, the right of the teachers to make their arguments heard and to receive protection from the state, as occurred in the first period, is harmed. A hearing, in this case, is a pointless exercise that is ineffective, unnecessary and takes away resources from the state, from the teachers, and from their employers. Furthermore, it is a mistaken interpretation of the legislator's intention and leads to a further fragmentation. This case, apart from being an example of absolute fragmentation among the intentions of the legislator and the state actions, demonstrates that inter-institutional coordination is not sufficient to maintain the spirit of the law. The public's interests must be noted and integrated into the state actions.

This example demonstrates a consensus on the one hand, and on the other shows the ways in which the distortion of the law developed. This same inequality, at its various levels, is ingrained in the fragmented state actions, based on multiplying the power of the state, both as employer and regulator, through the alliance formed with the nearest government ministry. This doubled power quiets the voices of the teachers and thus further reduces the power of a gender-based group employed in a women's profession, whose status is low in the hierarchy of the labour market.

The Fragmented Action of the State Players— Employment Services

The most significant damage to fair behaviour toward women appears in the fragmentation of the Employment Services, which clearly demonstrates the conflicted interests between the modi operandi of various state bodies.

Findings comparing the rates of women who were dismissed during pregnancy and were aided by regulation and those women were not and received unemployment benefits from Employment Services regardless demonstrates significant discrepancies between applications to the Employment Services as opposed to the interventionary system. Cross-checking data from the Employment Services with those from the resolution system reveals the enormous gap between the number of women who were assisted through the resolution mechanism following a request to dismiss them during pregnancy, and those who used the unemployment benefits when they were dismissed during pregnancy.

Women dismissed during pregnancy who turned to the employment services compared with the rate of those who used regulation between 1998-2007

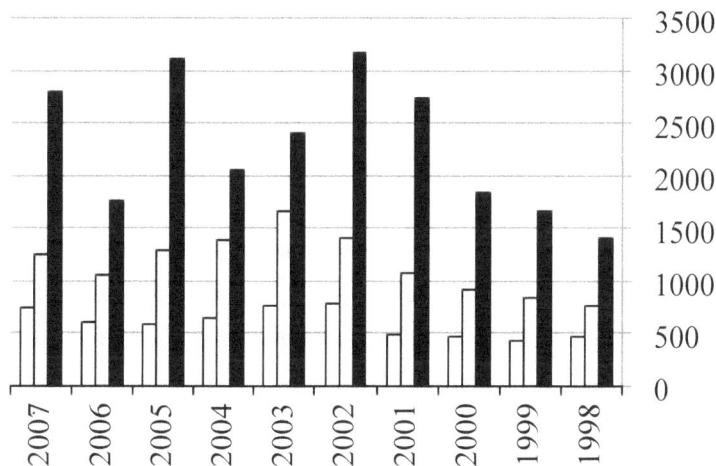

■ National Insurance Institute, those seeking employment during pregnancy
■ Applications to the Ministry of Industry, Commerce, and Employment
□ Ministry permission for dismissal

Figures: Resolution bureau, ministry of industry, commerce, and employment, employment services and national insurance institute, 1997–2008.

The divergence between the rates of women dismissed during pregnancy who employed (grey) regulation, and those who did not and despite this received (black) unemployment benefits from Employment Services demonstrates that yearly, over 60% of the women apparently renounced the legal rights granted to them by the state. Furthermore, by utilising their right to financial aid through social security from the National Insurance Institute while they are pregnant, these women lose their unemployment payments after delivery. If they had applied to the Ministry of Industry, Commerce, and Employment according to the law, they likely would have received state protection and would have increased their chances of receiving a salary from the employer, at least until their delivery. The main significance of this figure lies in the scope of criminal employers who do not submit requests for dismissal according to the law. Along with this, the numbers point to close to 8 million NIS that the state takes out of its treasury every year[94] in order to pay benefits to women. This sum could likely be saved if the Employment Services clerks would refer information on law-breaking employers to the Ministry of Industry, Commerce, and Employment. However, a gloomier picture emerges in an interview with National Insurance Institute clerks who were exposed to the following figures:

> There is a lack of coordination or cooperation among the clerks from the Ministry of Industry, Commerce, and Employment and those from the National Insurance Institute and the Employment Services and there always has been. This phenomenon exists in the enforcement of the Minimum Wage Law

---

94 According to estimates by the National Insurance Institute's Research Department.

as well, however, in that case, the loss of income reaches billions of shekels per year, so an estimate of 8 million NIS does not really upset us.

(Interview with representatives of the National Insurance Institute's Resource Department, April 2010).

The lack of coordination and cooperation are an inseparable aspect of the continuing fragmentation over the years. State clerks are used to this sort of behaviour. Furthermore, it does not seem to occur to them to undertake any action in order to render the state's work more efficient. The discrepancies point to fragmentation between clerks at the Ministry of Industry, Commerce, and Employment and those of the Employment Services, who in fact grant benefits to numerous women who have been dismissed and whose rights were not exhausted within the regulatory system of the state. The divergences in the institutional attitude to pregnant women are a function of various areas of actions, following which a series of different institutional and ideological interests and patterns of action develop and at times conflict. These are manifested in the mechanisms within which the abstract policy, stated in laws and regulations, is implemented. These inherent conflicts are influenced by a different approach to the public reputation of various apparatuses, located within the government ministry meant to represent a unified ideology and policy. Now, while the players responsible for social rights may aspire to assist pregnant women when they are dismissed, other political players may act in order to make it easier for employers to advance their interests. Thus, damage is done to the intention of the legislator to minimise gender-based inequality in the labour market.

In interviews and conversations with women who were dismissed during their pregnancy, there were repeated examples of threats by the employer, who informed the pregnant woman that if she uncomplainingly accepted the dismissal she would receive unemployment benefits—while if she chose to fight the dismissal, they would do all that was in their power to make her life miserable at work. An example of this may be seen in A.'s statement:

> I worked at an insurance agency for four years. My manager heard indirectly that I was pregnant and requested that I go to his office, in order to inform me I was being dismissed. ... He offered me a letter of dismissal that I could take to Employment Services and receive the unemployment benefits due to me. ... I am familiar with the law and told him it was not legal. He said no problem, but if I stayed I should take into account that he would not make my life easy. ... I had no choice; I tried to contact the Ministry of Industry, Commerce, and Employment, but I tried for days with no response. I am turning to you to see if you might be able to help me.
>
> (Telephone conversation, March 2010)

As we see from the conversation with A, the possibility of receiving unemployment benefits, dependent by law on an employee being dismissed, reduced the woman's incentive to fight the illegal dismissal process, as at least in the short term the family income would not (supposedly) be harmed significantly. This "incentive" that the state grants women who do not appeal their dismissal is further strengthened by the permanent custom of the Employment Services—despite it being subject to the Ministry of Industry, Commerce, and Employment—not to require pregnant women to appear at the employment bureau on a regular basis as other unemployed workers do.

The logic that characterises the actions of the Employment Bureau is accepted welfare logic. Given that the chance of finding work for a woman in the advanced months of pregnancy is highly unlikely, because the burden on the clerks at the bureau is heavy and the positions are few, and because of the further physical difficulty placed upon pregnant women who are forced to appear at the Employment Bureau, they can be relieved of this problem and paid an allowance that will allow them economic survival in the meantime. In order to make things easier for the pregnant woman, the Employment Bureau does not ask to see the authorisation granted by the state for her dismissal, nor do they report women who apply for unemployment benefits to the Enforcement Bureau. In this way, in fact, the state encourages illegal dismissals and takes responsibility in place of the employer, as the law intends. Furthermore, this policy conflicts with the intention of the legislator to keep women within the labour market.

Of all the figures presented thus far, there is a group of women who were dismissed during pregnancy and did not turn to the Ministry of Industry, Commerce, and Employment, nor to Employment Services, because they may not have completed the probationary period, as prescribed by the National Insurance Institute.[95] In the chart below, two groups are presented: the women who appealed to the Ministry of Industry, Commerce, and Employment, and who applied to the National Insurance Institute; and those who were dismissed during pregnancy and did not accept help from the state. The figures were received from the Resolution Bureau of the Ministry of Industry, Commerce, and Employment, from Employment Services, and from the National Insurance Institute, in comparison with human resources survey data from the decade between 1998 and 2007. As mentioned, in the human resources survey there is no direct question along the lines of, "Were you dismissed during pregnancy?" however, cross-checking data from the question, "Were you dismissed in the past year?" with that of "new mothers"— women who gave birth in the past year—provides an estimate of the scope of the phenomenon.

---

95 According to the criteria of the National Insurance Institute for age and employment periods.

Graph: Scope of women dismissed during pregnancy in relation to those who received aid from the state between 1998-2007

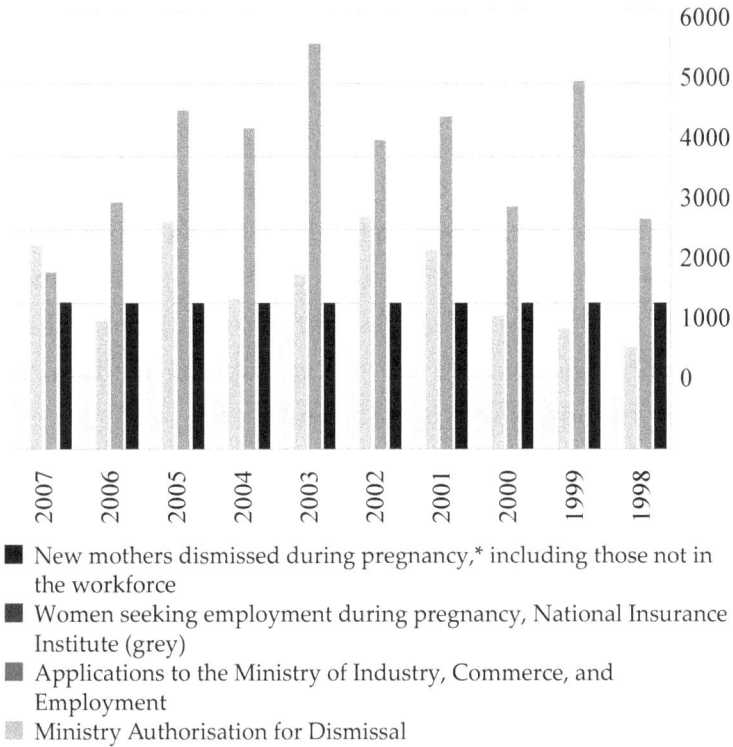

New mothers dismissed during pregnancy,* including those not in the workforce

Women seeking employment during pregnancy, National Insurance Institute (grey)

Applications to the Ministry of Industry, Commerce, and Employment

Ministry Authorisation for Dismissal

Employment services data, human resources survey, statistics bureau, resolution bureau of the ministry of industry, commerce, and employment: 1998–2007

* Women not in the workforce who were dismissed during pregnancy

It emerges from these figures that the average number of women dismissed who received or did not receive help from the state is 4,069 per year from 1998–2007. Of these, a smaller average applied to the National Insurance Institute (2,293), and a much smaller average turned to the Ministry of Industry, Commerce, and Employment (1,159). According to this figure, close to half of all women dismissed are not dealt with at all by the state. These significant differences in the scope of the phenomenon in relation to applications to state institutions point to only a partial employment of the law by these state institutions. On the other hand, the data indicates discrimination of thousands of women yearly on the basis of gender, with no treatment and no guidance, and even worse—no appropriate punishment for the employers who acted against them.

The use of unemployment benefits as a replacement for state protection for some women decreases their financial dependence upon the family unit and allows defamilisation. This protection pattern goes against the intention of the legislator in the second period, which seeks to ensure the continued employment of the women during her pregnancy and immediately following—not from specific economic intentions but to ensure the opportunity for self-fulfillment and continued employment. Beyond this, because motherhood (particularly of small children) is seen in the labour market as a situation that distances the employee from the image of the "ideal worker," women who were dismissed during pregnancy are exposed to a period of unemployment with no benefits after their maternity leave. In this case, the professional logic guiding the Employment Services clerks is in opposition to the logic that the state sought to instill in the protective mechanisms it developed. It emerges that the fragmentation found in the Ministry of Industry, Commerce, and Employment also characterises the lack of inter-ministerial cooperation with the National Insurance Institute, and these lead to uncoordinated, inconsistent, and fragmented state action. The spirit of the law—promotion of gender-based equality and keeping women in the labour force—is therefore not manifested in its implementation, and we see here a clear example of the development of state action that conflicts with the intention of the legislator.

Chapter Summary

This chapter reviewed the ways in which the acts by state mechanism for the protection of pregnant employees developed over the past 60 years. Through the focus of the chapter on Bourdieu's "field theory" and on theories of the state in action, we found that the development of a system for the prevention of dismissals during pregnancy was accompanied by an increasing ideological distancing between discourses, which deepened the power struggles within the field. We demonstrated that in the first 30 years, the system acted in a homogeneous manner and through inter-institutional coordination, through cooperation and consensus. The voices of the women were not heard in the field, and their inferior status within the preventative mechanism was symmetrical with their status in the labour market. They received patronal, patriarchal treatment and protection for their physiological situation for reasons other than promotion of equality. The second period, however, reflected changes in the cultural, political, and state arenas. We discovered that struggles within the field created changes that expanded the power of women in the labour relations field—power that was influenced by their growing participation in the labour market—making the issue of dismissals during pregnancy into part of the public discourse. Nonetheless, along with the expansion of neoliberalism and its influence within the political and economic arenas, protection of pregnant employees became a complex issue, at the core of which was a struggle between the women, who were represented by women's organisations and by the legislature, and their employers, who were empowered by the Ministry of Industry, Commerce, and Employment (now the Ministry of the Economy). The new captains and clerks espouse conflicting ideologies of neoliberalism and deregulation, while the veterans employ "patriarchal inertia."

We demonstrated that the legislators themselves acted at times in a fragmentary manner, which proves the inherent conflict between two discourses: neoliberalism and the promotion of human rights, and reduction of gender-based inequality. Here I sought to argue that the peak of the fragmentation occurs precisely with regard to the teachers. They are employed by a government ministry that is meant to care for their rights, however, because they are in fact in the early years of their employment, they lack the protection of the employees' union and find themselves in a labour market that is intent upon lowering the cost of employment, exposing them to the worst kind of discrimination. This fragmentation demonstrates how the decrease in the power of the unions along with flexible employment neoliberalism-style have harmed one of the groups most associated with women's professions. These findings show the manners in which the discrepancies form between the written law and its de facto implementation, as well as the ways in which inequality emerges.

Until now we have dealt with the labour relations field, in which the system's work and its players—whose location within the field determines its actions—function. In the next chapter, we will continue to examine further gaps in the implementation of the law; those created in the interaction of the state and its clients.

Chapter 5

The Law in Action—How Did the Women's Labour Law Become the Employers' Defence Law?

After we have studied the background to the development of the Women's Labour Law and the mechanism for preventing dismissals during pregnancy, it is crucial to comprehend in depth the ways in which the discrepancies were created between the written law and its de facto implementation. In the previous chapter, we described the creation of the system for the prevention of dismissal during pregnancy and the players active within it. This chapter will look at the field being examined and will consider the argument that harming the universal ability of women to seek aid and assistance in the law is influenced by differences in status as well as by the lack of unity in the logic, in patterns of action, and in position descriptions, leading in turn to the non-uniform action of state clerks toward clients.

We have seen that the supervisors function under the influence of two central, opposing discourses. Understanding these logics could clarify the internal conflicts and the lack of uniformity in the actions of law enforcers. One discourse is the process of privatisation of the welfare state, in the neoliberal spirit, which sees the role of the state as a mediator between the business needs of the organisations and those of the employees. This logic is based on the "individualisation" of cases. Thus, in effect, it ascribes great importance to the process of interaction during the hearing, which allows for the influence of the deviation stemming from the dynamics of state clerks with clients of different backgrounds. The second logic is based on the discourse of social principles, based on the desire to care for the employment security of the female employees. This logic developed in part through the "patriarchal inertia," according to which the Women's Labour Law is social in essence, and it is the state's role to particularly protect women who require financial aid, even if only for a fixed period.

The theoretical framework which will form the basis for this chapter combines theories from various areas, in order to achieve a more detailed understanding of the dimensions within which the discrepancies are created between the legislation and its implementation. Each of the answers to the following questions demonstrates one dimension of the full picture, whose purpose is to understand the logic of the work of the mechanism as well as its consequences:

1. How does the complexity of the supervisor's role influence the implementation of the Women's Labour Law?

2. How do the habitus of the supervisors and the clients influence the process of interaction?

3. How do social, economic, and cultural capital affect the ability to get help and access to equality?

4. How does the protection of the state influence the status of women in the labour market, in the long and short term?

In theoretical terms, we will focus on the micro and macro ingredients that affect the de facto implementation of the formal law. I would now like to go through the theoretical base, which will support the findings displayed.

Attempts by welfare states to minimise gender-based inequality in the labour force through family welfare policy have raised numerous complicated questions in recent years. "Law in action" researchers, who work on the analysis of implementation of laws, have pointed to the problem inherent in the need to appeal to the courts to receive assistance in cases where the employer breaks the Law for the Defence of Equal Opportunity for Women. The high cost of going to court, along with the physical and emotional effort that the legal process demands, creates another system of status inequality, as women who manage to assert their rights are often of the educated middle classes.[96] In Bourdieu's terms, everyone apparently has the same access to the state's protection by law, however, in effect, the ability to manage is reliant on the habitus required in order to handle the compensation (authorisation/protection from dismissal) that the field allows. This ability is a factor that layers and duplicates the inequality as well as the social superiority of specific groups, through the lowering and exclusion of other groups (Bourdieu 2005a). Bourdieu defines "habitus" as a system of unconscious resolutions and structures that organise the manners of action and the understanding of the individual (Bourdieu and Passeron 1990). People, he claims, act according to their understanding, their desires, and their interests, however, these are submerged and formed in light of norms and social arrangements that are relevant to their social placement (status, gender, ethnicity, and so forth). In this context, we wish to examine how the habitus of women from various social groups form their interaction with the system that is directed to prevent their dismissal, and how this interaction influences the results of the process and their chances to preserve their place in the labour force. It is important to emphasise that the "power"

---

96 Bumiller 1988; Selznick 1961; Silbey 2001, 2003; Ewick and Silbey 1998; Kritzer and Silbey 2003.

in Bourdieu's approach acts as a social power, for the most part latent, operated by the creation of an impression of superiority and segregation over those affected (Whiteman 2007). The exertion of force explains the difficulty in social obility and the recreation of statuses and power relations from generation to generation. Therefore, I would like to examine how the power of the players in the field forms the sectorial relations among those who operate the process and their clients, and how these relations affect the logic of action in the regulator.

The "law in action" theory focuses for the most part on the sociodemographic aspects of those who seek assistance in the law and on the sectorial aspects of the legal system, which place obstacles before disempowered groups wishing to use the court system. Nonetheless, less emphasis is placed on the dynamics within the framework of the formal system and the micro level, and the question as to how this dynamic influences the results of the legal process has not been asked.

In order to examine the ways in which the interaction occurs between the state and the women seeking its aid, along with Bourdieu's capital theory I will also rely on the "street-level bureaucrat" theory presented in Lipsky's article (Lipsky 1980), mentioned in the previous chapter and in the theoretical section. Lipsky's main argument is, as mentioned, that decisions taken at the higher, more senior levels do not affect the implementation of public policy as much as those taken by the "street-level bureaucrats," who actually set the agenda through methods developed to deal with various situations of uncertainty and different work-related pressures. The conflict manifests itself in struggles between the individual clerks and the citizens who "challenge" the clients' requests or give in to them. Nonetheless, in order to examine the ways in which these pressures become possible, it is crucial to understand in depth the complexity of a bureaucratic position (system functionaries). Therefore, in order to more concretely present the jobs of all the relevant players in the field to the readers, we will employ Goffman's theory of symbolic interaction and the democratic approach that characterises it (Goffman 1990). This approach uses terms from the world of theatre in order to make sense of the situation and the roles played within it. According to this approach, the hearing acts as a stage; a space within which each of the actors tries, in turn, to play the most convincing role in order to leave the most believable impression upon his interlocutor. This influence is notable through body language, background, and interpretation similar to symbols, as well as through similar expectations toward people they have a reciprocal relationship with. In the spirit of this approach, it could be argued that despite the fact that the supervisors come with prior baggage, the situation during the hearing constructs the role of supervisor and the results of the process. The definition of the supervisor's role is rife with constant negotiation, influenced by the dynamics of the many actors on the hearing's stage. These negotiations happen between centre stage and behind the scenes.

One very important distinction Goffman makes with regard to social behaviour is that of the "front stage" versus "back stage." The initial interpretation, generally received, examines a person's (front stage) observed behaviour, against the personal/natural/subjective (back stage), which is free of the manipulations of the stage art. This is the authentic space, where people feel comfortable in front of their friends and relatives. According to this argument, back stage is the place where we prepare for social interactions about to occur, it is where we define the situation and how to act, define goals, and so on. The move to the front stage, to the situation itself; the "stage," leads to a change in behaviour. In moving to the front stage, the individual dons a mask he did not wear on the back stage. In contrast to this approach, which sees the back stage as a place with no masks, the second interpretation says that the individual removes masks and moves toward the front stage with no authentic self. In other words, the self is not located behind the scenes, playing a defined role on the front stage, but rather is located within the dynamic of the move between the back stage and the front stage. In this chapter, we will consider the argument that the complex role of supervisor is located within the dynamic between back stage and front stage.

Although the dramaturgical approach looks closely at

social dynamics, it focuses less on explanations of power struggles created by the interaction. Here we will use examples of Bourdieu's theories of capital and habitus in order to explain the discrepancies in access to the law among groups with varying levels of social power. The integration of the theory of law in action, the street-level bureaucrat theory, and the theories of symbolic interaction and capital facilitates a deeper explanation of the findings at the micro and macro levels, in ways which complement each other. Thus, we create a picture of the situation that is multi-dimensional, complete, and all-encompassing.

Researchers studying cases of pregnancy-based discrimination claim that they cannot examine the logic and considerations in the institutional processes themselves beyond the results that are publicised. These researchers complain of the lack of institutional authorisation to examine the conduct in hearings carried out within the framework of mediation of even the decision-making process and its results (Russell and Banks 2011a). Within this context, the content of the current chapter may be the first sign of things to come in this field. Through presentation of observational findings that describe the interaction between the supervisors operating the mechanism and the employer and employee, based on analysis of statistical figures from human resources surveys and a special survey created for the purposes of this study, and, in particular, based on the groundwork of interviews and observations during the course of the hearing itself, we will closely follow the daily work of the system aimed at preventing the dismissals of women during pregnancy and after giving birth in Israel, as well as the intended and unintended results of the manner in which the policy is implemented.

The Complexity of the Supervisor's Task: Director, Playwright, and Actor

The complexity of the supervisor's role may be described using the dramaturgical approach, according to which at the time of the hearing, each of the parties is located on the front stage, attempting to play the more convincing role before the supervisor. The supervisor's role as an *actor* on the hearing's stage requires her to rehearse before the performance; in other words, to read the contents of the file, to interact with her clients, to gather evidence, and hold the hearing. Further, as director, she must decide who made a more honest and convincing impression. Although in each of the hearings the same questions are asked at the same, monotonous rate at which the supervisor writes down her clients' positions, one could say no one hearing is exactly the same as the next. In other words, in Goffman's terms, although the role is already scripted for the play, in each performance there remains ample space for improvisation, influenced by the lack of a uniform procedure in operating the mechanism, and here the supervisor requires the talents of a *playwright.* As mentioned in the previous chapter, the system for preventing the dismissal of women functions with no specific guidelines such as those that dictate the operation of the Committee for Prevention of Dismissal during Reserve Duty. Most supervisors, upon whose discretion alone decisions are taken, received no appropriate legal training, and they are forced to decide alone in dozens of cases that pass through their hands each month while being under the pressures of time and the actors in the field: the legislature, women's organisations, and employers. In other words, the supervisors have the triple responsibility of the roles of director, playwright, and actors. I will argue that the weight of this responsibility leaves them drifting between the front stage and back stage, with no clearly defined role and with no clear pre-determined definition. I will further argue that the law acts as a sort of script that is interpreted within the framework of the interaction. I would now like to explain these claims.

The complexity of the supervisor's role is manifested in a reality where the prohibition to dismiss pregnant women leads to the situation where only in a few cases do the requests submitted to the Ministry of Industry, Commerce, and Employment directly address the women's pregnancy as the cause for dismissal. Even in those cases, the pregnancy is referred to only in circumstances where it prevents the woman from performing her job at all, and in these cases it is a judgement call. The term "judgement" has received extensive research attention, in legal research in particular, because of the questions surrounding the existence of normative judgment and the questions of its limitations. The significance of normative judgement means providing the opportunity to choose from several options, all of which are legal[97] (Bendor 2006; Barak 2004). The supervisor often finds herself in these situations. In other words, the Women's Labour Law determines that "a minister shall not authorise dismissal if in *his opinion*[98] it is related to the pregnancy." It is the job of the senior supervisor to examine several options and to exercise normative judgement, while determining to what degree the employer is justified in his complaint against the employee and to which extent the choice of the pregnant employee as a candidate for dismissal, in cases of downsizing or increasing efficiency, is directly linked to her pregnancy. "I have a lot of trouble with the article that mentions judgement. I sometimes do not sleep at night, examining whether there is or isn't a connection, but the few times I have been taken to court and had my judgement attacked just proved I had made the right decision" (interview with senior supervisor, February 2006). I heard these sort of statements from each of the senior supervisors over the years, "There is the employee's version, and there is the employer's version, and each claims their case is just, and I am in the middle and have to decide who is right, but in any case, this is a lose-

---

97 When there is a single legal option, it is a matter of judgement and when there is more than one, it is a matter of normative judgment.

98 Author's emphasis.

lose situation" (February 2004). Even in later years, one of the senior supervisors complained to me, "It is impossible to withstand all the pressure and on all of the fronts, and to satisfy everyone. And I alone am responsible; I hardly have anyone to turn to" (May 2012). These quotations demonstrate the difficulty found in the position and thus the burden of responsibility that falls on one actor alone.

The requests placed before the senior supervisor may be divided into dismissals due to problems with the employee's performance (inefficiency, inadequate performance, theft, embezzlement, and so on), and problems related to the state of the business, and are presented as part of an unavoidable efficiency drive, which applies to all of the labour force (business closing, bankruptcy, quota reductions, and so on). From figures collected in 2002 from all the hearings held on the matter of dismissal of pregnant women, it emerged that in 28% of the cases in which the dismissals were authorised, permission was granted within the framework of an agreement—as opposed to 26% of the cases in which the dismissal was authorised due to the business closing or other economic factors that were unrelated to the pregnancy. In 17% of cases, dismissal was authorised due to labour relations problems, 20% of dismissals were by the Ministry of Education, and the rest were human resource employees or seasonal workers (Toshav-Eichner 2003).

In this context, it is interesting to see the large

discrepancies in the women's approaches as opposed to those of the employers with regard to the cause for dismissal. When asked in a survey, (2006) "Why do they want to dismiss you?" the majority (60%) responded that the reason was related to their pregnancy, while when asked, "What were you told by the organisation was the official reason for dismissal?" according to the employee's reports, this reason was almost unanimously (1%) denied by the employer. On the other hand, it was argued that the cause was the employee's performance (36%) or downsizing due to financial difficulties in the workplace (64%). It should be emphasised that these findings are quite similar to the official figures presented by the Ministry of Industry, Commerce, and Employment (2003–2010), according to which the rate of dissatisfaction with an employee's performance ranged from 20-30%.[99] These issues point to the complex judgement required by the supervisors when coming to a decision. I would now like to examine in depth the dimensions of this complexity.

---

99 Figures from the Ministry of Industry, Commerce, and Employment website, debates in the Committee on the Status of Women.

Dr. Nirit Toshav - Eichner

The Construction of a Non-uniform Role: Between Neoliberalism and Sociality

According to the dramaturgical method, it could be said that on the stage of the hearing, the meeting between each of the actors—the employer on one hand and the employee on the other, with state representatives—becomes a constant negotiation characterised by alternating various strategies of managing impressions. The situation between the supervisor and the actors at a hearing constructs the behaviour toward them and influences the manner in which the supervisor undertakes her task. The role of the supervisor is constantly under construction to match the events during the hearing. I will now explain this.

In the absence of a focused system of preparation and uniform policy in the area of dismissal prevention, the subjective manner in which the supervisors perceive their role is a central actor in the way in which they perform it. From the interviews and conversation with supervisors, a lack of clarity and non-uniformity emerge with regard to the description of their role and its definition. There are supervisors who see the welfare system as a universal body that does not require investment of economic resources, that should bypass the courts, and in particular as a body meant to supply information to the employee about how she needs to act in relation to the employer. Alongside them, there are those who see the system as a social body in essence, whose aim is to allow women to express themselves

248

and protect them at a specific point in their lives when it is difficult for them to find employment. Then there are those supervisors who present a feminist worldview that espouses the integration of women into the labour force. The lack of uniformity is also evident in the views of these supervisors with regard to women's careers and the need to protect the integration of women into senior positions. On the other hand, perhaps due to the bureau's location within the (former) Ministry of Labour and Welfare, the supervisors employed for many years in the ministry see the Women's Labour Law—and in particular the article prohibiting dismissal during pregnancy—as a social law whose purpose is to provide protection first and foremost for the welfare of weak employees. The lack of clarity in the understanding of the position can be exemplified by one of the supervisors, a woman with a feminist background, who mentioned she had studied women's studies and said of herself that she had a particular affinity to the special needs of women. Nonetheless, after she was promoted from supervisor, at the start of her term as senior supervisor, a sharp increase occurred in the number of permits (2006), as we see in the following chart:

15 Years of Dismissal Permits Authorised by the Ministry of Industry, Commerce, and Employment 1999–2013

Years	Requests submitted to the Ministry of Industry, Commerce, and Employment	Dismissal authorisations by the Ministry of Industry, Commerce, and Employment	Percentage of dismissal authorisations from all submissions
1999	828	419	50%
2000	907	460	50%
2001	1,070	489	45%
2002	1,407	782	55%
2003	1,657	761	45%
2004	1,394	643	46%
2005	1,280	571	44%
2006	1,048	591	56%
2007	1248	731	58%
2008	1,413	660	47%
2009	1,855	898	48%
2010	1,188	561	69%
2011	944	632	67%
2012	933	759	81%
2013	1,176	917	78%
Yearly average	1,223.2	658.2	56%

Percentage of permits (including the Ministry of Education) of all requests for dismissal during pregnancy as submitted to the Ministry of Industry, Commerce, and Employment 1999–2013

Ministry of Industry, Commerce, and Employment figures, and from debates in the Committee for the Advancement of the Status of Women

The senior supervisor explained that the increase in permits given in 2006 stemmed from the increase in cases where the employers had hired lawyers, who then looked for any way to achieve authorisation. This led to many difficulties that interfered with the senior supervisor's attempts to assist the women. This supervisor strongly supports the system, which is, in her words, "quick, free, provides counselling for women, guidance, instruction, protection before the pregnancy, with no need for the court" (interview with the supervisor, February 2008). However, not all of the supervisors provide counselling, as seen in a conversation with one of them following a hearing held for a clerk in a communications firm, "I could have helped her, but I am not obligated to counsel, it is not my job. We also do not have time; there are other people in line. She is meant to prepare by herself. ... What does she want? Money! I cannot pay her until the delivery" (conversation post-hearing, April 2009). Upon leaving the hearing room, after more than a half hour of testimony in which the employee cried, the supervisor said, "There will be authorisation in this case." In response to the question, "So why did you give her such an ample stage?" she replied: "Because she has the right to argue; if it had taken much longer, I would have cut her off" (Post-hearing conversation, May 2009).

These cases demonstrate the lack of continuity in the system's approach through its operators. There are supervisors who move from the front stage (from the automatic protocol of asking questions) and assist the employee with maskless suggestions on the back stage. In the spirit of the dramaturgical approach, one could say that on the one hand, in some interactions the clients are prepared, and they are given enough time to manage the impression that they wish to leave, and on the other hand, there are interactions in which the clients do not receive this "back stage time." Furthermore, it could be said that the time in which the women receive guidance beyond the known administrative process is an informal time that takes place with no masks and may create a closeness between the supervisor and the employee. It is plausible that a certain inequality is created toward those employees who do not receive this time, and I will address this presently.

Apart from this, the chart's findings indicate the way in which the neoliberal spirit is reflected in the statistical data that points to a significant increase in the permits granted in 2003-2010. I will present three possible factors that may explain the findings. The first explanation is based on the argument that the senior supervisor raised, according to which more employers are aided by lawyers, and thus the system has a harder time refusing their requests. The second explanation is related to the first, but in addition, there is a deeper understanding of the role of the supervisor in the hearing stage. In one of the Knesset sessions during the period mentioned, an argument erupted concerning the lack of balance between the employers (who are represented) and the employees and the claim was made that even if the woman is accompanied by a lawyer, they are not permitted to intervene. The senior supervisor, Ms. Sarit Yehudai, was asked to explain:

> It is true, and this is an emotional and unpleasant situation. There are lawyers here who were with the clients, with the employees when the testimony was taken, and they saw that our supervisors were *very nice and pleasant and tried to make the situation very pleasant and friendly*.[100] These are factual questions that only the employee may answer. These are not legal questions, and there is no need for intervention or testimony by the lawyer.
>
> (Protocol from the Knesset Committee, Session on the Committee for the Advancement of the Status of Women 135, March 12, 2012)

In the senior supervisor's statement, we note a reflection of the social approach to women. The hearing stage is seen by her as an arena in which there is a need to be "'nice, pleasant, and friendly", however, in reality, behind the scenes, when the masks are removed, the supervisor recommends authorising the dismissals in most cases and thus denies the employees their livelihood.

The third explanation of the rise in permits granted could focus on the increased trust the employers place in the system. The employers, who are witness to the consistent

---

100 Author's emphasis.

rise in authorisations given, adopt the logic that says that by using power within the field, one can win a "prize." Thus, over the years the powers are redistributed; it seems as if the administrative process changes the Women's Labour Law into an employers' protection law, and in doing so it distances itself greatly from the intent of the legislator. This claim gains strength in light of the argument that took place in the Committee for the Advancement of the Status of Women, between the attorney Shir-El Nakdimon, of the Women's Lobby, and the senior legal supervisor of the Ministry of Industry, Commerce, and Employment, Ms. Sarit Yehudai:

> **Nakdimon**: I find the matter of authorisation percentages disturbing. ...
>
> **Yehudai**: But we presented the segmentation: 60% due to the proven, harsh economic situation, and 30% due to dissatisfaction. ...
>
> **Nakdimon**: In cases that landed on my desk, we saw that the proven, harsh economic situation is some scrap of paper that an accountant came up with. ...
>
> **Yehudai:** We trust the confirmation by the accountant, this is absolute evidence. ...
>
> (Knesset Committee Protocol, Session of the Committee for the Advancement of the Status of Women 135, March 12, 2012)

Thus, we witness patterns of action that shape the work of the system for the prevention of dismissal during pregnancy, as well as the ways in which the employers find the system eased for them; by pressuring the supervisors with stories of economic difficulties. To support this claim is a statement by one of the supervisors in the nearby Enforcement Bureau:

> I am familiar with these authorisations. They are all shady deals between the employer and the accountant. In the end, the accountant also gets his salary from the employer and does not want to endanger that. The easiest thing would be to declare bankruptcy, change the name, and there you go, a new business with new employees.
>
> (Interview with supervisor at the Enforcement Bureau, May 14, 2014)

It is notable then, that the supervisors are located in the middle, between the pressures of the employers and those of the women, who are at times represented by women's organisations. It appears, however, that the pressure brought by the women's organisations has not had the desired effect of recompense in the field, given that in the following year (2012), the rate of permits granted increased even further and with it the power of the employers. One could, therefore, conclude that the supervisors' "niceness" was taken advantage of by the employers, who manage to place further pressure on the supervisors, expanding their power, and thus further weakening the power of the women in the field.

The Course of the Hearing and the Degree of Equality Shown Therein

Apart from the non-uniform instruction from the supervisor, and apart from the lack of clarity in her position, the length of time to be dedicated to each hearing was never defined. The impression is given that the length of a hearing is dependent upon the matters that come up in it, but also upon a shared or conflicting background between the participants. In other words, the hearing may become shorter when the participants' backgrounds are distant from that of the operators of the law, and a longer time will be set for a hearing in which there is a common background.

It should be emphasised that no link has necessarily been found between the length of a hearing and its results. However, as the time granted for hearing testimony grows, further findings are more likely to emerge, which in the end may affect the decision. Similarly, there may be a shift toward the back stage as we discussed earlier. An example of this argument can be seen in a hearing held by one of the supervisors, a woman from a secular background, who is educated, and the mother of three children, living in the centre of the country. Toward the end of a hearing for a religious physical education teacher from Beitar Ilit, which took about 10 minutes, the teacher said that she hoped that the fact that she had travelled quite a distance "helped to save my job." At the end of the hearing, the supervisor's body language showed anger and discomfort. When asked about this, she replied, "It's the Ministry of Education, it should take a half a minute at the most to give authorization, the dismissal is administrative. I have no time for this." (Observation and interview post-hearing, March 2007).

In the spirit of the dramaturgical approach, it could be said that the different backgrounds of the supervisor and the client affected the negotiations between them, and the role played by the employee did not leave enough of an impression on the supervisor. This then influenced the amount of time that the supervisor was willing to assign to the hearing. This assumption is supported by what took place in a similar hearing that was held right after the one described above. In this meeting, the supervisor's body language was relaxed and empathetic toward a secular teacher from the centre of the country with a background similar to her own. After a hearing that lasted 20 minutes — twice as much time as had been granted to the religious teacher — the supervisor said, "She is so nice. It's too bad I cannot help her." (Observation and post-hearing interview, March 2007). The two cases emphasise how the background influences the length of interaction and how it is conducted. Even so, notwithstanding the cases of the teachers employed by the Ministry of Education, the system is unable to employ discretion, given that the conduct before the state mechanisms is meant to act as a further factor in the empowerment of the employee. The impression left upon an employee who is received pleasantly and empathetically by the state's representatives, when the supervisor is supportive—"I am sure you will find employment immediately" (hearing observation, March 2007)—will be more positive than that of an employee who is quickly questioned in an atmosphere of time pressure. At the same time, beyond these cautious assumptions, the argument could be made that because the length of time for each hearing is not defined, there is an option to expand the limits of interaction and to grant a wide stage in the sense of "one case at a time," which has become entrenched in the system.

This phenomenon also appears in the case where the supervisor, who identified with the employee coming from a similar background to her own, granted her precious time at the expense of other employees waiting for their turn outside the hearing room. The supervisor allowed the employee—from the Ministry of Education, a nice, educated, secular girl from central Israel—to express herself continuously for 45 minutes about her relationship, and how it had been affected as a result of the request to dismiss her during pregnancy. The supervisor displayed great sympathy and spent time on matters not directly related to the hearing. When asked why, she answered, "The women need this hearing in order to unload the painful burden of the dismissal. I am here for that as well." (Observation and post-hearing interview, May 2007). In this case, we note that the similar background of the participants in the interaction has an influence on the level of empathy displayed toward them and on their empowerment by the state's system. On the other hand, in cases in which there is less empathy toward the situation or the woman, the time becomes significantly shorter and the interaction remains, for the most part, on the front stage.

The length of the hearing has a strong influence on the ability of the participants to construct a full and complete impression. The limited time may harm their ability to take advantage of all the rights granted within the framework of the law. Thus, the law's enforcement is in fact harmed when, in attempting to hasten the women or the employer, the testimony is not fully gathered. Further, a hearing that is shortened prevents the supervisor from empowering the employee within the framework of the state's intervention.

A Social Approach to Disempowered Women

Although ultimately, the different approaches toward strong women, as opposed to those seen as weak lead to the defence of many disempowered women whose cases are brought before the system, the concern does not always lead to ensuring the integration of the dismissed women into the labour force in the long term, and this may skew the decisions of the supervisors in favour of women with limited resources to act. From the observations (until 2010), it arose that in close to half of the cases the supervisor did, in fact, attempt to assist the women. The issue appears to be dependent on the time available to her, on her goodwill, and on the empathy she feels toward the women. The different attitude of the supervisors to their own role and to their clients demonstrates the inconsistency in their actions toward different women.

Thus, for example, following a hearing on a request for the dismissal of a civil service clerk whose (part-time) income was 1,700 NIS monthly, the supervisor said, "We will protect her, her husband was dismissed. … The Women's Labour Law … takes into account the financial situation of the entire family unit." (Post-hearing conversation, July 2005). Although the supervisor was not certain that the dismissal, in this case, was in fact caused by the employee's pregnancy, her social situation made her worthy of the law's protection, from her point of view, and this is in contradiction to the intent of the legislator to protect only women who were dismissed because of their pregnancy.

In one instance, a case was brought before the supervisor concerning the manager of a shoe store whose income was the main household wage. During the hearing, the employee burst into tears, saying, "My husband is a student and just began working in computers. I have a mortgage, and if I am dismissed I will lose the house."

When the employee left the hearing, the supervisor said, "Although the employer's request to dismiss her was not directly tied to her pregnancy, the employer had already been interviewed, and no permission was granted, so they will take her back at work. She is not in a good situation." (Observation, June 2006). This case also demonstrates the social approach, according to which the supervisors view the system as a welfare tool whose purpose is to assist the employees and their family units, and not necessarily to integrate them into the labour market.

A further expression of the pattern of thought that sees the state as a social system acting as an aide to women in need appears in the behaviour of the supervisors toward the requests of state institutions and large non-profit organisations to dismiss pregnant employees.[101] This approach was explained by a senior supervisor, "Institutions such as government ministries, WIZO, and Na'amat do not receive permits, and sometimes even when there is no connection to the pregnancy, the authorisation is withheld. ... The state needs to protect citizens from an inability to support themselves financially in the family unit." (Interview with senior supervisor, December 2006).

Employment in government institutions is seen here by the supervisors as a sort of welfare mechanism that must not be harmed, even if the dismissals are unconnected to

---

101 These are generally employees without permanent positions.

the pregnancy itself. The view is that the state and these non-profit organisations do not fall under market rules, and this will not be harmed if they employ women, even when these women are not a good fit and are not crucial to the system.

This logic is expressed in the following hearing, which was held for the CEO of a non-profit organisation during the economic crisis. The employer wished to dismiss several employees, among them a pregnant worker with five years' seniority. The supervisor asked, "Why specifically her?" and the employer responded, "We have no need for her specific field, we are downsizing other areas as well. We have no choice, otherwise we will have to shut down." The supervisor requested details of each field, and at the end of the hearing said, "He was stuttering a bit and they are piggybacking on the economic situation." (Hearing, February 2009). It could be concluded from this hearing that the suspicious approach toward the employer stems from the recognition of the association he heads as a body whose purpose is to employ women no matter what their condition is, and not one whose goal is financial profit. In this context, one could mention the "deep pockets principle," which works on relative principles. For example, if the supervisor refuses to grant a permit to an employer in a steady financial position, they will suffer less harm than an organisation with no means (Poitevin 1989). In an analogy of the "deep pockets principle," this case exemplifies the refusal that was handed down due to the association being a non-profit organisation, whose principles include (according to the supervisor's view) the employment of women, and it will supposedly suffer less than an organisation whose goal is profit.

It should again be emphasised that it appears from the observations that in most cases the desire of the supervisors to protect women hurt by dismissals—even in cases where pregnancy is not the direct cause of the dismissal—stems from a deep, true wish to help an employee in trouble. This social approach, however, has a problematic significance with regard to the efficiency of the protection in general. On the one hand, when the employers sense that pregnant employees are protected even in cases where the dismissals are not based on the pregnancy, their trust in the system is weakened, and they may avoid turning to it in future cases or worse, they may avoid hiring women of fertile age, out of concern that their autonomy will be limited if they wish to fire them for problems at work or financial trouble. Proof of this can be seen in studies from recent years, in which, as we said, the employers' trust increased when the permits were granted more freely and as the welfare approach decreased.

A Neoliberal Approach for Strong Populations

No less problematic is the significance of the social approach from the point of view of the women who request assistance and are not seen by the supervisor as in need, or as active in preventing their dismissal. In these cases, in particular, when the figures are not unequivocal, the supervisors tend to send those women who are seen as strong to the lawsuit channel through the labour courts. Thus, for example, one supervisor said, "They generally manage up to the point where they realise that they could lose their jobs, and then those who can manage it financially will go to court in order to get compensation." (Post-hearing interview with the supervisor, April 2009). This sort of statement demonstrates how responsibility has been shifted from those well-to-do women who deal with the system. This type of approach directly damages the ability of the system to provide equal assistance for all of its clients.

The supervisor's approach to less needy women also came up in cases that occurred during the economic crisis. "They suffer less from it. They see the crisis as the cause of dismissal and do not take it personally. It is not so bad as they will rest, and the husband in high-tech will bring in income. They also cry less." (Interview with supervisor, January 2009). This approach is similar to the welfare approach, according to which the role of the state is to protect the weak, but we note from the supervisor's comments what the role of the state is in regard to the "strong." I was further told by one supervisor during a period of economic slowdown, "She will take a slightly longer vacation as her husband makes enough for that." (February 2009, telephone conversation). According to the supervisor, for women with strong economic capital, being removed from the labour cycle is seen as positive, and this approach is far from the intent of the legislator as it is an approach which significantly harms the efficiency of law enforcement and the de facto implementation of the spirit of the law.

These statements exemplify the lack of clarity, the contradictions and the lack of uniformity found in the approach of those who operate the system. In cases where there is no connection between the dismissal and the pregnancy, the weak employee received protection, and the stronger employee, whose economic situation is better, received the "neoliberal" treatment in which the market forces take care of themselves without intervention by the state, relying on the high salary of a partner, or turning to the courts, which requires investment of resources.

The logic of the supervisor's actions is therefore influenced by the reciprocal relations that occur in a specific, daily situation with her clients in the field, which affect her decision-making and create the discrepancy between the law and its de facto implementation.

Interaction Stage: Dealing with Employers

Goffman argues that the purpose of the actors on stage is to construct the most convincing impression in keeping with the "situation definition" that circumstances dictate

(Goffman 1990). "Behind the scenes" they rehearse and prepare their versions prior to going on stage so that the performance at the hearing will be believable to the supervisor. The question arises; how do the clients prepare, and how does this preparation, in fact, affect the interaction? In this context "law in action" researchers argue that the manner of behaviour between those who exercise the law and their clients has an equally strong influence. The results of this interaction are likely to divert the equal enforcement of the law. The very fact of being aided by the law is not to be taken for granted and in itself mediates through social capital (Ewick and Silbey 1998; Silbey 2001). We will now consider these arguments.

In order to gain an in-depth understanding of how the employers are treated, we will first present some of the more notable characteristics as they appeared in the survey findings, and we will try to analyse the approaches of the pregnant workers' employers as they appeared during observations. We will also present the employers' positions toward employment during pregnancy in general, in order to understand their point of view in the matter. We will further address the employers' experiences of interaction with the supervisor. Before all of these, however, I would like to examine the employers' access to the law and the degree of deterrence by the law before they seek assistance from it.

It is clear that the most significant influence of the law is that it is a norm in the field that inhibits dismissals and sees it this as an illegal option from the start. In informal conversation with employers which took place during the years of the study about the phenomenon of dismissal during pregnancy, I was often told that "by law it is impossible to dismiss during pregnancy." On the one hand, this sort of statement demonstrates a lack of awareness of the law or a lack of understanding and on the other hand, it emphasises that we have no ability to estimate the number of women whose dismissals were prevented despite the fact that were it not for the appropriate legislation, the employer would have wished to dismiss them. These comments about the employers' awareness of the law were raised in the Knesset by Attorney Keren Bar Yehuda, a representative of the College of Lawyers, who said, "There is also a real need to bring this information to the employers. There are many employers who do not want to be lawbreakers, and if they had this information they would take steps according to the law" (Knesset Committee for the Advancement of the Status of Women, protocol 135, March 12, 2012).

Although analysing the level of effectiveness of the law was beyond the central goals of this study, the human resources survey figures from the Central Bureau for Statistics give us an estimate regarding the effectiveness and deterrence of the legislation. While 3.4% of the women aged 20-40 who are not new mothers reported they were dismissed from their work, only 1.7% of the new mothers were dismissed during this period. The blatant difference between the chances of women in the two groups (new mothers and those who are not) to be dismissed were unchanged when we observed other sociodemographic characteristics of the survey participants, including age, number of children, education, and workplace (private or public). This finding suggests that whether directly (through the state mechanism) or indirectly (by the creation of a norm), the legislation prohibiting the dismissal of pregnant women does, in fact, reduce the dismissal of pregnant women and new mothers by 26.7%, in comparison with the dismissal of women of comparable ages who are not new mothers. It is important to note in this context that the fact that new mothers, who are protected by the law, are dismissed at a lower rate that other young women teaches us that the protection for women in the initial stage is insufficient. It is worth emphasising that the discrimination toward women who are mothers of small children, or those who employers see as potential mothers in the near future, is present and is often fulfilled following the period in which the law protects the employee. Nonetheless, this matter was not examined in the current study.

This finding is important because it points to the fact that the power of the law—even when it is latent in the field and is not clear enough to certain employers— prevents employers from dismissing workers during pregnancy. Thus, if the law is more effectively enforced, the effectiveness and deterrence will increase as well. I would now like to look closely at the practices of women whose employers are not deterred by the law and seek their dismissal during pregnancy.

From the survey presented in the methodological section, for women whose employer wishes to dismiss them, findings showed that two-thirds of the managers who turn to the committee in order to receive permission to dismiss a pregnant employee are men (64%), and the rest women (36%). The average age of the male employers is 38.8 years old, an average nearly three years lower than the female employers (42 years old on average). Nearly two-thirds (65%) belong to the private sector; high-tech firms, insurance firms, banks, gas and oil companies as well as marketing companies, retail, and grocery shops. Among those requesting permits for the public sector are hospitals, universities, municipal councils, and government ministries such as the Ministry of Education, Housing, and Welfare.

I would now like to examine the argument that the employer's characteristics influence the supervisor's decision—a claim that arose in the past in the book when discussing non-profit organisations.

Within the framework of the observations of interactions during hearings, it was noted that one of the supervisors— from a secular background—showed great empathy for cases of women dismissed by religious employers, who are often themselves fathers to families with many children.

A religious employer, with an electrical contracting firm employing eight people, requested to dismiss a religious employee who had been working there for three years and upon returning from her maternity leave reported another pregnancy. The employer arrived at the hearing with his daughter who works with him, and her baby.

> I told her, I understand you have a problem, you have a baby. … I told S. you will soon have five children, why not focus on the home like any mother in Israel. You want to build a family at the expense of your work. … She told me, you cannot fire me. Every time she brings up another law which protects her.
>
> (Hearing, October 2007)

After leaving the hearing room, the supervisor said:

> Despite the employer's claims, the employee has the right to the protection of the law, and this protection will be granted her and the dismissal forbidden. When he has the legal opportunity he will fire her immediately after her maternity leave, however, in my opinion, given that the employer is religious, his request to dismiss the employee is particularly serious. He himself arrived here with his daughter and her baby and talks about the employee's family. What a nerve!

(Post-hearing interview, October 2007)

In this case, the supervisor herself assumed that preventing the dismissal would not make it possible for the employee to stay in her place of work after returning from maternity leave. She emphasised the social aspect that guarantees the employee a salary—even if minimal—during pregnancy rather than the broader aim of leaving the employee within the labour cycle. Furthermore, the employer's approach to hiring the pregnant employee angered her, in particular, based on her assumption that he himself was the father of a large family. Beyond all of this, it is possible to assume that the difference in backgrounds between the supervisor and the employer influenced her reaction to his version, as given during the hearing.

In order to gain an in-depth understanding of how the employers experience the interaction with the system, a number of the employers who participated in the hearings were interviewed. In all of the interviews,[102] comments were made that the supervisor was business-like and attentive and that it was clear that she tried to see the entire picture.

This was the testimony given by A., one of the interviewees, a human resources manager with a high-tech company in which 75% of the employees are ultra-orthodox women who give birth yearly. A., like the supervisor at the hearing, is a secular woman in her thirties, well-spoken and educated. The manner in which the employer portrayed her

---

102 Five in-depth interviews were held with employers who acted through the prevention system.

claims when trying to receive a permit to dismiss an ultra-orthodox employee with two and a half years of seniority exemplifies the claims of the law in action as well as the theory of symbolic interaction, on the shared background and its effect on reciprocal relations among actors:

> We have many ultra-orthodox women in the organisation, and as such they give birth every year. I know they see this work as a source of income for their families, given that the husband is learning. When I sought a dismissal a year ago [2010] I was uncomfortable with it, but I had no choice, and I turned to the Ministry of Industry, Commerce, and Employment. I needed to bring documents, but we do not have a set system for employee evaluation, as we see these employees as a cheap production line, like workers in India. They live and work in Jerusalem, so they are both cheap and available labour. In the company we see this as a win-win situation; they make a living, and we do not need to put out large resources for the egos of high-tech employees, and all that comes with it. Apart from the female employees, we also have a higher, narrow level of engineers who we do take care of in terms of salary and benefits, and the women then are the worker ants whose work does not require too much training. They do not seek benefits, they want the salary, and even if they do not earn much, they need every shekel. Because we do not have a proper evaluation system, I had to go to each team leader

and prepare a file for the employee. At the hearing, I felt that the supervisor listened to me and wanted to properly understand all of my considerations for dismissal. We were given the authorisation because the employee really had not proved herself in terms of production. They had to give us the permit. These are women who, no matter how you look at it, the law will always protect. They are always dealing with pregnancies, maternity leaves, and births. I should not be permanently stuck with a bad employee.

(Interview, November 2011)

This example highlights the manner in which the quality of work by pregnant women is seen by their employers, in particular, ultra-orthodox women who are seen as cheap labour by the employer. Nonetheless, the results of the interaction are even more important. This case and the previous one present a request for permission to dismiss due to pregnancy, which is against the law. While in the first case the employer upset the supervisor with his attitude and his request was denied, in the second case, the interaction with the human resources manager ended with a permit. It could be said, extremely cautiously, that the similar backgrounds shared by the supervisor and A., the human resources manager, contributed to the decision, even if it was not the main motivation. This assumption relies on the principle that the decision is affected by negotiation and by the backgrounds from which the participants in the interaction come. It is certainly possible that the human resources manager presented her reasons for dismissal in terms that line up with the supervisor's views, which is a logic influenced by the neoliberal discourse.

This assumption is strengthened in light of the following case: a hearing held for an ultra-orthodox manager, the owner of a chain of gyms, who has employed an ultra-orthodox secretary for the past five years. The employer claimed that he was interested in dismissal because he was not satisfied with her performance, and while saying this he banged his fist on the table and said loudly, "I am tired of always paying. She gives birth over and over and I need to pay money, money, money. If I do not get the permit I will need to pay more money for a service I never received from her, she's a bad employee!" (February 2008). When he left the hearing room the supervisor said, "Did you see how scary he is? I am not the person to deal with this, he needs to go to court with her. I cannot issue him a permit over this sort of conflict" (February 2008).

In the three cases presented here, the religious/ultra-orthodox women were employed for over two and a half years by the organisations, by employers who felt financially damaged by their fertility patterns at work. The employers testified, as expected, that the employees were not performing well, however, while the two religious employers created an unpleasant atmosphere of threats and discrimination, and their requests were denied, the submission by the human resources manager, from a similar background to the supervisor's, was granted. These cases exemplify how knowing how matters ought to be presented during an interaction with the state affects the outcome of the process, not only for the dismissed employee but also for employers. The influence of the participants' different backgrounds in the interaction and their level of preparedness to handle the system affect the results of the operation. A lack of uniformity in the role of the supervisors themselves could improve the chances of clients who have prepared to influence the decision of the system.

This argument is strengthened by the logic of individualism, explained through the comments of the supervisor as a logic that guides her to see "each case individually." Thus, for example, one supervisor stated in an interview, "We examine each case on its own merit; there are no rules as to when to permit or to refuse" (March 2011). This logic conflicts with the argument of a welfare approach, according to which disempowered female employees are treated with a social approach, and, as in many cases, the logic rests upon a social discourse that tips the scales in favour of the employee. Nonetheless, in the interactions we observed with the human resources manager, despite the employee being an ultra-orthodox woman without means—"an ant, cheap, available labour"—the employer's "performance" influenced the supervisor and the weak employee received no protection. This case conflicts with statements regarding the social consideration that acts as a significant standard when making decisions. This non-uniform spirit is encouraged by the individualist approach common among supervisors. One could assume that as far as they are concerned, this is the way to bypass the impact of the lack of clarity in the definition of their role, and they therefore prefer to approach "each case individually." Thus, for example, cases were noted in which the supervisors were unable to overcome the influence of their own personal backgrounds or their clients'.

Below is the case of another supervisor, who is ultra-orthodox. In the interview I held with her she expressed empathy toward an ultra-orthodox employer who was interested in dismissing an ultra-orthodox daycare assistant who had become pregnant outside of matrimony and, she emphasised, boasting, the decision to grant permission to dismiss the pregnant employee:

> Despite my background, and my sympathy toward the pregnant employee, I granted the permit because of the complaints from parents at the daycare centre where the woman worked that the pregnancy outside of marriage would damage the values upon which they educated their children. Once I would have pitied the employee and identified with her, but today I understand that she cannot stay at the daycare centre in this situation.

> (Interview, February 2006)

In this case the permission for dismissal was given contrary to the spirit of the law. The supervisor admitted that the woman was dismissed as a direct result of her pregnancy. It must be assumed that the supervisor did so because of her values and background, as well as an identification she felt with the values of the parents. As she stated, "I understand those parents as their children will ask how the employee is pregnant when she hasn't got a husband" (interview, February 2006). In this context, it could be said that the supervisor from an ultra-orthodox background was influenced by it and by the values upon which ultra-orthodox education is based. In said situation, she authorised the dismissal and ignored the fact that the request for dismissal stemmed directly from the pregnancy. This finding clearly matches the claim that there are people and situations that may lead those who operate the law to act in an irrational manner, and that prejudices affect their behaviour toward citizens from specific backgrounds (Ewick and Silbey 1998; Kritzer and Silbey 2003). Furthermore, this case strengthens the dramaturgical approach; the singular dynamics of each performance structures the role of the supervisor, which is in constant negotiation, dependent upon events occurring at the stage of the hearing.

This case bolsters the argument that the role definition occurs in keeping with operations in the field. In one conversation the supervisor expressed her concerns and said, "There are special cases. For example, it was very important to me to protect the employee here. It was someone close to the minister who approached us directly, and the bureau contacted us. I did backflips for this; we interviewed anything that moved within range of the employee and in the end we refused." It could be assumed that the pressure brought to bear by the office of the minister affected the work of the system as well as long-term handling of the file. When she was asked whether all cases are handled this way she responded, "I wish I had the time to spend like that on every single case. I have one supervisor who tried to mediate, but unfortunately, not all of my manpower is like that, and right now we are sorely short of supervisors" (September 2012). It ought to be noted that the claim of short-staffing and an inability to manage time-limitations has been raised by all senior and regular supervisors in the system. It may be very cautiously assumed that if in each case the system had spent significant time gathering evidence and testimonies strengthening the women's arguments, it is likely that the decisions would have been different in several cases.

This case exemplifies the power relations in the labour relations field, according to Bourdieu's theory. When latent power was employed, the supervisor "did backflips" in her own way, however, she also mentioned that she does not have the resources to do this in most cases. Further, using power explains the lack of mobility within society and the paralysing effect on status and power relations from one generation to another. One must assume that there were always women with the sort of social capital that would allow them to influence the power system within the field; those same women could come offstage, and go behind the scenes, and gain "field prizes" in the form of guidance and empowerment, as opposed to other women, who lack the habitus required to use their power.

If so, it would appear that given that the system lacks a clear definition for the senior supervisors' role as well as for the length of time each hearing is meant to take— apart from a definition of the effort required for effective "dealing" with each case—deviation becomes possible. This has a de facto effect on the results of the game, which stem from the players' backgrounds and from the power employed against each of those responsible for implementing the law.

The Legalisation of the Interaction

Let us focus on other actors and examine to what degree their influence is felt regarding the interaction in the labour relations field. We will use Mondlek's (2004) definition of legalisation as a phenomenon in which norms and patterns of legal action trickle into other areas of life. In Israel this trend is manifested in a number of ways; by the increasing need for the mediations and decisions of courts and lawyers in settling labour relations issues, in many other areas of legislation, and in the growing use of legal terminology outside of the legal field. In the past decade, we have witnessed the process of "legalisation" of labour relations—multiple petitions to the labour court, for private conflicts between employers and employees as well as in collective disputes. The reasons for this are varied; the expansion of the labour market, the process of globalisation that requires a more efficient and competitive market, increasing powers granted to the courts, and a change in the norms that characterise the labour relations system. The labour relations field is influenced by the aforementioned factors, and this is manifested in the lessened ability of the parties to reach an agreement (Bank of Israel report, 2004, Employment and Salary chapter).

Within the framework of the discourse of law in action, the claim is made that the rules of the law are influenced not only by the backgrounds of those who participate in the interaction but also by the worldview of the lawyers who act, in many cases, as cultural agents mediating between the disputants and the legal world (Trubeck 1980). Furthermore, the claim was made that the contribution of the law to what occurs within the legal field is highly significant, and its repercussions become part of the social reality within which relations occur among those involved in the legal process. The argument could therefore be made that the legalisation of the interaction within the framework of relations between the state's clients and the legal system limits the capabilities of those who exercise the law and reduces their autonomy of judgment, given that some of them lack the appropriate legal background. In addition, the presence of a lawyer during the course of the hearings has a direct and indirect influence upon its results. This argument emerges from the senior supervisor's statement:

> More and more employers arrive with lawyers, and this makes my decision more difficult as they try to attack and find loopholes every way possible. Even the women who can't afford it are equipped with lawyers, which makes things more complicated and slows down our work. More lawyers are entering the market. They don't have work, so they "hitch a ride" on the labour laws and inflate the cases, get their clients "heated up," and create a reality that is much harsher and more complex. It is almost impossible to arrive at a decision without it being attacked from one of the sides [either the employer or the employee].

(Interview, February 2008)

The findings presented at the opening of the chapter, along with findings from the survey we carried out, strengthen the argument that more and more employers, and in recent years women as well, employ the services of lawyers. Despite the fact that the system is meant to be equal and available to all, in 2002—the year the survey was performed—it was found that more than a third (34%) of the women cared for by the system used the services of a lawyer. Women who use a private lawyer come mainly from the socioeconomic middle- and upper-middle classes, and they belong for the most part to independent professions. It was further noted that 39% of the group of women who received protection from the state had employed a private lawyer. Of this group, 70% expressed satisfaction with the service they received from the lawyer, for example in negotiations they carried out with the employer, with the correspondence with the Ministry of Labour, or with the professional instruction they received. There were those who claimed that the fee was too high for them, and that they nonetheless used a lawyer. This is in contrast to the 28% of women who did not use a lawyer and received assistance from the system. It should be noted that the survey findings do not reveal a clear influence upon the results of the hearing being caused by assistance from a lawyer. However, despite the fact that the quantitative findings are unclear, the qualitative results that emerged from observations and interviews offer other dimensions to the phenomenon, which are important to study and understand. The presence of lawyers in hearings with those who exercise the law has become a regular part of this work, and it creates a new reality that may influence the manner in which the hearing plays out, as well as its outcome.

Let us examine the argument that having a further player enter the field supposedly relieves the supervisor of the burden of advising and aiding the employee. In cases in which there are no lawyers involved, the employee is liable not to fully assert her rights according to the law, and the gender-based inequality increases. It should be noted that during the hearings, inequality toward the women as opposed to the employers was seen—an inequality that manifested in the rule that allows lawyers accompanying employers to participate in the hearing and be heard during the proceedings, while a lawyer accompanying employees is forbidden from speaking. This emerged during the hearing mentioned below (December 2008). A marketing manager at a retail company, with one year's experience in the organisation, said, "The lawyer explained the law to me. They had dismissed numerous employees because of pregnancy, and they tried to fire me as well six months ago."

> **Supervisor**: If you want to keep your job you need to go back to work. Go back and try not to fight with them.
>
> **The supervisor adds**: Did they mention performance to you?
>
> Employee: No.
>
> **[The lawyer tries to interrupt but the supervisor does not allow it]**
>
> **Employee**: I am just very emotional.
>
> **Lawyer nonetheless interrupts**: She has no social security. I know you often mediate, and we would like to reach an agreement.
>
> **Supervisor**: You can request a permit for the day of birth, which is what generally happens in a compromise.
>
> (Hearing observation, December 2008).

This example demonstrates how the presence of a further actor may, on the one hand, expropriate the state's responsibility to offer alternatives such as compromise, counselling, or assistance, while on the other hand appropriating the woman's responsibility to maintain her position independently. Thus, through her personal capital, she may manage to maintain her position, but she replaces her reliance upon the state with reliance upon another element, the lawyer. This again raises the question of the equality of the process before the law. Although the lawyer is forbidden from intervening during the proceedings, at times they ignore this request, and in many cases at the end of the hearing they speak with the supervisor. This discussion may apply power in the end and influence (albeit indirectly) the supervisor's judgment as to whether to protect the employee or permit her dismissal.

The influence of the lawyer's latent power was revealed in a further interaction at the centre of which was a high-tech employee accompanied by a lawyer. When the supervisor stated during the course of the hearing that the lawyer could not respond, the employee protested that each minute was costing her money, and she asked the lawyer why he had bothered to appear at all at the hearing. His response was "this could help us further along, in court" (Hearing observation, March 2000).

This case exemplifies the common claim at the core of the law in action discourse; formal tribunals are at best effective for a limited number of cases. They act as an active threat, functioning on the edges of social interaction, and indirectly, in order to affect future negotiations (Macaulay 1984). One could say that despite the fact that the lawyer's participation in the hearing is limited during the interaction, it could help the employee by applying latent power and pressure upon the supervisor, as well as in future representation in court. This is precisely what was explained by an lawyer in the national labour court, "There is no doubt that there is an inflation of lawyers and they sometimes do extremely bad work, but they speak legalese, and today I see more and more women arriving with counsel."

When asked if she recalled a specific case that could support her statement, she replied:

> There was a case where the employee had been through treatments in the past and did not mention it to the employer. She became pregnant, went on leave without permission, and was dismissed. The employer, a lawyer himself, dismissed the secretary because she did not have permission, not actually because of the pregnancy. The senior supervisor left her in her position because she was convinced that she was a good and dedicated employee, and no hearing was held. The employer sued, and from 2005 until today, the case has gone from the regional to the national labour courts, and in the final hearing in 2012 it was closed, after Justice

Rosenfeld suggested the parties reach a monetary compromise.

Lawyers arrive prepared, after all the accompanying processes they have performed with the employee, or with the employers in hearings before the Ministry of Industry, Commerce, and Employment and through correspondence with the organisations. Although I am a lawyer at the national court, and I receive relatively few cases related to the regional level, there is no doubt that there is an over-legalisation of the field. There was a time when we did not get any files at all.

(Interview, July 2012)

The lawyer's comments give credence to the argument that the processes of legalisation are trickling down to the area of dismissals during pregnancy. The explanations according to which the lawyers "speak legalese" fit the dramaturgical approach, which maintains that the reciprocity between actors from a similar background may influence the dynamics between them. These explanations also strengthen the claim of inequality toward those citizens who are unable to hire professional counsel to defend them. The example given by the lawyer shows that the judge in fact ruled on a case that could have ended within the framework of the system, instead of at a trial that dragged on for years and ate up vast amounts of time and financial resources from the participants.

A further expression of this may be seen in the hearing discussed below, during which there were clear repercussions noted from the legalisation of the field as well as in the "lawyer norm" that affects the level of assistance given by those who apply the law. At the centre of the interaction is an employee from a technological services company, an industry and management engineer, according to whom "the project I worked on ended; there are no more contracts, and when I underwent fertility treatment I did not tell anyone."

> **Supervisor**: They have to continue paying until they have permission.
>
> **Employee**: They are not paying.
>
> **Supervisor**: Tell him to give you back your position.
>
> **Employee**: I want to work.

At the end of the hearing, the supervisor said, "If she had said that she was undergoing treatment she could have squeezed out a bit more. Likely enough, if she had had representation, she would have known this" (Observation and interview post-hearing, June 2009).

Here the supervisor chose not to supply this information, despite the fact that the system is meant to provide information to the employee, according to the senior supervisor during that period. The supervisor did not complete her task, and relied on the "lawyer norm," which did not apply to this employee and thus in effect she did not assert all of her rights.

Therefore, it appears that the legalisation of the area has become a norm in the field, to the extent that explanations of the law by those who wield it have been abandoned, and instead this role has been transferred to the responsibility of the lawyers. Thus, women and employers who are not represented by legal counsel are, on the one hand, harmed, and on the other, they do not receive full instruction from the state.

This claim is reinforced in light of statements made by the senior supervisor in 2012:

> Anyone with enough money to fund it arrives with a lawyer. There are women who are not represented, who say nonsense during the hearing, as well as employers, particularly small-scale ones, who absolutely defeat themselves. If they have not had any instruction, they could really make mistakes. We cannot sit one on one and explain as we do not have the time.

> (Interview, September 2012)

The supervisor's comments reflect a picture of inequality being created, and fit the micro approaches that act as the theoretical basis for this chapter. On the one hand, there are large organisations represented by batteries of lawyers. This group includes women with the financial, and one can assume, cultural capital, who have been instructed by their lawyer how best to leave the "right" impression on the hearing stand. On the other hand, there are also those women who "say nonsense," and small business employers who may lack the resources to engage appropriate representation, and thus their impression is less effective before the system. In this way, two de facto types of population are created before the very system that is meant to be universal in its service to all its clients. Below are comments by the senior supervisor for human resources at one of the largest organisations in Israel:

> Today I use our lawyers for every single little lawsuit. I have an entire battery. A year ago, for example, a human resources employee was dismissed, and about a month later she came to us and said that the dismissal was invalid because she was pregnant. At the Ministry of Industry, Commerce, and Employment they granted us permission, and the employee would not give in and took us to court. Our lawyers made such fools of her lawyer that the judge waved the permit and said to the lawyer and the employee, there is a permit here from the Ministry of Industry, Commerce, and Employment, what else do you want? In this case she was a temporary medical secretary here. We would not even think of dismissing our permanent employees. In any case, I use our legal bureau more and more.

(Interview, September 2012)

This strengthens the arguments concerning legalisation of labour relations as well as regarding the clear hierarchy of larger employers. One could say that the strong financial status of an organisation represented by a "battery of lawyers" improved their ability to manage the impression they made on the Ministry of Industry, Commerce, and Employments, or before any labour court. Thus the inequality increases toward women who are not represented, or less effectively represented.

How Compromises Are Reached

Despite the instruction in the Women's Labour Law Section 9a, according to which the system of intervention will examine each case and a decision will be made whether to permit or refuse the request for dismissal, there are cases that end in compromise. In 2002 close to a quarter of the cases ended in compromise, while a decade later, in 2013, out of 1,176 cases, 12% ended in compromise, as opposed to 6% in 2012. In official documents from the Ministry of Industry, Commerce, and Employment, the section is defined thus, "12% of cases ended with the agreement of the employee."[103] Presumably, in these cases the employers were unable to prove deficiency, as did a third (32%) of the employers in 2012, and 18% in 2013. It is likely that they tried and were unsuccessful in proving financial difficulties as did more than half of the organisations in 2012 (56%) and two-thirds in the following year (66%).

---

103 Ministry of Industry, Commerce and Employment website, under Department of Resolution and Enforcement, www. moital.gov.il

Sometimes, the compromise ends with the file being closed, which generally leads to a payment in accordance with the woman's rights (dismissal compensation and the woman's salary for the months left until birth plus the 60 days she is due protection from dismissal following a return from maternity leave), but not with a return to the workplace as the legislator intended. This is shown, for example, in the following comments by the supervisor:

> If once a file has been opened and we are informed that a compromise has been reached, I do not dig too deep. I have no legal mandate to examine these matters beyond what I am meant to do. I am not permitted to examine whether there is or is not a link to the pregnancy. If we are told that there is a compromise, as far as I am concerned, the file is closed. I also do not check whether the agreement is fulfilled, or the content of the agreement.

> (Interview with supervisor, February 2011)

> Once the employer and the employee have succeeded in reaching an agreement, the file, insofar as we are concerned, is closed. I have no mandate to interfere, despite the fact that at times the employer and the employee come to me with the agreement, and then I can suggest a permit from the date of giving birth, and this is a sort of compromise between them. Each of them gives in to the other a bit. The employee generally receives

a salary but stays at home until the birth. Some of them are happy with this.

(Conversation following observation, February 2008)

In one of the observations, the employee said, "I do not have enough days for social security so I hope you will help us reach some agreement." At the end of the interview, the supervisor said, "What does she want? I cannot pay her until the birth" (Conversation post-hearing, May 2009).

Despite these comments by the supervisor, there were cases in which the interaction ended differently. In one hearing, a lawyer accompanied an academic employer with a managerial position. His comments show prior knowledge, "I can offer an 'off-the-record' compromise. I know that you often perform this sort of mediation." The supervisor's response, "I agree that you can write that you are prepared for a permit for the date of giving birth" (Observation, March 2009). This means that the employee receives her salary until the birth and will then be dismissed. In other words, the state is permitting the law to be broken, because in fact, the employee is protected by law from dismissal until several months after her maternity leave. In the case before us, a compromise was reached by stepping off of the formal stage to the "off-the-record" one, behind the scenes.

It should be noted that the supervisor did everything possible to prevent the lawyer from speaking, however, despite her best efforts, his pressure and stubbornness led her to agree. This case fits the "from the bottom up" policy theory, according to which pressure brought to bear by citizens—in this case the employer's lawyer—influences the implementation of the policy and tips the decision in a direction other than straightforward law. This case also exemplifies Lipsky's theory (Lipsky 1980), which points to "street-level bureaucrats" as those with the influence to implement public policy more than decisions by the upper strata that sets policy. We have already explained that civil servants in the field, according to Lipsky, set the agenda through their dealing with uncertain situations and work pressures, and that the conflict is expressed in the struggles between individual civil servants and the citizens who pressure them. Lipsky further explained that the civil servants are influenced by stereotypes that they create regarding the clientele. These claims may be seen in a variety of ways. First, we have seen the power of the supervisor and her ability to help beyond what is required by the law. Second, the pressures exercised upon the supervisor show how, in the spirit of the dramaturgical approach, the power relations between the various actors influence the interaction between them and finally upon the successful impression, which tips the scales.

These findings also back the claims by law-in-action researchers, that the ability to benefit from the law is not obvious and depends on the participants' backgrounds. This argument is exemplified in the case of the catering employee with limited personal capital, who was unable to influence the supervisor, as opposed to the case of the lawyer who represented an employee with extensive personal and financial capital, whose pressure succeeded in affecting the decision.

Despite the fact that Israel employs a universal system of intervention that is meant to provide assistance to all women, over a third of the women do not settle for the state's protection and purchase "professional protection services." This figure creates two sorts of populations who function as a stratified factor that reflects the inequality and the social superiority of certain groups, and thus also the inferiority and exclusion of others. In other words, the findings prove that despite the fact that regulatory systems are open to provide assistance for women and employers from all manner of professions and economic classes, their accessibility is not equal for the general population. It is actually the large organisations, on the one hand, and well-established women on the other who increase their chances of receiving the state's protection by employing socioeconomic-cultural capital. Thus, in effect, the discrimination occurs toward less well-established populations and organisations, which is a discrimination that creates two types of citizens and employers. The first is type A, who increase their chances of "managing impressions," as opposed to type B, who experience an expansion of inequality. It is therefore worth taking a deeper look and examining how informal actors, whose assistance is not dependent upon financial resources, affect the chances of women to leave a more effective impression.

How Did Women Experience the Assistance from Informal Actors?

Theoreticians who study "the law in action" claim that only observation of events found beyond the field of law can illuminate the social reality that lies beyond the formal legal process (Trubeck 1980). With regard to these arguments, we have shown that alongside the formal administrative process of the protection given by the state, there are extra-state practices that supply counsel and instruction to women who were dismissed during their pregnancy or following maternity leave, including women's organisations and the new Histadrut.

It should be emphasised that the findings of regression were not clear vis-à-vis the efficacy of using all of these sources of help or employing a lawyer. Nonetheless, it may be said that the very fact of assistance contributes to guidance regarding how to deal with the regulation, as preparation for a hearing, to empowerment or legal defense during the state process and afterward, as well as in minimising the sense of uncertainty—all without cost (apart from the services of the lawyer, as discussed in this chapter).

Assistance from Women's Groups

As discussed in Chapter Two, from the mid-1980s women's organisations began to offer help in cases of dismissals during pregnancy, and bodies including the Women's Lobby encouraged women to protect their rights as salaried employees. This activity is complementary to the enforcement of rights and their anchoring in the legislation. At the basis of the women's organisations' activities lies the concept that salaried employment acts as a factor in reducing dependency and inequality. Staying within the labour cycle means a chance to remain involved in society and to continue developing social skills (Tamir and Nagar 2007).

Findings show that of those who dealt with the regulations, close to 36% used the services of women's organisations, and close to two-thirds subjectively reported, unrelated to the outcome, that this assistance was effective. Aid for women is provided in the form of guidance, and for a small number of them in the form of legal representation. Even those who do not receive legal representation are instructed by the organisations over the phone vis-à-vis how to deal with the state system. The legal counselors in these organisations report an increasing rise in complaints linked to dismissal during pregnancy, "Most of the women have no idea that they can complain and sue" (Lawyer Odelia Levi-Ettinger, Representative of the College of Lawyers, Protocol no. 160, February 14, 2005). Similar claims arose in Knesset committees from 2010 onwards.

In light of these figures, which reveal that more than two-thirds of women seek assistance, and that some make use of information received from women's organisations during their hearings, it is unsurprising to hear this sort of statement from the senior supervisor at the end of a hearing, "It smells as if the women's groups gave her instructions beforehand" (February 2008). We thus hear statements from the women such as, "The Women's Lobby told me I cannot be accompanied to the hearing" (telephone conversation, February 2011), a comment which demonstrates the women's preparation for interaction with the welfare system. In each of the meetings of the Committee for the Advancement of the Status of Women and Gender-Based Equality, some of which were presented in the book, the women's organisations staunchly defended their empowerment in the field. This explains the comments by a representative of the Women's Lobby, Shir-El Nakdimon:

> So, it is true that we really do not want to say that every woman who has ever become pregnant will be protected for life, but in fact, an employer who tells an employee during her pregnancy "of course you will be dismissed," should also be dealt with by the law. … I spoke about the issues of status and of the warning of the sort, "You will be dismissed on the 61st day," and how protection for the employees may be handled in this area as well.
>
> (Knesset Committee for the Advancement of the Status of Women, Protocol 165, March 12, 2012)

These quotes demonstrate the ways in which the matter has been debated over the years by the Committee for the Advancement of the Status of Women. In accordance with this, one could cautiously assume that if the women's organisation as an actor is not physically present on the stage of the hearing before the state, its power influences the dynamics in the field vis-à-vis expansion of the power of women against the state.

Seeking Assistance from the Histadrut

A game change in the rules of the labour world along with the weakening of professional unions, as mentioned in earlier chapters, left many employees open to discrimination by their employers. The reduced power of the Histadrut in the mid-1990s left a vacuum of lack of protection for the workers. Nonetheless, the "New Histadrut," which was established from the ashes of the old one, intends to act as a resource for all employees. "It is true, there were years in which we were not heard, but now we want to give more support to employees and protect them from the growing exploitation by employers who do not provide appropriate conditions" (Interview with the Director of the New Histadrut, February 2010).

Despite these statements, we are witness to the fact that notwithstanding the findings, which show that 40% of the women whose dismissals were sought during pregnancy requested assistance from the Histadrut, nearly half of them reported that the help was ineffective, and that they received comments typical of the old Histadrut, "If you are not a member, you will not receive protection", or "Your organisation is not a member so you will not get protection" (survey findings, 2006). One woman even claimed that the representative who she had consulted slapped her face, and she did not sue because in her condition she did not have the strength to commence a new battle.

Despite the fact that the regulation mechanisms are open to providing equal assistance to all women, there are women who nonetheless try to increase their chances of being defended, and who employ other bodies for this purpose. There are however, of all the women participating in the survey, some who requested help from non-state actors and claimed the assistance was effective, and more women who sought assistance from women's organisations (67%). This is in relation to half of the women who received help from the Histadrut and were satisfied with it.

We will now examine who these women are who have successfully entered the labour relations field.

Assistance and Unequal Access—Who Manages to Enter the Field?

"Law in action" researchers claim that the very fact of assistance from the law should not be taken for granted, and it is itself mediated by social capital (Ewick and Silbey

1998; Silbey 2001). Further, the argument exists that apart from the extensive heterogeneity in the manners of the operation of the various state actors in their design and implementation of systems to prevent dismissals, there is also a significant difference in the ability of citizens to receive assistance from the state mechanisms. This matter lies at the core of this field. Not only did the ambiguity manifest in the state systems, but also the differential chances of those seeking aid to receive appropriate legal representation explain the failure of legal interventions to prevent the forbidden discrimination.[104] According to this approach, the differential access to legal aid explains the marginal influence of the extensive and advanced legislation for the prevention of discrimination in the labour force. These studies highlight the importance of the state systems working to enforce the laws,[105] and not just the mere existence of said laws.[106] In recent years, "law in action" literature extensively documents the variations in the *accessibility* of the legal system to different groups, and it raises the fact that members of socially weaker groups, the economically disadvantaged, ethnic groups, and those who are not citizens have a harder time exercising their rights in the various legal tribunals. This

104 Bumiller 1988; Selznick 1961; Silbey 2001, 2003; Kritzer and Silbey 2003.
105 Laws including equal wages, equal opportunities, prevention of discrimination.
106 Lofstrom and Gustafsson 1991; Bellace 1991; Ferber 1991; Mandel 2004.

is due to a lack of knowledge of the law and of the rights due to them, as well as a lack of financial, social, and cultural resources that facilitate access to courts of law, quality legal representation, and the ability to be heard within the framework of legal proceedings. Therefore the principle of equality is damaged under the law[107]

---

107 The principle of equality before the law is based upon an approach that states that laws must apply uniformly to all citizens of the state, and their implementation must occur without bias, in the sense of "one law for rich and poor." The rule of law in the State of Israel, as in most rule-of-law states in the world, is based upon the principle of equality before the law. This principle is based upon equal fairness toward all citizens without prejudice against background, religion, race, or gender. Nonetheless there are judges who claim that there are times when the term equality before the law carries a double meaning in Israel. First, because there is no constitution in Israel, the Knesset is responsible for passing egalitarian laws and thus protecting equality is dependent upon the Knesset self-policing itself. Second, the executive branch can enforce equality-based laws in an unequal manner, by discriminating on the basis of background, race, religion, or gender. This kind of discrimination is forbidden and unacceptable, however, given that people are not equal, there is, at times a need to exercise discretion which may contradict the principle of equality. In order to address this conflict, legal workers argue that "for each and every matter there are considerations that are relevant to the matter and external considerations that are irrelevant to the matter." (High Court/ 95387 Poraz v Mayor of Tel Aviv, Zamir 1991, High Court/ 98169, Bergman v Minister of the Exchequer).

for these groups.[108]

Access to the Law

Researchers and legal workers agree that citizens' level of accessibility to the courts is unequal and depends, in many cases, on their sociocultural capital (Bogosh and Don Yihyeh 1999). Sociocultural capital is defined as the sum of all resources a woman possesses, including social connections, academic references, goods owned, trust in the state system, background, and personal abilities. In a similar context, Bourdieu argues that the cultural capital acts as a stratifying factor that reflects the inequality in a society, and that understanding the various types of capital will contribute to an understanding of the structure and function of the social world (Bourdieu 1986).

As stated, at the core of the "law in action" discourse is the argument that the chances of disempowered groups for assistance in the legal system are significantly smaller than those of the stronger groups. The establishment of a universal state mechanism for the prevention of dismissal of pregnant women in Israel was intended to reduce the importance of the social and economic resources available to a woman when defining her chances of protection from dismissal during her pregnancy. The "law in action"

---

108 Bogosh and Don Yihyeh 1999; Bumiller 1988; Selznick 1961; Silbey 2001, 2003; Ewick and Silbey 1998; Kritzer and Silbey 2003.

argument has been examined by comparing the rates of applications to the system for the prevention of dismissal at the Ministry of Industry, Commerce, and Employment and the rates of application for unemployment benefits, which are more accessible, provide financial aid according to one's entitlement, and do not require one to deal with a hearing.

A comparison of the number of those who turn to the system for prevention of dismissal at the Ministry of Industry, Commerce, and Employment with the number of applications for unemployment benefits, and with the human resource figures on new mothers who were dismissed reveals minimal differences in the accessibility of the various population groups to the two state systems. For example, new immigrants formed 16.5% of all new mothers dismissed, and 17% were those who turned to the Ministry and to the Employment Services, as we will detail later. In addition, despite the notable differences that we discovered among women in the various education groups, both women with university education and those who had not completed secondary school received treatment from the prevention system at higher rates than the rate of the population who were dismissed during pregnancy. While the rate of women lacking secondary education among those dismissed during pregnancy accounts for 4.2% according to the human resources survey, the rate among those turning to the Employment Services is 6.5%, and among those handled by the prevention mechanism they account for 17%. Women with a university education accounted for 26.5% of those dismissed during pregnancy, and 36% of those were dealt with by the prevention system. These figures indicate that despite the difficulty apparent in the general number of applications for help from the system for the prevention of dismissals, among Jewish women it was more difficult to identify a clear pattern of discrimination or differences in the accessibility to state mechanisms between those groups normally seen as weak and strong. The case of Arab women, however, is starkly different. While the rate of Arab women among those new mothers dismissed stands at 6.4%, the rate among those assisted by the system for prevention reaches less than 1%, while the number of those seeking assistance from the Employment Services in order to receive unemployment benefits was especially high, reaching 11%. In the methodology chapter, a description is given of the survey within which these figures appeared.

I would now like to present some explanations of the statistical findings noted. First let us focus on the immigrants' group. Studies show that new immigrants from the 1990s are more highly integrated than their counterparts in the population in the secondary work sector in Israel, and they are found in part-time and temporary positions through contractors and human resource companies (Nadiv 2005). Further, the birthrate among immigrant women from the former USSR is lower than the birthrate of those born here (Okun 1997). Based on this figure alone, one can surmise that their chances of becoming pregnant and being exposed to pregnancy-related dismissal is lower than that of women who have been in Israel for longer. On the other hand, the high rate of immigrant workers in the secondary employment sector, and their high rate in jobs involving physical labour, cleaning and maintenance work, could foretell that when they do become pregnant their possibility of dismissal will be higher than long-term employees. In further studies it was noted that employers in the secondary sector were less likely to follow labour laws, including providing full information about rights and labour laws (Ho et al. 1996). If so, the assumption could be made that those who employ the immigrants would request fewer permits for dismissal during pregnancy, and that the immigrants would be less aware of their legal rights than employees with more experience in Israel. However, as we have said, in a survey conducted for the purposes of this study, it was noted that new immigrants account for 16.5% of all new mother employees dismissed and 17% are the employees who turn to the Ministry of Industry, Commerce, and Employment and to the Employment Services. This finding is supported by a conversation with the senior legal supervisor:

> Immigrants come to us occasionally, and they are not always familiar with the law. I cannot really characterise whether there is a phenomenon of immigrants being more or less aware; there are those who know the law and those who know less—

it depends where they come from. ... The more educated ones come to me once they have done their homework, protected by a battery of lawyers. They are aware of the law and are familiar with it. The uneducated ones may be familiar with the law. If they are not, we explain it to them, although they are not meant to come to us if they know the law.

(Telephone conversation with the senior supervisor, 3.6.12)

From comments by the senior supervisor concerning accessibility for immigrants, it seems that there really is no clear pattern for the behaviour of the immigrants regarding the system, and in this context it could be said that the findings do not match up with the research arguments concerning reduced accessibility for disempowered populations to legal aid.[109] Nonetheless, her statement represents her clear position on the various dimensions of the system's patterns of action and she is, therefore, important to our discussion.

The approach that posits that the range of those who are capable of dealing with the system is greater than that of the weaker population, based on the senior supervisor's experience of many years in the field, is not borne out by the numbers. While the rate of women with no secondary

---

109 Bogosh and Don Yihyeh 1999; Bumiller 1988; Selznick 1961; Silbey 2001, 2003; Ewick and Silbey 1998; Kritzer and Silbey 2003.

education among those dismissed, as seen in the human resources survey, is 4.2%, their rate within those women who turn to Employment Services is 6.5%, and among those handled by the intervention mechanism, they reach 17%. One possible explanation for this could be found in the seniority variable in the labour force. It may be that women who are mostly employed in jobs that do not require expertise have not spent enough time in the labour force in order to have accumulated sufficient seniority—the training period required by social security laws—and therefore apply to the intervention mechanism in order to try and maintain their ability to make a living, without which they will end up with no income at all. The validity of this explanation may be seen in the hearing held for G., a cafeteria cook employed by a catering company, who had accumulated only 8 months of seniority. During the course of the hearing, she said to the supervisor:

> I would ask you to please be considerate of me. If you do not defend me I will not be able to go to the National Insurance Institute—I do not have enough seniority, and since a second company bought out the catering company where I work, I will lose out. They took all of the male employees who work as porters; just not me, because I'm pregnant.

> (Hearing observation, April 2009).

This case demonstrated, first of all, the distressing situation the uneducated worker finds herself in. Secondly, the case sharpens the discrimination for the pregnant employee vis-à-vis the other employees. This discrimination further strengthens the weakness of her sociocultural capital, which stems from her lack of education and in this case from her being female.

The case of H., a salesperson for a clothing chain, also paints a picture of the distress and the uncertainty an uneducated employee finds herself opposed with when faced with the system. Below is a small part of her statement during the hearing, which lasted far beyond the average time:

> After I gave notification of the pregnancy, they suddenly informed me that they did not need me. I arranged some merchandise on the shelf; I didn't feel well, so I came down to get a drink of water, and right then the department manager came in and told me to go home. The next day they sent me an SMS saying not to come to work. Since I became pregnant they had me working on much more difficult tasks.
>
> (Hearing observation,, May 2008)

Half an hour after the hearing, the employee came back into the room while the supervisor was involved in another hearing and asked, "Why did they even send me to you?"

At the end of the interrupted hearing the supervisor commented, "It will be a refusal. She annoyed me with her

stupidity and waste of my time. I need to get her focused."
This case demonstrates how the low status and lack of
knowledge of the uneducated employee is reflected in her
limited ability to manage the rules of the field. On the one
hand, the state seeks to protect this sort of employee and
enters them into the field, however, on the other hand, her
lack of knowledge upset the supervisor. Instead of being
understanding and explaining the rules of the game to the
employee in order to give her more mobility and expand
her knowledge and power, the supervisor maintained her
limited power.

Of the hearings observed, it emerged that the
testimonies of educated employees flowed and were better
understood than those of the uneducated employees. The
employees' cultural capital acts as a factor in improving
chances of better expressing oneself within the system.
Having said that, despite notable differences seen among
women of varied educational levels, the human resources
survey demonstrated that both women with a university
education, and those who did not complete their secondary
education were treated within the state system at a higher
rate than their percentage within the population of women
dismissed during pregnancy in the labour market. These
figures establish that despite the difficulties, as discussed
in the previous chapter, of general levels of applications for
assistance from the system for the prevention of dismissals
among Jewish women, it is difficult to pinpoint a clear
pattern of discrimination or distinction in accessibility

to the state mechanisms among those groups generally considered weaker and those groups which are strong. These findings do not fit the arguments by the law in action researchers.[110] One could say, however, that the unique nature of the universal system redesigns accessibility to the process while simultaneously reflecting the power of the weaker populations, and thus it does not make the system more egalitarian but rather maintains the gaps that had existed prior to entry into the field. It is nonetheless worth examining groups that do not possess the "appropriate" habitus and are therefore excluded a priori from the field.

Ethnic Groups against the State: Assistance versus Exclusion

The case of Arab women clearly supports the argument standing at the centre of the "law in action" discourse: the ability of ethnic groups to access state institutions and legal tribunals is much smaller than that of other groups in the country (Silbey 2003; Ewick and Silbey 1998). While the percentage of Arab women among the new mothers dismissed stands at 6.4%, their presence among those women who employed the prevention mechanism is less than 1%, and their rate among those employees who turned to the Employment Services in order to receive

---

110 Bogosh and Don Yihyeh 1999; Kritzer and Silbey 2003; Bumiller 1988; Selznick 1961; Silbey 2001, 2003; Ewick and Silbey 1998.

unemployment benefits is particularly high, 11%. Given that only one Arab employee was included in the survey carried out among women whose cases were brought before the state system, one suspects that the low percentage reflects the low rate of willingness among this population to participate in the survey and not necessarily a low rate of application to the ministry's system. Notwithstanding this, the ministry's supervisors were asked to estimate the number of Arab women whose cases were brought before them, and according to their assessment, the rate of Arab women within the total of cases does not exceed 1%. As the supervisor said, "Arab women come in dribs and drabs, but those who do arrive are aware, educated, those with resources, the ones with seniority" (Telephone conversation, June 3, 2012). Despite this, 11% of all women who apply for unemployment benefits during their pregnancy are Arabs, who turn to Social Services and the Employment Services. Explanations for this may be rooted in several possibilities which complement one another. Given that the test for receiving unemployment benefits is formal, and because the Employment Services mechanism is more accessible geographically and socially to the Arab sector than the state protection system, that only holds hearings in large cities and at times only in Tel Aviv, the distance may act as a barrier for Arab women in seeking assistance from the ministry's system. One could therefore assume that sociodemographic characteristics, along with sociocultural capital characteristics such as places of residence, knowledge of Hebrew, education, knowledge of the law, and trust in the state system reduce the ability of Arab women to receive aid from within the state system and affect their ability to apply to the Employment Services system. One of the supervisors we interviewed, who is very familiar with employment patterns in the Arab sector, claimed:

> The Arab employees who are dismissed during their pregnancies are loathe to bring the matter before the state system because their employers are for the most part people from their surrounding community, and by turning to the state system it could harm their future employment chances, and even their social situation.
>
> (Interview with a supervisor in the Enforcement Bureau, June 2009)

In the spirit of the dramaturgical approach, one could posit that the interaction taking place upon a foreign stage, in a language that is not one's mother tongue, discourages the women from dealing with a system whose operators are from a background different to their own. These findings support Bourdieu's claims concerning unequal opportunities to enter the field and compete for its prizes. It appears that the habitus of Arab women does not allow them to appear on the hearing's stage and does not even allow them to enter the theatre. This sort of approach raises many questions concerning the manner in which the state's assistance to all its citizens is seen and supports the arguments of "law in action" researchers, according to which the legal solutions are not equally accessible to all sectors of the population.[111]

In the next section I would like to examine the active practices of those women who were able to enter the hearing stage.

Women in Action

In order to fully comprehend how one operates within the state, apart from the accepted sociodemographic characteristics, we chose to examine the practices of action that women employ in order to receive the state's protection. Women's practices of action stem from within their socioeconomic and cultural capital, with Bourdieu further arguing that the practice is a place within which habitus is expressed. At the heart of the practice is the social context in its symbolic sense; a place in which the individual can act. The practices are not fully "objective," because they leave room for action—but they are also not completely "subjective," as they are influenced by the construct and from within it (Richer 2006). Bourdieu addressed the options and manners of operation for individuals with free (though limited) choice. His argument was, as stated,

111 Bogosh and Don Yihyeh 1999; Bumiller 1988; Selznick 1961; Silbey 2001, 2003; Ewick and Silbey 1998; Kritzer and Silbey 2003.

that the field is a sort of competitive market in which various forms of capital (economic, cultural and social) are employed. Those who fulfill spaces in the field seek to improve or maintain their positions, and to place the hierarchical principles that favour them. It is impossible to enter the field without adopting its rules, however, from the moment one enters it, the rules may be changed. In other words, each field has its own rules, but they are not sacred, and they may be fought over and altered.

Within this context, the argument that women who decided to actively work to maintain their position in the labour market were more successful at it than those who did not try their strength, will be considered. The economic capital is financial wealth whose value can be realised in all parts of society, for example in employing the services of a lawyer, as we discussed in the previous section. The social capital is a network of long-term social relations, and it manifests itself in the area of the subject's social contacts. Cultural capital is manifested through knowledge, behaviour, tendencies, diplomas, and education (Grenfell and James 1998). According to this approach, pregnant women with the "required" habitus to increase their resources in the field—such as with cultural and economic capital—who were dismissed, will succeed in maximising their chances of receiving the state's protection and return to the labour market faster, as opposed to women who lack this sort of capital. These claims will be examined in this section.

In keeping with the various theories from the area of law in action, we analysed a series of independent variables, listed in the methodological chapter. To these background variables we added the woman's response to the question to what degree she had been active in preventing her dismissal herself (acted, did not act). This question does not necessarily reflect the level of action actually undertaken, but rather the subjective feeling of control which women have in their fate or in their desire for said control.

Non-linear regression, which we carried out in order to examine the influence of multiple variables on the decision of the state system whether to protect the employee or agree to the request for dismissal, reveals that the sole variable that significantly and clearly explains the willingness of the state system to protect the employee whose case is before it is her willingness or ability to work in order to receive this protection.

In order to examine the assumption that personal capital variables would increase the chances of receiving the state's protection, the dependent variable—the state's protection—was checked against the independent variable, through several regressions.

The table below presents the results of the logistic (non-linear) regression, and the multiple variable regression for the analysis of the influence of personal characteristics upon the employee's chances of receiving the state's protection from dismissal.

The link between the woman's actions and receiving protection from the state, according to background characteristics and active practices*

Independent Variable: Was defended (refusal)	1	2
Acted to prevent dismissal (action)	11.586	14.166
	(0.00)	(0.00)
Seniority	-	1.113
		(0.29)
Age	-	1.065
		(0.25)
Working partner	-	0.513
		(0.33)
Assistance from women's organisations	-	1.504
		(0.41)
Organisation size	-	0.888
		(0.53)
University education	-	1.186
		(0.74)
Assistance from a lawyer	-	0.999
		(1.00)
N observations	100	97
C index for nature of compatibility	68.3%	
Likelihood ration	18.18	
P. value	<.0001	

*Survey findings 2006

Findings from the analysis reveal that not a single one of the background variables affected the chance of receiving protection from the state, apart from the women's actions to prevent their dismissals. The rate of the chances of women who acted to receive protection from the state is 11 times higher than that for those who did not state that they undertook to act on this matter. The strong link between the actions of the women and the defense they received would raise the argument that assertiveness and activeness, rather than the protection of the state in itself, are what lead to a woman, who has received said protection, remaining within the labour force.

Nonetheless, the inclusion of the action variable in the regression that examined all of the factors listed as affecting the fact of remaining within the labour cycle revealed that the clear influence of the state's protection remained extremely clear and stable, and even increased for those women who acted, with a ratio of 14 times higher or more, as opposed to those who did not act. We have therefore demonstrated that in contrast to the clear request of the state—to separate the active desire of pregnant women to remain in the labour force and the state's defense of these women—it was clear that the practice of action by these women strongly affected the defense provided for them by the state. In other words, in contrast to the legislature's intent, the state does not act strongly enough to protect those women who are less aware of their rights, or, for various reasons, does not act intently enough to prevent their dismissal. It was noted that all women who decided to actively operate to maintain their status within the labour market were more successful in this in relation to those who did not attempt it. Thus the ability of women to fight for the prizes in the field (protection from the state) was manifested. It is clear that the women's ability was characterised by an autonomy that was made possible by the space of action which the field grants the actors (Grenfell and James 1998). Furthermore, these findings are in line with Bourdieu's argument that entry into the labour relations field is not to be taken for granted. One cannot enter the field without operating according to the norms within it, though once the field has been entered the rules may be changed. In other words, each field has its own rules, which may be challenged and altered (Richer 2006).

Alongside this claim, we will try to explain the findings by presenting the argument at the core of the "bottom up" theory, according to which citizens will influence new policy as long as they are dissatisfied.[112] We have shown that women who did not accept the request to dismiss them were prepared to act in order to affect the state's decision, in order to keep their source of income. The question arises, which actions did these women choose to prevent their dismissal? It was found that in response to the open questions posed to the survey participants,

112 Merritt and Merritt 1985; Altshuler and Zegans 1997; Lynn 1997; Glor 1997; Golden 1997.

such as "How did you act?" the primary answers were, going to the employer (17%), and appealing against the dismissal before the Ministry of Industry, Commerce, and Employment (37%). In accordance with the street-level bureaucracy theory, it was noted that state clerks tend more to defend those women who themselves requested assistance, in those cases where the employer did not apply for a legal permit, with the pressure on the clerks coming solely from the women. Other patterns of action mentioned were, application to women's organisations, lawyers, or the Histadrut in order to receive assistance, as well as writing official letters to the employer or to other parties. Nonetheless, as mentioned, the statistical link between the claim of a woman who acted to prevent her dismissal and her response to direct questions about seeking a lawyer, women's organisations, or help from the Histadrut did not reveal a clear connection between the phenomena.

Pie chart: Women who acted to prevent their dismissal according to application type and results

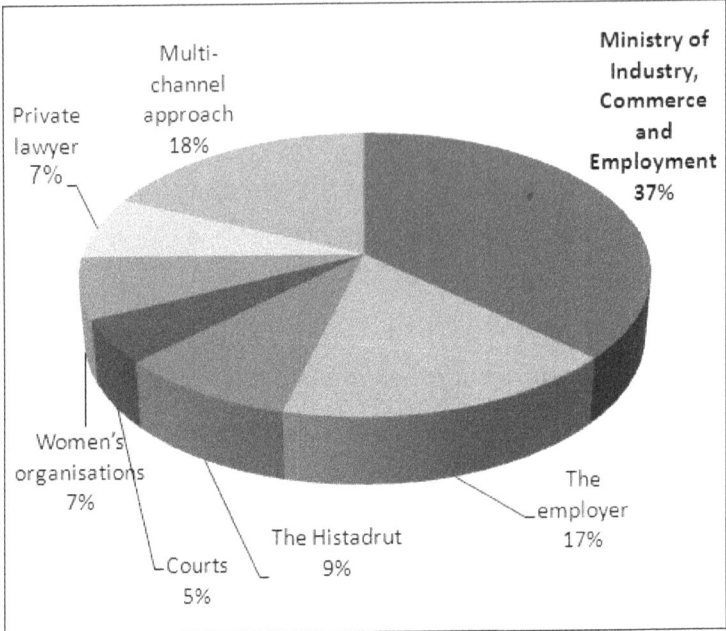

Survey figures 2006
*A multi- channel approach refers to action taken with more than one body.

It is worth mentioning that these findings also support the qualitative results that emerged in the framework of the observations of hearings for many women with a lower status in personal and financial capital: women who were uneducated, who came from a low socioeconomic status, and those whose jobs were as salespeople, dishwashers, cooks, or secretaries, and women who arrived at the "hearing field" well-prepared, assertive, aware of their legal rights, and determined not to lose the prize (meaning their source of income). I will remind the reader here that Bourdieu distinguished between three types of capital: economic, social, and cultural. Economic capital is monetary wealth, and its value can be realised in all areas of society. Social capital is a network of long-term social relations and is manifested in the area of the subject's social contacts. Cultural capital is manifested in research through knowledge and awareness of the secrets of the law and its de facto implementation (Grenfell and James 1998). Through presentation of the cases below, we will examine the argument that pregnant women who were dismissed, as long as they possess cultural capital, will succeed in maximising their chances of operating within the state.

R., an 18-year-old supermarket cashier, arrived for the hearing with her mother. The supervisor asked the mother to wait outside.

> In my previous pregnancy I had a Caesarean section, because there were complications. I cannot work 12, 14 hours during pregnancy. … They want to dismiss me because of the pregnancy. Everyone knows that as soon as you are not working as well, they want to fire you.

The supervisor said to her, "You need to return to work if you want to keep your job." Her response shows that she arrived prepared:

If my mother had not known what the law says they would have dismissed me too. I am a great worker! They threw me out just because of the pregnancy. They throw out anyone who comes for close to a year so they do not have to pay severance. ... They only paid me for the days I was not there after my mother said I could sue them.

(Hearing observation August 2, 2005)

This quotation demonstrates how an employee with the sociocultural capital Bourdieu would define as low status was able to change her social/family capital and move from the network of connections she is located in to a cultural capital of knowledge of the law. In an attempt to explain this case using Bourdieu's theory of capital, one could assume that the employee would not have been made aware of the law if not for her mother drawing her attention to it, and she would then have found herself outside the labour market, as she claimed had happened to other employees with her low status. According to Bourdieu, capital brings capital, and it may be gathered and exchanged. This employee exchanged her social capital for ownership of cultural capital that was manifested through knowledge passed to her by the mother, which helped the employee compete for the state's protection of her livelihood.

The following example, of H., a 22-year-old student in a shop, reflects how an employee with the habitus typical of low status gathered cultural capital, which allowed her to know her rights and to understand how to present her case at the hearing.

> **H.**: I received an SMS that they were dismissing me. I was transferred to another place, and they lowered my wages and my benefits—all after I had announced I could no longer climb ladders and arrange merchandise, because of the pregnancy.
>
> **Supervisor (who had already held the employer's hearing)**: Did you see the letter of complaint?
>
> **H.**: If they had complaints about me, why didn't they dismiss me a year or two ago? Why only now when I am pregnant?
>
> (Hearing observation, March 2008)

The employee's comments demonstrate knowledge of the law and its implementation. It is likely that she would not have mentioned her seniority unless she knew it was an important factor in deciding whether to permit her dismissal during pregnancy. It is even more likely that had she not been aware of the law, she would not have claimed that the employer was using the pregnancy as a pretext for dismissal. It appears here that possession of cultural capital that is manifested through knowledge aids the employees in operating within the field even when they lack economic capital.

The case below, concerning M., also demonstrates knowledge of the law and rights, despite her being a

25-year-old food server with only 10 months' seniority at a food plant.

> I cannot keep working because my cervix is effaced, but I checked if I could sign on for unemployment and I am missing a month or two. I hope you will help me come to a compromise with them.

(Hearing observation, February 2009)

These cases support the regression findings and confirm, qualitatively, the findings that a woman's entry into the field is not to be taken for granted, but that once she has entered she has space to manoeuvre and gather cultural capital—even if only short term—in the form of prior preparation, knowledge of the law and assertiveness, which are possible within the framework of the limited autonomy the field grants its players.

Accordingly, it is worth explaining how it is possible that the action of women alone is the only clear variable influencing the chance to receive protection from the state. Relying on sociological theories at the micro level, it could be said that a number of factors affected the women's chances—without relying on their resources or the background from which they come—to receive protection from the state. The first is that the dismissal case is decided by the state, in other words, the women have entered the "field." The fact of their entry into the field, according to Bourdieu, allows the actors to compete for its prizes. In other words, whoever lacks the habitus needed to engage the assistance of state institutions will not be able to compete for the permit. Second, upon entering the field, some autonomy is granted to the actors in the manner of preparation for handling the "performance" on the hearing's state. Third, acting against the threat of dismissal occurs through desire, ability, and initiative, which stem from the wish to maintain a source of income.

Even so, these findings raise concerns regarding implementation of the law. In contrast with the state's clearly stated purpose to separate the ability of pregnant women to fight for their places in the labour force and the state's protection, findings demonstrate that this ability strongly affects the protection granted to them by the state. In other words, in opposition with the intention of the legislature, the state is not acting actively enough to protect women who are less aware of their rights, or who for various reasons are not actively operating to prevent their dismissals. These findings join the tapestry of discrepancies found between the law's implementation and the written law.

Toward the end of the chapter, it is important to understand the long-term consequences of the state's decision upon the labour profile of women who experienced dismissal during pregnancy.

Dr. Nirit Toshav - Eichner

How Is the Women's Employment Profile Affected after They Experience Dismissal during Pregnancy?

In the spirit of Bourdieu's theory of capital, pregnant women who were dismissed, and who possessed the habitus necessary to gain the field's resources, will succeed in returning more quickly to the labour market than women who lack this capital. According to this theory, even in cases of dismissal during or because of pregnancy, the chances of an employee with sociocultural capital to find employment are greater than those of an employee with limited sociocultural capital. In addition to the argument that the employee's habitus is what indicates who will succeed in returning to the labour field and who will fail, the explanations suggested at the individual level are also linked to the question of motivation. How eager is the employee to return to the labour cycle after giving birth? We should note that all participants in the survey declared themselves interested in returning to the labour cycle, or that they were interested in being reintegrated into the labour force once they had become desperate. Therefore, the desire to reintegrate is not a sufficiently significant explanation for the women's employment status four years after their dismissal.

First I would like to present two findings that emerged from the research, which explain the potential influence of preventing dismissal on the future integration of new mothers into the labour force. An analysis of the human

326

resources survey comparing new mothers and women who are not new mothers reveals clear differences in the chances of both groups to return to the labour cycle after being dismissed. While 95.35% of those dismissed in the general female population aged 20–40 who are not mothers returned to the labour force after their dismissal, 88% of the new mothers who were dismissed were reintegrated into the working world by the time the survey was carried out. This figure demonstrates that new mothers have a more difficult time returning to the labour cycle after dismissal than those who are not new mothers. It is important to note that the sampling included only women who wished to return to work and not those who reported leaving the labour cycle of their own free will.

The survey carried out within the framework of this study among women whose cases were heard by the Ministry of Industry, Commerce, and Employment reveals even more interesting findings, within the range of four years from dismissal. In the theoretical statistics' findings it emerged that among women whose employer sought to dismiss them, those who still worked in the same place on the day of the interview were employed following the dismissal, as expected, during the four years up to the interview date. On the other hand, women who worked somewhere else on the day of the interview worked more than half of the period (58% of the time), in other words, they were employed for over two of the four years following dismissal. However, those who were not working on the day of the interview worked, on average, during more than a third (35%) of the period, in other words, less than a year and a half following the dismissal during pregnancy. If this is the case, the argument can be made that the fact of dismissal during pregnancy reduces the length of employment for women by over two years on average out of the four years which have passed since the request for dismissal.

Within the framework of a further regression carried out, another dependent variable was chosen—"return to the labour market "—out of a wish to examine the long-term influence of women's behaviour when dealing with state institutions. The assumption was that women who were defended—even if they were dismissed after the protective umbrella failed to safeguard their status— would return to the labour market quickly due to the sense of empowerment they felt. The independent variables examined in relation to the variable were: whether the woman was defended, had a university education, had a working partner, her age, and her seniority—as listed in the chart in the methodology chapter, in which all the variables, method of encoding, and research function for the choice of variable were presented.

For the purposes of checking the long-term results of the system's decision, the assumption was that the personal capital variable would increase the chances of returning to the labour market after dismissal.

In comparisons between groups of women whose dismissals were authorised by the state system and groups of women whose dismissals were not authorised, we discovered that the relative chances of those women whose dismissals were prevented and had participated in the work cycle during the survey (four years after the request to dismiss them) was three times greater than those of women whose dismissals were authorised. However, as we stated, this discrepancy alone does not necessarily prove the influence of the prevention mechanism upon the integration of the women in the labour market, and a more distinct test was therefore carried out. In order to estimate the level of influence of the state's involvement upon the return to the labour market (the dependent market variable), the independent *"refusal"* variable was chosen (whether the woman was defended or not), along with several other independent variables that might influence the chance to return to the labour market, such as, for example, the partner's employment status—whether employed or unemployed—which could cause the female employee to make an effort to return to the market (if her husband is not working). Furthermore, economic theories generally suppose that the individual characteristics of the employee, or their "personal capital"[113] (Per 2011)—which are manifested in variables such as education and employment experience—are the main factors that form

---

113 Defined as the sum-total of the individual's skills, whether natural (age, gender etc.) or acquired (education, seniority).

the individual's chances to return to work or find new employment in the case of dismissal. According to these theories, in the case of dismissal during pregnancy, the chances of an employee with personal capital finding new employment are greater than those of an employee with limited personal capital. In order to estimate the contribution of the state's actions to prevent dismissal to the employment status of the employee in the years following the attempt to dismiss, we also noted further personal capital variables that were likely to influence the chance of finding employment, including education—whether academic or not—as well as the consecutive variables of age and seniority.

Findings for the logistical regression to examine the variables which explain the factors that encourage the woman to remain in the labour market (the *"market"* variable) after a dismissal process teach us that, even after examining these individual variables, the influence of the state-supplied defense was seen to be significant and clear. The chances of women whose dismissals were prevented by the state to be employed four years afterward, whether by the same employer or another one, were 2.8 times greater than those women who had not been protected by the state, even after we took their education into account.

Further, in keeping with the assumption at the core of the personal capital theory and Bourdieu's theory of capital, a woman's education (cultural capital) is in fact the most influential variable vis-à-vis her chances to reintegrate into the labour market after her employer sought to dismiss her. The chances of employees with a university education of reintegrating into the labour cycle was found to be 3.82 times higher than employees with no academic education, even after taking into account the question of whether the state had defended them from dismissal, their age and seniority at work, and their partner's employment status. Not a single one of these variables demonstrated as clear an influence upon reintegration, as we note in the chart below:

The influence of the state's defense upon chances to return to the labour market

The Dependent Variable Return to the labour market (market)	1	2
Defended or not (refusal)	2.593	2.822
	(0.03)	(0.036)
Education	-	3.820
		(0.012)
Employed partner		2.433
		(0.204)
Age		1.031
		(0.557)
Years of seniority		1.038
Observations		(0.685)
	85	85
C rate for compatibility	70.9	
Likelihood ration	2.763	
P. value	<.03	

Survey figures 2006

The findings that show that the state's defense helps women maintain their jobs or return more quickly to the labour market in relation to the women who did not receive protection support, somewhat at least, demonstrate the legislature's choice to invest efforts in the prevention of dismissals for pregnant women and new mothers, as an efficient strategy to promote the integration of women into the labour force. Our argument is that *the prevention of dismissals of pregnant women is an effective strategy in that it ensures their continued integration into the labour force* even after giving birth. Nonetheless, the great importance that can be ascribed to prevention of dismissal makes the issue of the present system's efficacy and its success in helping women remain within the labour force without dependence upon the social and economic resources available to them particularly important.

Chapter Summary and Conclusions

The purpose of this chapter was to continue examining how the discrepancies are created between the written law and its de facto implementation, through an understanding of the ways in which these discrepancies develop. We therefore sought to examine the argument that damage to the universal ability of women to seek aid and use the law is affected by status gaps and by a lack of logic, uniform patterns of action and task definitions, which in turn affect the management of non-uniform interaction between the state's clerks and their clients. Despite the Israeli system being egalitarian according to legal definition, we discovered that access to the law and the ability to use it are not to be taken for granted.

In this chapter we relied upon the macro "law in action" theory and the micro "capital theory," the dramaturgical approach, and the street-level bureaucracy theory. In keeping with these theories we discovered discrepancies between the spirit of the legislation and its de facto implementation. It emerged that in contrast with the law's instruction, the state regulation is not a universal mechanism, and the ability to employ it effectively is at times dependent upon putting on pressure and upon the social and economic resources of the person dismissed, or that of their employer. These gaps were created due to several factors, including a lack of training or a clear understanding of tasks, the influence of the participants' background upon the interaction, and legalisation of the labour relations field. I will, in summary, explain how these factors manifest themselves in the study's findings.

An examination of the interaction between the supervisors and the women and the employers revealed that two kinds of logic guide the supervisors during the hearings; the logic derived from the social-welfare discourse, and what we called "the patriarchal inertia." The latter sees the prevention of dismissal as a protective welfare mechanism that must be enacted, particularly for women from weaker groups. There is also a "particular case" logic—in other words, each group on its own—that seems to have developed as a way around the lack of uniformity in the understanding of the supervisors' role and in the system's operation. It was noted that the second approach seeks to see the state's role, through those who enact the law, as a means to bridge the conflict of interests (which is taken for granted) between the employers and the pregnant employees. It was nonetheless found that this approach could affect decision-making due to the influence from the participants' backgrounds during the interaction, which creates unequal results within the framework of the process. We found that in similar cases there could be differing results, and I therefore argue that joining the two logics could lead to damaging the state system's efficiency, along with the trust placed in it by employers and employees and its ability to contribute to significant change in the attitude of employers to pregnant employees. Furthermore, the supervisors' non-uniform behaviour during the hearings, stemming from a lack of uniform training, for example, structuring a different role for legal operators or differing priorities, could affect the decisions and in some cases even damage the principle of equality before the law. This, therefore, increases the inequality toward those who were less successful in leaving a good impression at the hearing stage, or who did not rehearse enough before going on stage, as is appropriate, or toward those who were not given full opportunity to express themselves on stage or behind the scenes. It is thus possible to say that the equality in the assistance was harmed.

It was noted that managing the impression by actors with a background similar to the supervisors affected reciprocal relations during the interaction and that during the hearing there was a constant structuring of the supervisor's role. In comparing women whose cases were heard within the state system and those who sought unemployment benefits during pregnancy, it was found that higher education and belonging to the Jewish sector increased the chances for a woman who had been dismissed to be dealt with effectively within the framework of the state mechanism both for the short and long term. Nonetheless, for women who did not deal with the system or who dealt with it without knowing the "rules of the game" — in particular Arab women, those without an education, those with a background different from the supervisor's, women belonging to the weaker populations—one can assume that their full rights were not used, if at all, and for them, the inequality expanded even more.

Moreover, due to the legalisation occurring in the labour relations field in Israel, we described the entrance of a further player into the field in the form of the lawyer. This presence was found at times to supplant the state's authority to provide full instruction and assistance on the one hand, and increase the gap between citizens and employers in their chance of receiving full protection from the state, on the other.

I noted that in all of the hearings I observed for research purposes, not once was an effort made to help the employer better prepare himself to employ a pregnant employee. On the contrary, women were sometimes instructed by the supervisors to return to work "and try to be good girls, not to cause trouble, at least until the birth." Further, even in cases in which the state intervened to prevent dismissals, no attempt was made to follow up on the employees' reintegration at work or on her fate once the protective legal period was over. According to the supervisors, the law is very narrow and allows them to authorise dismissals or to refuse the employer's request, and what happens afterward is already outside the boundaries of their responsibility. In their words, "a woman who is harmed should turn to the courts" (interview with the senior supervisor, January 2008). The employers do not receive any instruction or explanation concerning the advantages of employing mothers or pregnant women, and there is no organised attempt to undermine the prejudices which lead to the dismissals during pregnancy or prevent the next attempt at dismissal. Moreover, it has in fact been noted that with the growth of neoliberalism there is an increase in the employers' trust in the system, and findings show that the law protects employers more than it protects women. It therefore appears that the supervisors' friendly manner, which is interpreted by women as empathy, acts for the employers as a further pressure tactic.

Findings confirm the complexity of policies for the protection of pregnant women. On the one hand, the state's intervention in preventing the dismissal of women appears to be an effective strategy that reaches its goal to keep women within the labour cycle. On the other hand, despite the state's desire to create a universal system to serve all its clients without any connection to their resources or the level of their determination to receive the state's protection, it is clear that the clerks are influenced by the pressures brought to bear upon them and thus tend to protect women who operated more actively to prevent their dismissals. It was noted that the very fact of the willingness and ability to act to protect her rights significantly increases the chances for a woman whose case is handled within the framework of the state to receive protection from dismissal. The long-term repercussions of decisions by those who implement the law point to varying lengths of employment among women who received defense as opposed to those who were not defended. Results of the decision whether to protect a pregnant employee or to permit her dismissal are particularly notable in the case of uneducated women. The complex repercussions of this decision emerge after the dismissal, with her extended exclusion from the labour market, and in the spirit of Bourdieu, in the reflection of the gender-based inequality in the field.

I would like to posit that the legalism of the interaction with the employer and the employee increased the unique strategy of each case on its own; however, in this approach—due to a lack of a permanent process with uniform operation—there is a constant deviation in setting the boundaries of the hearing. This deviation is directly influenced by the impression and pressures employed by its participants. Thus, in effect, the full significance of the system to prevent dismissals during pregnancy according to the spirit of the law never reaches its full potential— to minimise the gender-based inequality in the labour market. This has created discrepancies between the written law and its de facto implementation.

Chapter 6

Debate and Conclusions

This book seeks to provide an in-depth examination of one of the harshest punishments meted out to mothers — dismissal during pregnancy. Our purpose was to look at the discrepancy between the formal policies and their de facto implementation, while focusing on the case of dismissal during pregnancy in the State of Israel. We further wished to consider to what degree the regulatory system for the prevention of the dismissal of women during pregnancy reflects the legislative intent to prevent these dismissals, and how this regulation is experienced by pregnant women who were dismissed by their employers. We investigated the manners in which the fragmentation developed, in order to explain the ways in which inequality is created. We focused on achieving these goals through relying mainly on theories of "the state in action," the "law in action," and Bourdieu's capital and field theories.

The Regulation Axis-Logic of Action by the State Protection System

The state regulation responsible for protecting pregnant women in the labour market sometimes functions in a fragmentary manner. This fragmentation increased toward the end of the last century and has continued doing so up through the second decade of the current one. As argued in the research discourse of "the state in action," the fragmentation is primarily influenced by political interests (Li 2002). We are witness to a welfare system operated by a ministry seeking to create a reputation for economy and power, and ignore its responsibility to care for those damaged by society (Lein 2000). Actions by the Ministry of Industry, Commerce, and Employment that operate the welfare system, Employment Services, and the National Insurance Institute, are characterised by a lack of internal and external coordination, and by differing and even conflicting patterns of action. The fragmentation stems from conflicting interests, a different attitude to public reputation, and from different goals. As a result of these, deviation from the spirit of the law occurs. Although to a certain degree the law deters employers from dismissing pregnant workers, as we discovered, there are large discrepancies in the range of applications to each of the state support systems and the regulation is not used to its full potential. These inherent conflicts have led to harm to the clients — in this case pregnant women who the employer seeks to dismiss. In theory, these findings are in agreement with arguments by researchers of the state in action, who focus on the lack of coordination and irregularities among the various state apparatuses regarding implementation of the law.

The state's fragmentary actions influence the differential in the ability of the women themselves to find aid in the law, which may in the end affect the inequality within the actions of the state regulatory system. In this context it is worth considering the most blatant finding; the positive influence of the state's defense upon the chances of those women whose dismissals were prevented to return to the labour market. These chances were nearly three times higher than those of women undefended by the state — and we should mention that we noted their education. Findings indicated that the rate of women who received protection and participate in the labour market is significantly higher than that of women who were undefended (55% as opposed to 36%). This finding shows that the state's protection is influential beyond time and location. The conclusion could be drawn that the state's protection creates a strengthening, support, and empowerment for the women, therefore increasing their self-confidence and allowing them to continue integration into the labour market. Nonetheless, the finding that stands out the most is the rate of chances for those women who acted in order to receive the state's protection—this figure stands at 14 times higher than for women who did not state that they had taken action on their own initiative. The strong, clear influence of this variable remained stable even considering other variables such as personal capital, including education (academic), age, seniority, welfare needs (partner's employment), organic variables (organisation size), as well as variables related to assistance received by the employee during the hearing within the framework of the state system (whether they were helped by a lawyer or by women's organisations). It is clear that the state system tends more to protect women who themselves requested assistance, in cases when the employer did not request legal authorisation.

If so, then in contrast to the intention of the legislator, the state does not operate actively enough to protect employers or women who are less aware of their rights, or who, for various reasons, do not act decisively enough to prevent their dismissal. The lack of a clear definition of the supervisors' role, along with the lack of instruction regarding the rest of the interaction with the clients, leads to deviation in the role and may influence the state's actions for equality. Furthermore, with the entrance of a further actor—in the form of a lawyer—into the field, some of the responsibility to instruct and assist the employee is removed from the supervisor, and thus, even though assistance from a lawyer does not clearly increase the chances of a women to receive protection, in cases where lawyers are not involved, the employee is more likely not to fully exhaust all her legal options. Thus the state, through its actions, increases inequality among this population of women.

By understanding the regulation axis, it emerges that the actions of the state clerks are influenced by non-uniform approaches concerning the nature of the system. It was further noted that there are numerous cases in which the "patriarchal inertia," which characterised the system's actions in its first years, affects actions during the neoliberal period too, and it is seen by its operators as a social system. Within this framework there is a concentration on background data and on the actions of the employee whose case is being dealt with, instead of on preventing the dismissal of pregnant women in general. This approach helps some women—those who are particularly active or who seem the most in need of assistance—keep their jobs, and it also helps in cases in which there is some doubt regarding the link between the pregnancy and the request for dismissal. However, at the same time, when it is a case of women who are perceived as strong, or with little motivation to prevent the dismissal, the system places them in danger of dismissal even when there is a strong connection to their pregnancy. The state's refusal to use their databases in order to locate employers who dismissed women illegally could be explained in part through this ideology. Women who did not report their illegal dismissal are seen as not requiring the state's intervention, and thus do not go out of their way to involve the state—even when this involvement is in line with their own interests (such as savings in benefits). Nonetheless, in recent years an approach has emerged known as "prosecutability of the case," which seeks to consider each case individually. This approach depends strongly upon the habitus of the participants in the interaction, and may therefore increase the inequality toward a specific population. Furthermore, the approach relies upon characteristics of a social welfare system toward disempowered women, and takes a different, neoliberal approach toward stronger women who appear to be able to look after themselves. Therefore, it is a way of bypassing the lack of clear and constant policy patterns in the state's actions.

As we look at the question of the link between fragmentation, the ability to receive help and the deviations in judgment which may expand the gender-based inequality, we argue that the lack of coordination between the various apparatuses leads to non-uniform state action, which damages the ability to instill and implement the spirit of the law and its principles, thus, in effect, expanding—even if indirectly—the gender-based inequality. Thus the actions of the state-as-employer were presented in the case of the teachers from the Ministry of Education as an example of the influence of fragmentation between the state action and the spirit of the law, directly affecting the increase of gender inequality within the population of female teachers. In a different state action toward the same populace, located in the "pink ghetto"

(Gebel and Giesecke 2011), the state in effect discriminates among citizens; a discrimination based on professional background, which affects how the law is employed equally while directly increasing the inequality toward the population of teachers. Furthermore, the most blatant example presented of the effect of fragmentation upon the creation of gender-based inequality is the conflict between the Women's Labour Law, which protects pregnant employees, and the Manpower Contractor's Law Section 12a, which permits dismissal of any employee (even pregnant) during their probationary period. Here we note that the state in effect goes along with breaking a law that it passed itself. Worse still, injury is done to a weak sector within the labour market—that belonging to the secondary labour market, which is devoid of rights. As we stated, this is a direct outcome of neoliberalism.

Market Axis, the Employers and Organisations versus the Regulator: Neoliberalism versus Welfare Logic

The approach of some Israeli employers located within the framework of our study are in line with that of employers who participated in a survey of employers in Britain (Mori 2002), in which the explanations given by employers for the discrimination of women due to pregnancy focus mainly on the woman's responsibility to the home, which is a central factor in her life. These employers were concerned that the workplace was seen by women as being of secondary importance—an approach that could tip the balance of the employer's judgment prior to hiring these women. Thus, just as in the case of the employers who dismiss pregnant workers, it appears that the state system also takes it for granted that women, whether pregnant or post-birth, are a lesser workforce, and that the question of whether to continue employing them is neither financial nor professional but rather welfare-based. Despite the fact that the supervisors themselves are interested in preventing the dismissals, it is clear that they see the system as a social welfare mechanism intended to protect the employee "during the period in which it will be difficult for her to find employment," rather than as a broad social and economic mechanism whose purpose is to change the attitude of employers to pregnant employees and mothers, and to increase the integration of women—particularly those from weaker sectors—in the labour cycle.

It appears that this basic premise is what stands at the core of the extensive fragmentation and the internal conflicts that characterise those who operate the law in Israel for the prevention of the dismissal of pregnant women. The fragmentary nature of the state's operations are notable in the establishment of a bureau, which on the one hand is tasked with enforcing the implementation of the law, and on the other is prevented from using existing data on the employers who break it. It further manifests itself in the demand from government ministries and non-profit organisations to continue employing pregnant employees even when the dismissals are unrelated to the pregnancy, bolstered by compromise deals that permit dismissals with the state's blessing in places where the employer has harmed the employee not only by attempting to dismiss her during pregnancy but also by creating an atmosphere in which it is impossible for her to continue working.

The existence of the alternate, non-interventional welfare mechanism, which allows pregnant women who have been dismissed to receive unemployment benefits, while the employer is not required to pay their salaries during pregnancy and is not punished for illegally dismissing a pregnant women, is a blatant expression of the fact that the state is willing to pay the heavy cost of the woman's salary through unemployment benefits from social services, in order to avoid harming the autonomy of the employer to dismiss an employee and the woman's ability to support herself and her family. This approach became much stronger once the Ministry of Labour — which was responsible for enforcing the labour law — was merged with the Ministry of Industry, Commerce, and Employment, which is responsible for representing the interests of employers (in 2003). According to this approach, in order to protect the employers' interests, and in order to prevent excess harm to employees, which could interfere with industrial peace, the state took some of the debts previously shouldered by the employers (such as subsidizing the welfare and health systems) upon itself.

Paradoxically, this approach, which guided the greater part of the state's actions in the field of labour relations until 1985, was strengthened significantly following the plan for economic stability, despite the neoliberal approach, which left a large amount of the arrangements in the labour relations field to the market powers.

The peak of the fragmentation occurs within the conflict between Section 9a of the Women's Labour Law, which prevents dismissal of pregnant women, and the Manpower Contractors' Law, which allows the dismissal of any manpower employee within up to eight months of their employment. The de facto result of this conflict between laws is manifested in dismissals during pregnancy, which are permitted at the state level.[114] The supervisors themselves have stated that dozens of women are dismissed each year while pregnant according to the law's instruction.

The system functions asymmetrically with employers with regard to the employees, for example, in the ability to include a lawyer in the hearing and give him the right to speak. The habitus and character of an organisation influences the decision whether to permit or refuse dismissal of a pregnant employee. Further, the interaction between the supervisor and the employer is significant, and is at times affected by the employer's background.

---

114 This conflict has double meaning and thus has been discussed in both analyses.

Over the years, more and more employers have used the services of private lawyers, "learned" how the state acts, and tried to bypass or to fight it.

One could assume that the sharp increase found in the past decade in formal applications and informal dismissals during pregnancy could stem from the reality of uncompromising competition for resources and control in the neoliberal economy. The explanation could be given that this reality has led employers who wish to dismiss a pregnant employee to find themselves in three polarised power struggles: first, against the employee; second, against the state; and third, against the organisation's members— the employee's colleagues. While in the first two their control is limited, the third is within their control and may, at times, be used (even unofficially) in the struggle against the employee. Therefore, previous studies found that a harmful attitude from the employee influenced the way they were treated by their colleagues in the organisation.[115] Thus, in effect, a new front opens, of social pressure brought on by members of the organisations, demonstrated by the employee's rejection, either openly or subtly. Because high rates of violations of the law were noted among employers, along with discriminatory comments, it is impossible to characterise the causes with certainty. One must assume

---

115 Buzzanell and Liu 2007; Cockburn 2002; El-Sawad et al. 2004; Gatrell 2005, 2007a, b, 2008; Hausman 2004; Haynes 2006a, b, 2008a, b.

that the employers prefer to avoid dealing with the second power circle (the state) and thus find a way—whether through a financial compromise or by employing the third circle (members of the organisation)—to convince the employee to leave the organisation. If so, we can summarise that within the context of the market axis, the habitus of participants in the interaction as well as the nature of the organisation both have an effect on the decision whether to authorise the request to dismiss a pregnant woman. These claims are in line with the theory of "law in action."

Up until 2010 the neoliberal reality in the labour market was apparently manifested in a less significant manner through the state's actions toward employers within the regulatory framework, and it is clear that the welfare approach characterised the state's attitude to certain employers. Nonetheless, beyond the limits of regulation, with its support for "compromise" or in other cases by turning a blind eye to the illegal activities of the employers, the state in effect granted the employers the power to continue affecting the outcome of the power struggle against the employee. It thus handed them control over the employee's decision to accept the compromise and turn directly to the Employment Services, without seeking assistance through regulation. In the past four years, however, the neoliberal spirit has been present in the significant rise in permits granted, and it appears that rather than the law protecting pregnant women from dismissal, it protects the employers from pregnant women.

If so, on the employers' axis there were discrepancies between the legislators' intent to keep women within the labour market and minimise gender-based inequality and the fragmented enforcement of the law, which is based on the conflicting logic of neoliberalism and allowing market forces to act freely. This is despite the welfare-base paternalism manifested in discriminatory, harmful, and even illegal organisation action, whose results are a continuing inequality toward women mediated by the state.

The Women in Action Axis

There are high rates of women who are dismissed during pregnancy and do not seek assistance from the state system. Women from a more privileged social class have economic and cultural capital, which allows them to better cope with the demands of the state mechanism by paying for legal assistance and presenting their claims in a manner that appears more reasonable to the system's representatives. Even if it was not found clearly in the defense by women employing lawyers, the assistance is in fact mediated by the personal and financial capital that may help the employee in her operations with the organisational and state bureaucracy. The result is that the cultural capital manifested in the different status, which characterises women who face the system, acts as a stratifying factor that reflects the inequality and social superiority of certain groups and the low status and exclusion of others.

By focusing on those women who did not seek assistance from the regulation, we sought to present a slightly different angle on the issue of *the choice* of these women, and we tried to examine whether they had logic separate from that of those women who chose regulation. It emerged that, on average, about half of the women who dealt with the system received protection and were therefore able to maintain their position in the labour market. It should be noted that within the study, it was not possible to include the causes for not dealing with the system within the total of all women dismissed during pregnancy. Nonetheless, one possible explanation for this could be that there are women who, right before becoming mothers, are not interested in working for the organisation. There are those for whom giving birth is an opportunity to leave a job which perhaps is unchallenging, or they may prefer to spend all their time caring for their family. Debby Bernstein (2008) wrote, among other subjects, about women's work in the first decades after the state was founded. In her work she describes a depressing picture of marginal work, for short hours, in order not to harm the woman's position as caregiver for her family. Bernstein posits that women were supposedly offered a choice—whether to work and where— however, this choice was predetermined and mediated by the patriarchal institution that controlled it. In a sharp switch from the "paternalistic homogeneity" to the neoliberal period, we still see a lack of representation of women—particularly Arab women—against the system. We found, however, that the fact that they do not seek assistance from the system does not necessarily mean they do not seek help from alternatives such as the financial safety net offered by the National Insurance Institute and the Employment Services. Nonetheless, we noted a large amount of women who were dismissed during pregnancy and did not seek help from the state at all. One could assume that they were not eligible or that they were unaware of their right to receive assistance and thus dropped out of the labour market, with some not returning even several years later.

With reference to these issues, we will focus our discussion on the assumption that in the current period, neoliberalism has made its way into individuals' decision-making as well. There are therefore women who choose not to seek help from the welfare system and prefer to settle for the social mechanism of the non-interventional social security through the National Insurance Institute, which permits what is perhaps a more autonomous range of choice. In other words, in the neoliberal period there are women who prefer *maintaining* their financial rights over *interventional protection* regarding their place on the labour market's economic spectrum. They choose to relate to the state as an "enabling state" (Young 2003), whose main characteristics are expressed through the reduction of roles that the state can/wishes to take upon itself, and in particular through reduction of the interventional support system in the lives of the inhabitants. Given that the "enabling state" hands over numerous services to non-state bodies (non-governmental organisations, for example), it in effect works for the most part as an actor operating meta-regulation through legislation—setting standards and oversight. Therefore, "protection" of the economic rights of those women is less pressing for them, while permitting autonomy within the limits of the space. It permits a non-interventional safety net and gives the state a position as gatekeeper which is less intervening and more safeguarding.

The state, in its role as protector, seeks to defend, but occasionally misses its mark. It "pushes" too much and this enforces solutions which are not always accepted, creating resistance on both sides. The question thus emerges: Did those women, who sought only unemployment benefits but not state protection, do so out of a preference not to be helped by an overly protective regulation? Are we lacking "protection," which allows broader limitations of freedom to manoeuvere on the one hand, and on the other provides a social welfare network that will permit defamilisation and economic strength? In keeping with Young's statement, we should ask: What is the best path in terms of the state? We have shown that the system continues to function according to patriarchal and sometimes corporatist logic, while neoliberalism is expressed at times when employers take advantage of the law and continue the inequality toward women mediated by the state. A question emerges from this whose answer lies beyond the scope of this book: Does the state need to pay attention to levels of symmetric and egalitarian "enabling" between the employers and the employees, and if yes, how? Further, the issue of choice also needs to be examined in depth, given that cases were presented that definitely supported the idea of a social safety net in the form of maintaining rights. Even so, many "social" cases were presented as well, where the state's protection aided in addressing economic difficulties, even if only in the short term. Moreover, the mere act of preventing dismissal significantly improves the chance to receive protection by the interventional mechanism. The ability granted to women to defend their rights could initiate an empowering process for some women, sharpening their awareness of their rights, unrelated to the results of the state decision. Women who were given state protection, even if they were dismissed in the end, had nearly three times as great a chance to find their way back into the labour market as women who were not defended. If so, one could say that this possibility is withheld from the women who do not seek assistance from the system, and are similarly denied the chance to experience the empowerment granted by the system to some women. The argument could be made that for them, the gender-based inequality increases.

Conclusions: Integration of the Three Axis: State, Market, and Women

The final section of the research dealt with the integrative combination of findings that emerged within the framework of the three axes—the state, the organisations, and the women—in an attempt to find the level of dependence between the fragmentation and the inequality. In the fragmentation noted in the case of the state as employer, despite the fact that the state apparatuses functioned in a coordinated and cooperative manner, there was in fact fragmentation in opposition to the spirit of the law. When within the framework of the inter-ministerial agreement the Ministry of Industry, Commerce, and Employment was granted the possibility of permitting administrative dismissals of teachers with no chance of a hearing, which other women have a right to, the teachers were in fact discriminated against, and the purpose of the law—to keep women within the labour market—was harmed. In this case findings showed that the fragmentation and gender-based inequality maintain a directly dependent relation, as a result of which damage is done to a most clearly gender-defined profession- teaching.

Another case that was presented involved the fragmentation created by the lack of coordination between ministries, among the Employment Services, and the National Insurance Institute security, in conjunction with the Ministry of Industry, Commerce, and Employment.

In this context we described the development of the approach to pregnant women who had been dismissed. At the beginning of the second period, women were forced to blindly follow universal bureaucratic procedures meant for all unemployed people seeking to visit the employment bureau three times weekly. In later years, however, we note a trickle of "gender-based action" absent of "gender logic." This action manifested itself through the easier terms granted to pregnant employees—although the clerks were struck by "patriarchal inertia," within whose framework the policies were enacted. This made the granting of benefits easier, as there were no attempts to encourage the employees to fully use the law within the system that could help them remain in the labour market, as the legislature intended in the promotion of gender-based human rights. In this context, the roots of the fragmentation stem from the lack of cooperation and non-transfer of data among the various institutional bodies. This fragmentation influenced the increase of gender-based inequality.

This conclusion is further strengthened by findings that showed that the state's protection primarily assists educated women and those who made the effort to prevent their dismissal. Despite this, weaker women— Arabs for example—with a more limited personal capital, turned to the non-interventional mechanism of National Insurance Institute benefits. In an attempt to locate the degree of dependency between the fragmentation in the state's actions in this case, and the inequality manifested therein, we found that this fragmentation was particularly sharp, given that it not only increased the gender-based inequality for weaker populations but through its actions actually enforced the social inequality toward those sectors who were forced to deal with daily discrimination in all aspects of their lives. This argument gains further strength in the face of the conflict created between the Women's Labour Law and the Manpower Contractors' Law. Within this framework, dozens of pregnant women belonging to the secondary group and discriminated against within the dual labour market find themselves excluded from the labour cycle by law, with no rights, and no ability to receive protection from the state. For these women, blatant discrimination and inequality of the worst sort are created. One must assume that they are part of the third of women who did not act within the state system, as apparent from the chart below, which clearly illustrates the discrepancies between the law and its de facto implementation:

Women excluded versus women assisted between 1999–2007

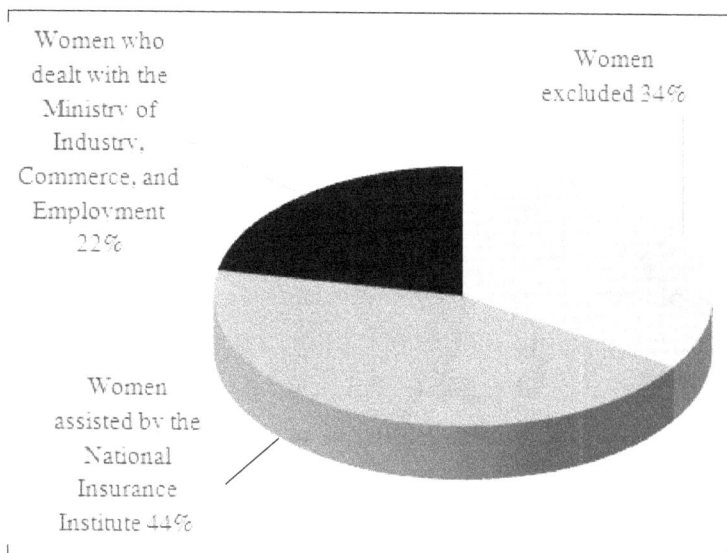

Women who dealt with the Ministry of Industry, Commerce, and Employment 22%

Women excluded 34%

Women assisted by the National Insurance Institute 44%

Figures from the 2006 survey, manpower survey data, Employment Services and National Insurance Institute data

This chart, which summarises the findings presented in previous chapters, shows that in fact, less than one quarter of the women dismissed during pregnancy operated within the system that is meant to examine, according to the law, all requests for dismissal during pregnancy. These findings are a clear indicator of the gaps between the law and its de facto implementation.

Despite the importance of the fragmentation we found in the state's operations, the crux of our work lay in the attempt to examine the logic of the state's actions in enacting the regulation under the authority of the Ministry of Industry, Commerce, and Employment. Current researchers claim that the inequality has an effect on the social and economic variables, which cause the sociopolitical instability, and in turn deepen the inequality (Crystal et al. 2006). These arguments strengthen our main claim, that the fragmentation in the state's actions limits the policy's ability to promote significant social chance and reduce inequality. In light of the findings, one can conclude that structural changes to political needs strengthen the chances of fragmentary, unequal action.

In other words, moving the Ministry of Labour—which runs the welfare system that examines requests for dismissals during pregnancy—to a ministry with an ideology of industry and commerce created complexity in enforcement. This complexity is manifested in various understandings of roles, as those who enact the law explained—in the conflicting and confused inter-departmental relations with the public and in the lack of any attempt to instruct the clerks. This lack of guidance has at times manifested itself from within the welfare-based "patriarchal inertia" that existed prior to the law being enforced, and not through any intent to reduce the gender-based inequality and keep the employee within the labour market, in the spirit of promoting gender-based equality, as the legislator intended. The non-uniform role definition of the job emerged through individual interpretations of "each case on its own," and the various interactions with the clients affected the decisions whether or not to permit dismissals or protect the employee. As we saw, despite the honest desire to use the law to the fullest, more than once judgment was affected by additional variables such as the presence of a lawyer, personal background, and previous priorities that affected the ability to allow full expression to clients during the hearing. The attempt to brand the Ministry of Industry, Commerce, and Employment as a strong economic ministry further reduces the importance of the welfare logic, diminishes the significance of the protective law for the population of women who need defending, and swings the balance toward the employer's economic logic, even if not blatantly so. Within all this we can conclude that the state's action is influenced by a range of interests, which are at times conflicting, at times less to the point and more political, and at times utterly lacking uniformity or coordination. This leads to fragmentation, which influenced the unstable "policy implementation," and from this point the path to the ability to access equal and uniform assistance according to the law becomes ever longer.

In summary the question arises whether in a neoliberal reality, in which individual choice is supposedly strengthened, there is still a place for an intervening regulatory system. The answer to this is complicated. The state's defense does help women maintain their place in the labour market, however, the "policy implementation" requires several changes. The very protection granted by the state contains a process of female empowerment and confidence-boosting, which may accompany them for the rest of their employment and personal life. This process and its results require further examination, and for this, continuing research is needed.

The research presented in this book combined theories from several disciplines, and based them on quantitative and qualitative methodologies. In this way we exposed the discrepancies between the written law and the de facto translation into partial policy implementation for pregnant employees, as well as the inequality created from these discrepancies. We found that non-Jewish women, uneducated women, and those who do not act to prevent their dismissal were less successful in receiving the state's protection and paid the heavy price of dismissal, followed by difficulty in reintegrating into the labour market. We further found that most of the women who chose to act against the dismissals were notably successful at convincing the system's operators to grant them protection. The study was based on two main theoretical stages, "the state in action" and "the law in action." Results emerged in line with their main arguments, according to which fragmentation is created as a result of the lack of intra- and extra-institutional coordination, conflicting interests, varying approaches to the public reputation, and political strength. The inequality is created as a result of the influence stemming from the background of the interaction's participants, along with the influence of the individual habitus upon the level of accessibility and assistance in all of the state bodies. Even so, we noted that neither the state's actions nor the spirit of the law were helpful in assisting women maintain their status in the labour market. It was actually the women's actions themselves that significantly affected their chances of receiving the state's protection. This bears out sociological theories that claim that the rational choice and the agency of women given the opportunity to deal with the state led them to initiate actions that do not necessarily match their backgrounds or personal capital,[116] in order to maintain their status in the labour market.

Regarding the theoretical contribution, we sought to expand the research literature concerning the influence of pregnancy on the employment of women. We chiefly suggested an opportunity for ways in which the state acts in cases of dismissal during pregnancy, following the research that noted the inability to examine institutional behaviour in hearings carried out within the framework of mediation, even during the process of decision-making and its repercussions (Russell and Banks 2011a).

We also presented the "from the bottom up" theory from the field of public policy. These theories helped support the findings and were in keeping with the study's conclusions, according to which "the street-level bureaucrats" (SLB)

---

116 Eisenhardt 1989; Burt 2000; Blau 1964; Weber 1949; Gambetta 2000; Giddens 1976.

were those who in fact set the agenda, through methods they developed in order to handle various situations of uncertainty and work pressure. This in turn supports the argument that at times there are conflicts and struggles between the state clerks and citizens who "challenge them" and even defeat them. Another point supported is the conclusion that clerks function based on trial and error (Behn 1988). A change in policy could occur as a result of internal and external pressures (Howlett and Cashore 2009; Howlett 2005) and be influenced by the stereotypes that the clerks create regarding various clients, thus affecting the interaction between them (Lipsky 1980). This study is an example of the advantage of integrating theories from diverse disciplines, expanding understanding of the phenomenon, and deepening conclusions.

The state regulation meant to protect the jobs of pregnant women in Israel is only one of the welfare mechanisms intended to provide various services in an equal manner to diverse populations. These groups require state intervention during their private and work lives. Reinforcement of theories from varied discourses may challenge future research seeking to examine other welfare systems. Findings from this study could act as an empirical base when examining the influence of family welfare policies, including the Women's Labour Law and implementation of policies in Israel—not only upon the state's actions but also on repercussions of the act and its outcomes. The findings could expand the knowledge base regarding patterns of women's entry and exit from the labour market during pregnancy and after giving birth, as well as regarding the employers' approach to women's work, including parenting, motherhood, and pregnancy at work in this context. It would be interesting to examine the employers' approaches to employment of disempowered women, including ultra-orthodox, Arab, or uneducated women, particularly in light of their backgrounds according to which they are often seen as cheap, available labour, similar to female employees in India. Thus the theoretical and practical discourse expands with regard to the degree to which the welfare state contributes through interventional regulation.

A study of the fragmentation in the state's regulatory actions and its influence upon the creation of gender-based inequality toward pregnant women in a welfare state may be a possible model for examining further state regulations, in the scientific field in Israel and in comparative international research. Follow-up research could look at further regulations at the local level, and examine the state's actions in implementing egalitarian legislation, for example, a look at the state protection given to men during reserve duty, or the results of dismissal during pregnancy upon the personal and employment lives of women in general. Further, it is possible to examine the Israeli case from a comparative, international perspective, emphasising the cultural aspects, in order to provide a response to the following question: Is the fragmentation part of the dynamic in Israeli society and the political reality in Israel, or does it cross borders?

At the implementation level, the study's findings demonstrate the great potential inherent in the state's intervention in the prevention of dismissal of pregnant women, from the point of view of expanding the participation of women and mothers in the labour cycle as well as pointing out the need to administer the interventional mechanism in a more effective manner, and to accompany it with broad-based, uniform explanations concerning the advantages of continuing to employ women during pregnancy, not only for potential employers, but also for those who enact the law and for the women themselves (Toshav-Eichner and Frenkel 2011). Accompanying the dismissal prevention process with counseling and following up on the employee's reintegration into the work place could prevent the need for compromises, which grant the state's legitimisation of dismissals during pregnancy. In the long run, the number of employers seeking dismissals along with compromises, thus increasing the gender-based inequality in the labour market, must be reduced.

Based on the findings it is worth considering the effectiveness of the system, as well as the equality therein, and to examine ways to prevent the fragmentation of the state protection mechanisms for all women as well as for the organisations employing them. For example, a way must be found to increase awareness of the law and to make it more accessible to the populations at large. Efforts must be made to create a uniform understanding of the role of supervisor and to rethink the mechanism's place. If the Ministry of Industry, Commerce, and Employment (Economy) is the most appropriate address, then equality must be forged between employment and commerce and industry. Further, there must be better and more effective enforcement vis-à-vis employers who dismiss women illegally. Increasing deterrence and punishments on the one hand, and explanation of the advantages of employing mothers on the other, as well as coordination among the government ministries and clear instructions concerning the purpose of the system in order to avoid conflicting approaches by operators could create uniform and more equal state action. In addition, it is worth considering rewarding those who employ new mothers, for example by training them at the state's expense during their maternity leave in subjects that could contribute to the employer and the organisation.

In an attempt to find a more effective way to "implement policy," based on the habitus and capital theories, one could assume that in the habitus of the senior supervisors there is a logic stemming from "patriarchal inertia," and decision-making patterns that are limited by the field. During the interviews the senior supervisors complained several times that there are cases that keep them awake at night. In this context it would seem better to operate along two separate axes: on the one hand, to abandon the patriarchal logic, and on the other, to abandon the individual decision-making processes and adopt a new logic, for example, one involving gender-based thought. It would make more sense to adopt the cooperation characterising the first period, in which the relevant institutional bodies deliberated and made the decision together, and when the guiding logic was that which aimed to reduce the gender-based inequality.

Given that structural changes lead to conflict surrounding the institutional arrangement, and internalisation of the change among the clerks does not end with the completion of the institutionalisation period (Thelen 1999), it is worth thinking strategically and uniformly, in a structured manner, in order to ground all of the relevant parties before enacting the change, or at the most, at the stage of its inclusion. It is nonetheless worth emphasising that in cases of dismissals of pregnant teachers, the consensus established among the ministries created inequality, and it is therefore important to say that in order to maintain the spirit of the law, coordination is not enough. There is also a need to see eye to eye with the public's interest and to engage them in the state action.

In the reality that has emerged, there is a crucial place for a mechanism whose purpose is to help women remain within the labour world. However, there is a need to find a formula that will move with the spirit of the times and not reflect the patriarchal systems that protect only up to a certain point and then abandon the protected party to the will of an employer who does not want them. The senior supervisor has an overly heavy responsibility on her shoulders. The decision whether to refuse a request to dismiss or to permit the dismissal occurs under heavy pressure, and it is becoming ever more complicated in the increasingly neoliberal reality. It seems that in order to ease the burden of decision, the regulation must first be moved to a body with no conflicting interests such as those characteristic of the Ministry of the Economy. This body could, for example, refer to the model of protection for employees in reserve duty, even if only in the reduced context of a number of participants with legal roles who share the decision. This body should be inter-ministerial, independent, and must be responsible for all matters related to the protection of women's employment during pregnancy and after giving birth. It should function through planning, coordination, cooperation, and a uniform ideology, and be run less for constantly changing political motives based on the moods of the decision-maker. Furthermore, it is important to consider how according to the law, proof can be provided that once an employee returns to work, after the state chose to protect her position, she will not be harmed.

As a final comment of the book, it is appropriate to present a quote from a hearing carried out for one of many women whose employer sought to dismiss her during pregnancy:

I want to believe that the law gives me the right to fulfill my desire for motherhood, and it bothers me that despite my having done my best work, and the fact that I love my job, they still want to dismiss me. I would be glad if you [the state] could help me.

(Hearing observation, May 2008)

Bibliography

Acker, J. (1990). "Hierarchies, Jobs, Bodies: A Theory of Gendered Organisations," *Gender and Society* 4(2): 139-158.

Acker, J. (1995). "Decisions without Hierarchy: Feminist Intervention in Organisation Theory and Practice," *Sings* 20(2): 467-470.

Acker, J. (2003). "Hierarchies, Jobs, Bodies: A Theory of Gendered Organisations," In: Ely, R., Foldy, E. and Scully, M. (eds.), *Gender ,Work and Organisation*, Oxford: Blackwell, pp. 49-61.

Acker, J. (2006). "Inequality Regimes: Gender, Class, and Race in Organisations," *Gender and Society* 20(4): 441-464.

Adams, L., Winterbotham, M., and McAndrew, F. (2005). *Pregnancy Discrimination at Work: a Survey of Women*, IFF Research, EOC Working Paper Series, UK.

Adler, P. A., and Adler, P. (1994). "Observational

Techniques," in: N. K. Denzin and Y. S. Lincoln (eds.), *Handbook of Qualitative Research*, pp. 377-392.

Ajzenstadt, M., and Gal, J. (2001). "Appearances Can Be Deceptive: Gender in the Israeli Welfare State," *Social Politics: International Studies in Gender, State & Society* 8(3): 292-324.

Ajzenstadt, Mimi and Gal, Jonny (2001). *Gender in the Israeli Welfare State- Developments and Issues*, Jerusalem: The Centre for the Study of Social Policy in Israel.

Albrecht, J., Björklund, A., and Vorman, S. (2003). "Is There a Glass Ceiling In Sweden?," *Journal of Labour Economics* 21(1), 145: pp. 145-177.

Alfasi, Michal (2008). *The Work of Pregnant Women*, Bureau for Research, Planning and Economy, Ministry of Industry, Commerce, and Employment.

Almagor-Lotan, Orli (2012). *Dismissal of Pregnant Women and Women Undergoing Fertility Treatments- Update for 2012*, Knesset Centre for Research and Data, presented to the Committee for the Advancement of the Status of Women.

Altshuler, A. A., and Zegans, M. D. (1997). "Innovation and Public Management: Notes from the State House and City Hall," in: Alan A. Altshuler and Robert D. Behn (eds.), *Innovation in American Government: Challenges, Opportunities and Dilemmas*, Washington: Brookings Institution Press, pp. 68-82.

Amargan –Barnea, Amalia (1985). "Women Go Home," *Yedioth Ahronoth*, 27.10.85.

Anon. (1952). "What are the rights of the working woman," *Yedioth Ahronoth*, 30.7.52.

Anon. (2002) "Questions and answers with the worker's hotline," *Yedioth Ahronoth*, 8.10.02.

Anon. (2007). "Questions and answers with the worker's hotline: Is one allowed to dismiss a pregnant employee?"

Anush, Hagar (1997). "Amendment to a Chauvinist Law," *Yedioth Ahronoth*, 6.6.97.

Anush, Hagar (1999). "It's Not Worth Getting Pregnant," *Yedioth Ahronoth*, 16.5.99.

Avnimelech, Moriah and Tamir, Yosef (2002). *Ticking Welfare- Economy and Politics of Welfare in Israel.* Tel Aviv: Kav Adom, HaKibbutz HaMeuchad.

Bank of Israel (2004). *Work and Salary Report*, Research Department, Report.

Barak, Aharon (2004). *A Judge in a Democratic Society,* Haifa University Press.

Barak, Benny (2002). "There is an Exemption- There is no Consideration of a Master Plan Regarding Protective Laws for Pregnant Employees" *Yedioth Ahronoth*, 11.10.02.

Barak-Erez, Dafna (2010). *Administrative Law*, 2 volumes, Tel Aviv: Bar Association Press.

Bardach, E. (1977). *The Implementation Game: What Happens after a Bill Becomes a Law?*, M.I.T Press, Cambridge MA.

Bareli, Avi (2002). "From a Community of Workers to a Lonely Mass," *Another Country* 12, 2002.

Behn, R. D. (1988). "Management by Groping Along," *Journal of Policy Analysis and Management* 7(1): 643-663.

Bellace, J. (1991). "The Role of The Law Effecting Gender Pay Equality: A Comparison of Six Countries Experience," in: S. L. Willborn (ed.), *Women's Wages: Stability and Change in Six Industrial Countries*, Greenwich, CN: JAI, Press, pp. 21-31.

Ben Israel, Ruth (1998). *Equal Opportunity and the Prohibition on Discrimination in the Workplace*, Tel Aviv: Open University, Vol. 2, Chapters 6-8.

Bendor, Ariel (2006). "The Limits of Justice Barak (or Does Judicial Discretion Really Exist?)," *Law and Government (Mishpat u'Mimshal)* 9, 2005: 261-295.

Benko, C., and Weisberg, A. (2007). *Mass Career Customization: Aligning the Workplace with Today's Non-Traditional Workforce*, Boston, MA: Harvard Business School Press.

Bercovic, Nitza (2001). "Citizenship and Motherhood: The Status of Women in Israel," in: Yoav Peled and Adi Ofir (ed.) *Israel: From a Conscripted Society to a Civil Society?* Tel Aviv: Kibbutz Hameuchad Press, pp.206-243.

Bercovic, Nitza (2003). "The Globalisation of Human Rights and Women's Rights: The State and the Global Political System," *Theory and Criticism (Teoria u'Bikoret)* 23: 13-48.

Berenzon, Haim (1984). "Dismissal of a Pregnant, Temporary Employee," *Yedioth Ahronoth*, 25.12.84.

Berg, B. (1998). *Qualitative Research Methods for the Social Sciences*, Boston: Allyn and Bacon.

Berkovitch, N. (1999). *From Motherhood to Citizenship: Women's Rights and International Organisations*, Baltimore: Johns Hopkins University Press.

Bernstein, Debby (2008). *Women in the Margins*, Yad Yitzchak.

Bernstein, S. D. (1992). "Pioneers and Homemakers: Jewish Women," *Pre-State Israel Albany*: State University of New York Press.

Binyamin, Orli (2002). "Duality in Relations between the State and Women in Israel: the Case of Women Employed Through Manpower Companies in the Public Sector," *Society and Welfare (Chevra u'Revacha)*25, 4: 455-480.

Blair-Loy, M. (2003). *Competing Devotions*, Cambridge, MA: Harvard University Press.

Blau, F., and Kahn, L. (1995). "The Gender Earning Gap: Some International Evidence," in: R. B. Freeman and L. F. Katz (eds.), *Differences and Changes in Wage Structures*, Chicago: University of Chicago Press.

Blau, P. M. (1964). *Exchange and Power in Social Life*, Transaction Publishers.Bourdieu, P. (1986). "The Forms of Capital," in: J. Richardson (ed.), *Handbook of Theory and Research for the Sociology of Education*, New York, Greenwood, pp. 241-258.

Bogosh, Rina and Don Yihyeh, Rachel (1999). *Gender and the Law: Discrimination of Women in the Courts in Israel*, Jerusalem: The Jerusalem Centre for the Study of Israel.

Bourdieu, P. (1987). "The Force of Law: Towards a Sociology of the Juridical Field," *The Hasting Law Journal* 38: 814-853.

Bourdieu, P., and Passeron, J. C. (1990). *Reproduction in Education, Society and Culture* 4, Sage

Bourdieu, Pierre (2005a). "But Who Created the Creators?," in Pierre Bourdieu, *Questions of Sociology*, Tel Aviv: Resling, pp. 93-206.

Bourdieu, Pierre (2005b). "High Fashion: High Culture," in Pierre Bourdieu, *Questions of Sociology*, Tel Aviv: Resling, pp. 183-191.

Buding, M., and England, P. (2001). "Wage Penalty for Motherhood," *American Sociological Review* 66: 204-225.

Bumiller, K. (1988). *The Civil Rights Society: The Social Construction of Victims*, Baltimore: Johns Hopkins University Press.

Burt, R. S. (2000). "The Network Structure of Social Capital," *Research in Organisational Behaviour* 22: 345-423.

Buzzanell, P., and Liu, M. (2007). "It's 'give and take': Maternity Leave as a Conflict Management Process," *Human Relations* 60: 463-495.

Bygren, M., and Kumlin, J. (2005). "Mechanisms of Organisational Sex Segregation," *Work and Occupations* 32(1): 39-65.

Calavita, K. (1992). *Inside the State – the Bracero Program, Immigration, and the I.N.S*, New York: Routledge, p. 243.

Calloway, D. A. (1995). "Accommodating Pregnancy in the Workplace," *Stetson Law Revew* 25(1): 1-53.

Campbell, J. L. (2004). *Institutional Change and Globalisation*, Princeton University Press.

Carpenter, D. P., and Krause, G. A. (2012). "Reputation and Public Administration," *Public Administration Review* 72(1): 26-32.

Cockburn, C. (2002). "Resisting Equal Opportunities: The Issue of Maternity," in: S. Jackson and S. Scott (eds.), *Gender: A Sociological Reader*, London: Routledge, pp. 180-191.

Collinson, D. (2000). "Strategies of Resistance: Power, Knowledge and Subjectivities in the Workplace," in: K. Grint (ed.), *Work and Society: A Reader*, Cambridge: Polity Press.

Cotter, D. A., Hermsen, J. G., Ovadia, S., and Vannerman, R. (2001). "The Glass Ceiling Effect," *Social Forces* 80(2): 655-681.

Crystal, Tali, Cohen, Yinon and Mondlak, Guy (2006). *The Professional Union and the Growth of Economic Inequality in Israel 1970-2003*. Jerusalem: Van Leer Institute.

Dahan, Momi (2001). "The Rise of Financial Inequality," in Avi Ben Basat (ed.) *From Government Intervention to Market Economy: 1985-1998*, Tel Aviv: Am Oved, pp.610-656.

Dahan, Momi (2006). *Inequality*, Nitza Bercovic and Ori Ram (eds.), Ben Gurion University Press.

Davidov, Guy (2009). "Unbound: Some Comments on Israel's Judicially-Developed Labour Law," *Comparative Labour Law and Policy Journal* 30(2): 283-311.

Del Bono, E., Weber, A., and Winter-Ebmer, R. (2012). "Clash of Career and Family: Fertility Decisions after Job Displacement," *Journal of the European Economic Association* 10(4): 659-683.

Denzin, N. K., (1994). "The Art and Politics of Interpretation: The Stories We Tell One Another," in: N. K. Denzin and Y. S. Lincoln (eds.), *Handbook of Qualitative Research*, New York: Sage.

Denzin, N. K., and Lincoln, Y. S. (2000). "Introduction: The Discipline and Practice of Qualitative Research," in: N. K. Denzin and Y. S. Lincoln (eds.), *Handbook of Qualitative Research*, pp. 1-28, London: Sage.

Desai, S., and Waite, L. J. (1991). "Women's Employment During Pregnancy and after the First Birth: Occupational

Characteristics and Work Commitment," *American Sociological Review* 56(4): 551-566.

Deutsch, K. W. (1985). "On Theory and Research in Innovation," in: R. L. Merritt and A. J. Merritt (eds.), *Innovation in the Public Sector*, Beverley Hills: Sage Publication, pp. 17-35.

Dobrovitzky, Lital (2008). "A Question of Discrimination: a Guide to Employment and Dismissal During Pregnancy for Employers ," *Yedioth Ahronoth*, Finance Supplement, 13.2.08.

Doron, Avraham (1992). *The Welfare State in an Era of Returns*, Jerusalem: I.L Magnes, Hebrew University.

Doron, Avraham (1994). "Mothers' Insurance: Reciprocity among Legislation, Policy, Implementation and Enactment," *Society and Welfare (Chevra ve-Revacha)* 14, Ministry of Labour and Welfare and the Women's League for Israel, in cooperation with Social Work schools in Israel.

Duffield, M. (2002). "Trends in Female Employment 2002," *Labour Market Trends* 110(11): 605-616.

Duncan, K. C., and Prus, M. J. (1992). "Atrophy Rates for Intermittent employment for Married and Never-Married Women: A Test of Human Capital Theory of Occupational Sex Segregation," *Quarterly Review of Economics and Finance* 32: 27-37.

Dunstan, R. (2001). *Birth Rights: A CAB Evidence Report on*

Maternity and Parental Rights at Work, London: National Association of Citizens Advice Bureaux.

Dushnik, Liron and Tzabar ben Yehoshua, Naama (2001). "The Ethics of Qualitative Research," in Na'ama Tzabar Ben Yehoshua (ed) *Traditions and Trends in Qualitative Research* Or Yehuda: Dvir, pp. 343-368.

Dworkin, G. (1972). "Paternalism," *The Monist* 56(1): 64-84.

Edwards, M. E. (1996). "Pregnancy Discrimination Litigation: Legal Erosion of Capitalist Ideology under Equal Employment Opportunity Law," *Social Forces* 75: 247-269.

Eisenhardt, K. M. (1989). "Agency Theory: An Assessment and Review," *Academy of Management Review* 14(1): 57-74.

Ella, Sima (1989). "Women on the Ropes," *Yedioth Ahronoth*, Modern Times supplement, 9.8.89.

Elmore, R. F. (1982). "Backward Mapping: Implementation Research and Policy Decisions," *Political Science Quarterly* 94(4): 601-616.

El-Sawad, A., Arnold, J., and Cohen, L. (2004). "'Doublethink': The Prevalence and Function of Contradiction in Accounts of Organisational Life," *Human Relations* 57: 1179-1203.

EOC – Equal Opportunities Commission (2005). *Greater Expectations: Final Report of the EOC's Investigation into*

Discrimination Against New and Expectant Mothers in the Workplace, Manchester: Equal Opportunities Commission.

Equalities Review (2007). "Fairness and Freedom: The Final Report of the Equalities Review," http://archive.cabinetoffice.gov.uk/equalitiesreview/publications.html

Eshet, Gidon (1990). "The Woman and the Method," "*Yedioth Ahronoth*, 1.5.90.

Esping-Andersen, G. (1990). *The Three Worlds of Welfare Capitalism*, Princeton University Press.

Esping-Andersen, G. (1999). *Social Foundations of Postindustrial Economies*, New York: Oxford University Press.

Estivill, J. (2003). *Concepts and Strategies for Combating Social Exclusion*, Geneva International Labour Office.

Evans, P. (1995). *Embedded Autonomy – State and Industrial Transformation*, Princeton University Press.

Evertsson, M., and Grunow, D. (2012). "Women's Work Interruptions and Career Prospects in Germany and Sweden," *International Journal of Sociology and Social Policy* 32(9/10): 561-575.

Ewick, P., and Silbey, S. (1998). *The Common Place of Law: Stories from Everyday Life*, Chicago: University of Chicago Press.

Far, Michelle (2011). "Personal Capital," *Key (Mafteach)* 3: 131-150.

Farjoun, I. E. (1983). "Class Divisions in Israeli Society," *Society Khamsin* 10: 29-39.

Ferber, A. F. (1991). "Women in the Labour Market: The Incomplete Revolution," in: S. L. Willborn (ed.), *International Review of Comparative Public Policy*, A Research Annual: Women's Wages: Stability and Change in Six Industrial Countries, Greenwich, CN: JAI, Press 3, pp. 39-60.

Fogel-Bijoy, Silvia (1999). "Families in Israel: Between Families and Post-Modernity," in: Dafna Yizre'eli et al (eds.) *Sex, Gender and Politics*, Tel Aviv: HaKibbutz HaMeuchad, pp. 107-166.

Fogel-Bijoy, Silvia (2003). "The Secondary Earner in the Age of Globalisation, Women in the Israeli Labout Market," *Society- A Socialist Journal of Social, Economic, Political and Cultural Issues* 8, Yesod Press: 10-14.

Fogel-Bijoy, Silvia (2005). "If It's So Good, Why Is It So Bad: Gender Aspects of Neo-Liberalism in the Israeli Labour Market" in: Avi Bareli et al (eds.), *Society and Economy in Israel*, Jerusalem: Ben Tzvi Institute and Ben Gurion University, pp. 183-216.

Frenkel, Michal, Hacker, Dafna and Broide, Yael (2011). "Working Families in Israeli Law: Between Neo-Liberalism and Human Rights," in: Margalit Shilo and Gidon Katz (eds.), *Gender in Israel: New Studies on Gender in the Yishuv and the State,* 2 vols, Ben Gurion Institute Press, pp. 682-727.

Frenkiel, N. (1984). *The Up and Comers: Bryant Takes Aim at the Settlers-In*, Adweek, March 1984.

Gabizon, Ruth (2009). "The Hollow Hope: Can the Courts Bring About Social Change? A Critique of the Second Edition of Gerald Rosenberg's Book 2008" *Legal Deeds (Ma'asei Mishpat)* 2: 15.

Gambetta, D. (2000). "Can We Trust Trust," in: D. Gambetta (ed.) *Trust: Making and Breaking Cooperative Relations*, Oxford: Basil Blackwell, pp. 213-237.

Gatrell, C. (2005). *Hard Labour: The Sociology of Parenthood*, Maidenhead: Open University Press.

Gatrell, C. (2007a). "A Fractional Commitment?," *International Journal of Human Resource Management* 18: 462-475.

Gatrell, C. (2007b). "Secrets and Lies: Breastfeeding and Professional Paid Work," *Social Science & Medicine* 65: 393-404.

Gatrell, C. (2008). *Embodying Women's Work*, Maidenhead: Open University Press.

Gatrell, C. (2011). "Managing the Maternal Body: A Comprehensive Review and Transdisciplinary Analysis," *International Journal of Management Reviews* 13(1): 97-112.

Gebel, M., and Giesecke, J. (2011). "Labour Market Flexibility and Inequality: The Changing Skill-Based

Temporary Employment and Unemployment Risks in Europe," *Social Forces* 90(1): 17-39.

Geller, Lidia (1975). "Broad Support for the Proposed Law for the Equality of Women" *Yedioth Ahronoth*, 1.7.75.

Giddens, A. (1976). "Classical Social Theory and the Origins of Modern Sociology," *American Journal of Sociology* 81(4): 703-729.

Glazer-Raymo, J. (1999). *Shattering the Myths: Women in Academe*, Baltimore, MD: John Hopkins University Press.

Glenn, R. C., Goodstein, J., and Gyenes, A. (1988). "Organisations and the State: Effects of the Institutional Environment on Agricultural Cooperatives in Hungary," *Administrative Science Quarterly* 33(2): 233-256.

Glor, E. (1997). "What is Public Sector Innovation?," *The Innovation Journal* 2(1), article 1.

Goffen-Sarig, Anat (2004). *Do it Yourself—Civil Initiative as a Strategy for the Renewal of Education Policy in Israel*. The School for Public Policy, Hebrew University.

Goffman, E. (1990). *The Presentation of Self in Everyday Life*, New York: Penguin Books.

Golden, O. (1997). "Innovation in Public Sector Human Services Programs: The Implication of Innovation by 'Groping Along'," in: A. A. Altshuler and R. D. Behn (eds.), *Innovation in American Government: Challenges, Opportunities and Dilemmas*, Washington: Brookings Institution Press, pp. 146-174.

Gordon, D. M. (1972). *Theories of Poverty and Unemployment*, D. C. Heath and Company, Massachusetts.

Gordon, L. (1988). "What Does Welfare Regulate?," *Social Researches* 55: 609-630.

Gornick, J. C. (1999). "Gender Equality in the Labour Market: Women's Employment and Earnings," in: D. Sunsbury (ed.), *Gender and Welfare State Regimes*, Oxford University Press, pp. 210-242.

Gornick, J. C., and Meyers, M. (2003). *Families that Work: Policies for Reconciling Parenthood and Employment*, New York: Russell Sage Foundation.

Gornick, J. C., Meyers, M. K., and. Ross, K. E. (1997). "Supporting the Employment of Mothers: Policy Variation Across Fourteen Welfare States," *Journal of European Social Policy* 7(1): 45-70.

Gottschalk, P., and Smeeding, T. (1997). "Inequality, Income Growth, and Mobility: The Basic Facts," *Journal of Economic Perspectives* 11(2): 21-40.

Gotwin, Dani (2001). "The Dialectics of the Failure of Equality: The Israeli Left Between Neo-Liberalism and Social Democracy." *From Up Close (Mikarov)*3: 30-57.

Grenfell, M., and James, D. (1998). *Bourdieu and Education: Acts of Practical Theory*, London: Falmer.

Grinberg, L. (1991). *Split Corporatism in Israel,* Albany: State University of New York Press.

Gronau, R. (1988). "Sex-Related Wage Differentials and Women's Interrupted Labour Careers – the Chicken or the Egg," *Journal of Labour Economics* 6: 277-301.

Grover, S. L., and Crooker, K. J. (1995). "Who Appreciates Family-Responsive Human Resource Policies: The Impact of Family-Friendly Policies on the Organisational Attachment of Parents and Non-Parents," *Personnel Psychology* 48(2): 271-288.

Haas, L. (1992). *Equal Parenthood and Social Policy – A Study of Parental Leave in Sweden,* Albany: State University of New York Press.

Haas, L., and Hwang, P. (1999). "Parental Leave in Sweden," in: P. Moss and F. Devan (eds.), *Parental Leave: Progress or Pitfall?,* The Hague/Brussels, NIDI/CBGS Publications, vol 35: 45-68.

Hacker, Dafna (2008). *Parenting in the Law,* Tel Aviv: Hakibbutz HaMeuchad.

Harvey, D. (2005). "A Brief History of Neoliberalism," Oxford University Press.

Hausman, B. L. (2004). "The Feminist Politics of Breastfeeding," *Australian Feminist Studies* 19: 273-285.

Haynes, K. (2006a). "Linking Narrative and Identity

Construction: Using Autobiography in Accounting Research," *Critical Perspectives on Accounting* 17: 399-418.

Haynes, K. (2006b). "A Therapeutic Journey?," *Qualitative Research in Organisations and Management* 1: 204-221.

Haynes, K. (2008a). "(Re)figuring Accounting and Maternal Bodies: The Gendered Embodiment of Accounting Professionals," *Accounting, Organisations and Society* 33: 328-348.

Haynes, K. (2008b). "Transforming Identities: Accounting Professionals and the Transition to Motherhood," *Critical Perspectives on Accounting* 19: 620-642.

Haynes, K. (2010). "Other Lives in Accounting: Critical Reflections on Oral History Methodology in Action," *Critical Perspectives on Accounting*, 21(3): 22-23.

Hernes, H. (1987). *Welfare State and Woman Power: Essays in State Feminism*, Oslo, Norway University Press.

Herzog, Chana (2000). *Women in Israel*. Tel Aviv: Maxem F.

Hills, J. (2004). *Inequality and the State*, Oxford University Press.

Ho, L., Powell, C., and Volpp, L. (1996). *(Dis)Assembling Rights of Women Workers Along the Global Assembly Line: Human Rights and the Garment Industry*, 31 Harv. C.R.-C.L. L., Rev. 383.

Houston, D., and Marks, G. (2003). "The Role of Planning

and Workplace Support in Returning to Work after Maternity Leave," *British Journal of Industrial Relations* 41: 197-214.

Howlett, M. (2005). "What is a Policy Instrument? Tools, Mixes, and Implementation Styles," in: P. Eliadis, M. M. Hill and M. P. Houlett (eds.), *Designing Government: From Instruments to Governance*, Mc Gill-Queen's University press, pp. 31-50.

Howlett, M. (2009). "Process Sequencing Policy Dynamics: Beyond Homeostasis and Path Dependency," *Journal of Public Policy* 29(3): 241-262.

Howlett, M., and Cashore, B. (2009). "The Dependent Variable Problem in the Study of Policy Change: Understanding Policy Change as a Methodological Problem," *Journal of Comparative Policy Analysis* 11(1): 33-46.

Ilberg, Ella (1989). "The Female MKs are Better than the Male MKs," *Yedioth Ahronoth*, 24 hours supplement, 20.0.83.

ILO (2001). *Pregnancy Discrimination at Work*. Legal Review, International Labour Conference 89th session 2001 Geneva.

James, G. (2004). *Pregnancy Discrimination at Work, A Review*, University of Reading, Working Paper Series No. 14.

James, G. (2007). "Law's Response to Pregnancy/Workplace Conflicts: A Critique," *Feminist Legal Studies* 15: 167-188.

James, G. (2009). "Mothers and Fathers as Parents and Workers: Family-Friendly Employment Policies in an Era of Shifting Identities," *Journal of Social Welfare & Family Law* 31(3): 271-283.

James, G. (2011). "The Law Relating to Maternity Leave," in: T. Wright and H. Conley (eds.), *Gower handbook of Discrimination at Work*, Gower Publishing Ltd., pp. 47-56.

Jick, T. D. (1979). "Mixing Qualitative and Quantitative Methods: Triangulation in Action," *Administrative Science Quarterly* 24(4): 602-611.

Kennedy, E., and Mendus, S. (1987). *Women in Western Political Philosophy*, Brighton: Wheatsheaf Books, pp. 3-10.

Knjin, T., and Kremer, M. (1997). "Gender and the Caring Dimension of Welfare State: Towards Inclusive Citizenship," *Social Politics: International Studies in Gender, State and Society* 4(3): 328-361.

Kohl, J., Mayfield, M., and Mayfield, J. (2005). "Recent Trends in Pregnancy Discrimination Law," *Business Horizons* 48: 421-429.

Kolberg, J. E. (1991), "The Gender Dimension of the Welfare State," *International Journal of Sociology* 21: 119-148.

Korpi, W. (2000). "Faces of Inequality: Gender, Class, and Patterns of Inequalities in Different Types of Welfare State," *Social Politics* 7(2): 127-191.

Kotz-Bar, Chen (2002). "Thousands of Pregnant Women Fired Without Permits," *Ma'ariv*, Weekend Supplement, 9.8.02.

Kraamwinkel, M. (1992). "Women's Work and Law: New Perspective on the Labour Market Strategy," *New England Reveiew* 26: 823-824.

Kramer, L. A., and Lambert, S. (2001). "Sex-Linked Bias in Chances of Being Promoted to Supervisor," *Sociological Perspectives* 44(1): 111-127.

Kraus, V. (2002). *Secondary Breadwinners: Israeli Women in the Labour Force*, Greenwood Publishing Group.

Kricheli-Katz, T. (2012). "Choice, Discrimination, and the Motherhood Penalty," *Law & Society Review* 46(3): 557-587.

Kritzer, H., and Silbey, S. (eds.), (2003). *In Litigation: Do The "Have's" Still Come Out Ahead*, Stanford University Press.

Kymlicka, W. (1990). *Contemporary Political Philosophy*, Oxford Press, p. 238.

La Valle, I., Clery, E., and Huerta, M. C. (2008). *Maternity Rights and Mothers*, Employment Decisions No. 496, HM Stationery Office

Labour, Welfare and Health Committee (2002). Protocol (9.7.02).

Leighton, P., and Evans, R. (2004). *Pregnant Women at Work: A Survey of Small Business Employers in Wales*, Manchester: Equal Opportunities Commission 2004.

Lein, Y. (2000). "The State and the Business Coalition: The Case of the Stock Market Tax in Israel," in: M. Moutner (ed.), *Distributing Justice in Israel*, Tel Aviv University, Ramot, pp. 391-408.

Lewin, K. (1936). *Principles of Topological Psychology*, New York: McGraw-Hill.

Li, J. (2002). "State Fragmentation: Toward a Theoretical Understanding of the Territorial Power of the State," *Sociological Theory* 20: 139-156.

Lin, Yechezkel (2002). "The State, Business Elites and Coalitions: The Stock Exchange Tax as an Example," in Menachem Mautner (ed.) *Divisional Equality in Israel*, Tel Aviv: Ramot Press, Tel Aviv University, pp. 223-259.

Lior, Gad and Shibi, Chaim (2005). "They earn 22% less than men; an outline for increasing rules to protect women against harm caused by employers during pregnancy" , *Yedioth Ahronoth*, 8.3.05.

Lipsky, M. (1980). *Street-Level Bureaucracy*, New York: Russell Sage Foundation.

Lofstorm, A., and Gustafsson, S. (1991). "Policy Changes and Women's Wage in Sweden," in: S. L. Willborn (ed.), *International Review of Comparative Public Policy*, A Research Annual: Women's Wages: Stability and Change in Six Industrial Countries, Greenwich, CN: JAI, Press 3, pp. 313-330.

Lynn, L. E. Jr. (1997). "Innovation and the Public Interest: Insights from the Private Sector," in: A. A. Altshuler and R. D. Behn (eds.), *Innovation in American Government: Challenges, Opportunities and Dilemmas*, Washington: Brookings Institution Press, pp. 83-103.

Macaulay, S. (1984). "Law and the Behavioural Sciences: Is There Any There There?," *Law and Policy* 6(2): 149-187.

MacKinnon, C. A. (1984). "Difference and Dominance: On Sex Discrimination," in: K. T. Bartlett and R. Kennedy (eds.), *Feminist Legal Theory, Reading in Law and Gender*, Westview Press Boulder 1991, pp. 81-94.

Majone, G. (1994). "The Rise of the Regulatory State," *West European Politics* 17(3): 81.

Mäkelä, L. (2005). "Pregnancy and Leader-Follower Dyadic Relationships: A Research Agenda," *Equal Opportunities International* 24: 50-73.

Mäkelä, L. (2009). "Representations of Change within Dyadic Relations between Leader and Follower: Discourses of Pregnant Followers," *Leadership* 5: 171-192.

Maman, Dani and Rosenhek, Ze'ev (2009). *The Bank of Israel: Political Economy in a Neo-Liberal Era*, HaKibbutz HaMeuchad and The Van Leer Institute.

Mandel, H. (2009). "Configurations of Gender Inequality: The Consequences of Ideology and Public Policy," *The British Journal of Sociology* 60(4): 693-719.

Mandel, H. (2011). "Rethinking the Paradox: Tradeoffs in Work-Family Policy and Patterns of Gender Inequality," *Community, Work & Family* 14(2): 159-176.

Mandel, H., and Shalev, M. (2009). "How Welfare States Shape the Gender Pay Gap: A Theoretical and Comparative Analysis," *Social Forces* 87(4): 1873-1911.

Martin, C. J. (1989). "Business Influence and State Power: The Case of U.S Corporate Tax Policy," *Politics and Society* 17(2): 189-223.

Mautner, M. (ed.), *Divisional Equality in Israel,* Tel Aviv Ramot, pp. 223-259.

McDonald, P., and Dear, K. (2006). "Pregnancy Discrimination in Queensland: Internal Labour Market Issues and Progress to Formal Redress" (Conference paper), in: J. Bailey et al. (eds.), *Our Work...Our Lives: National Conference on Women and Industrial Relations,* 12-14 July 2006, Brisbane.

McRae, S. (1993). "Returning to Work After Childbirth: Opportunities and Inequalities," *European Sociological Review* 9(2): 125-138.

McRae, S., and Daniel, W. W. (1991). "Maternity Rights in Britain: First Findings from Maternity Rights in Britain: The Experience of Women and Employers," *Policy Studies Institute* 729, London.

Mendel, Hadas (2004). *The Repercussions of Family Welfare*

Policy Upon the Various Facets of Inequality Among Sexes: a Comparison of 20 Countries, a compulsory Ph.D essay, Tel Aviv University, pp. 4-19.

Merlino, L. P., Parrotta, P., and Pozzoli, D. (2012). "Assortative Matching and Gender," *Discussion Paper Series*, Vol. 6983, Forschungsinstitut zur Zukunft der Arbeit.

Merritt, R. L., and Merritt, A. J. (1985). "Innovation in the Public Sector," in: R. L. Merritt and A. J. Merritt (eds.), *Innovation in the Public Sector*, Beverley Hills: Sage Publication, pp. 9-16.

Mill, J. S., and Mill, H. T. (1970). *Essays on Sex Equality* (A. Rossi ed.), University of Chicago Press.

Mincer, J., and Ofek, H. (1982). "Interrupted Work Careers: Depreciation and Restoration of Human Capital," *Journal of Human Resources* 17(1): 3-24.

Mishler, E. (1986). *Research Interviewing: Context and Narrative*, Boston: Harvard University Press.

Mondlek, Guy (2004). *Labour Relations in an Era of Reciprocity*, The Israeli Centre for Democracy.

Moore, M. H., Sparrow, M., and Spelman, W. (1997). "Innovation in Policing: From Production Lines to Jobs Shops," in: A. A. Altshuler and R. D. Behn (eds.), *Innovation in American Government: Challenges, Opportunities and Dilemmas*, Washington: Brookings Institution Press, pp. 274-298.

Mori (2002). *Big Employers Childcare Survey*, Daycare Trust and BUPA. London: Daycare Trust.

Mundlak, G. (2008). "Israeli System of Labour Law: Sources and Form," *Comparative Labour Law and Policy Journal* 30: 159.

Mundlak, G. (2009). "The Law of Equal Opportunities in Employment: Between Equality and Polarization," *Comparative Labour Law and Policy Journal* 30(2): 213-241.

Nadiv, Ronit (2005). *Licensed Manpower Contractors*, Bureau of Planning, Research and Economics, Ministry of Industry, Commerce, and Employment.

Nitzan, Avital (1985). "Women in the Sights," *Yedioth Ahronoth*, Modern Times Supplement, 13.11.85.

Nosek, Hillel (2002). *Israel and the Start of the 21st Century: Society, Law, Economics and Media*. Tel Aviv: Tcherikover.

O'Connor, J. (1973). *The Fiscal Crisis of the State*, New York: St. Martin.

O'Grady, F., and Wakefild, H. (1989). *Women Work and Maternity: The Inside Story*, London: Maternity Alliance.

Okin, S. M. (1982). "Woman and the Making of the Sentimental Family," *Philosophy and Public Affairs* 11: 65-88.

Okun, B. S. (1997). "Family Planning in the Jewish Population of Israel: Correlates of Withdrawal Use," *Studies in Family Planning* 28(3): 215-227.

Oltzwer, Amos (2005). *Estimating Initial Costs of the Women's Labour Law, Amendment of the Early Announcement of Dismissal, 2003 p/1484,* Knesset Centre for Research and Data.

Orloff, A. S. (1996). "Gender in the Welfare State," *Annual Review of Sociology* 22: 51-78.

Padavic, I., and Reskin, B. (2002). *Women and Men at Work,* Thousand Oaks, CA: Sage.

Page, E. C. (2006). "The Origins of Policy," in: M. Moran, M. Rein and R. E. Goodin (eds.), *The Oxford Handbook of Public Policy,* Oxford University Press, pp. 207-227.

Pagonis, K. (2002). "Pregnancy Related Discrimination in Employment: Review of Employment Tribunal Decisions from November 1999 through April 2002," *Report for the Equal Opportunities Commission in London.*

Panagiotis, D. (2010). *The Fragmentation of International Trade Law,* February 18, 2010, TILEC Discussion Paper No. 2010-010.

Petersen, T., and Meyersson. E. M. (1999). "More Glory and Less Injustice: The Glass Ceiling in Sweden, 1970-1990," *Research in Social Stratification and Mobility* 17: 199-261.

Pichtelberg-Bermetz, Osnat and Harris, Ronit (2011). *Woman in Comparison to Men in the Labour World: Central Measures for International Women's Day, 2011,* Bureau for Research, Planning and Economy, Ministry of Industry, Commerce, and Employment.

Poitevin, M. (1989). "Financial Signalling and the 'Deep-Pocket' Argument," *RAND Journal of Economics* 20(1): 26-40.

Porter, N. B. (2006). "Re-Defining Superwoman: An Essay on Overcoming the Maternal Wall in the Legal Workplace," *Duke Journal of Gender Law and Policy* 13: 55.

Pressman, J., and Wildavsky, A. (1973). *Implementation: How Great Expectations in Washington are Dashed in Oakland*, University of California Press, Berkeley.

Radaï, F. (2002). "The Decline of Union Power – Structural Inevitability or Policy Choice?," in: J. Conaghan, M. Fischl and K. Karl (eds.), *Labour Law in an Era of Globalisation*, Oxford University Press, pp. 353-377.

Raday, Francis, Carmel, Shalev and Leiben-Kobi, Michal (1995). *The Status of Women in Society and in the Law*, Jerusalem: Shocken.

Rake, K. (2000). *Women's Incomes over a Lifetime*, Report to The Women's Unit, Cabinet Office, London: HMSO.

Ram, Ori (1999). "Between Arms and the Market—Israel in the Age of the Local World," I*sraeli Sociology* B(1): 99-145.

Ray, R., Gornick, J., and Schmitt, J. (2009). "Parental Leave Policies in 21 Countries: Assessing Generosity and Gender Equality," *Centre for Economic and Policy Research*, Washington D.C.

Regev, David (2004). "Even in the IDF an Officer was Dismissed While Pregnant," *Yedioth Ahronoth*, 11.0.04

Regev, David (2006). "Fired While Pregnant after 5.5 Months of Employment and will be Compensated," *Yedioth Ahronoth*, 11.7.06

Regev, David (2007). "A Bad Year for Working Women; in the Wake of the Women's Lobby Report Concerning Worsening for Female Employees in Israel; Discrimination against Mothers based on Pregnancy," *Yedioth Ahronoth*, News Supplement, 17.1.07.

Regev, David and Feingold, Hagai (2007). "Kicking the Soft Spot—66% if Complaints to the Women's Lobby Hotline are from Pregnant Women who have been Dismissed" *Yedioth Ahronoth*, 10.4.07.

Regev, Moti (2011). "Cultural Capital and the Field of Cultural Creation: the Work of Pierre Bourdieu," in Moti Regev, *The Sociology of Culture—General Introduction*, Ra'anana: Open University, pp. 275-319.

Reskin, B. F. (2003). "Including Mechanisms in Our Models of Ascriptive Inequality," *American Sociological Review* 68(1): 1-21.

Rimlet, Noya (2010) *Legal Feminism from Theory to Practice: The Struggle for Equality Among the Sexes in Israel and the United States*, Pardes Press and Haifa University Press.

Ritzer, George (2006). "Habitus and the Field" in: George

Ritzer, *Modern Sociological Theories*, Ra'anana: Open University, pp. 445-459.

Rodmell, S., and Smart, L. (1982). *Pregnant at Work: the Experiences of Women*, Milton Keynes: Open University Press.

Rosenberg, G. N. (2008). *The Hollow Hope: Can Courts Bring About Social change?*, University of Chicago Press.

Rosenfeld, R. A., Trappe, H., and Gornick, J. C. (2004). "Gender and Work in Germany: Before and after Reunification," *Annual Review of Sociology*, 30: 103-124.

Rosenhek, Z. (1999). "The Exclusionary Logic of the Welfare State: Palestinian Citizens in the Israeli Welfare State," *International Sociology* 14(2): 195-215.

Rosenhek, Z. (2002). "Social Policy and State-Building: The Dynamics of the Israeli Welfare State," *Journal of Societal and Social Policy* 1(1): 19-38.

Rosenhek, Ze'ev (1999). "Labour Emigrants in the Israeli Welfare State," *Social Security (Bitachon Sotziali)*, 56: 97-127.

Rosenhek, Ze'ev (2002). "Globalisation, Local Politics and Changes in the Welfare State: Unemployment Security Planning in Israel," *Work, Society and Law (Avoda, Chevra ve-Mishpat)* 9: 155-174.

Ross, C. E., Mirowsky, J., and Huber, J. (1983). "Dividing Work, Sharing Work, and In Between: Marriage Patterns and Depression," *American Sociological Review* 48: 309-323.

Rouse, J., and Sappleton, N. (2009). "Managing Maternity Fairly and Productively: Support for Small Employers," *International Small Business Journal* 27: 215-225.

Russell, H., and Banks, J. (2011a). *Pregnancy Discrimination in the Workplace: Legal Framework and Review of Legal Decisions, 1999 to 2008*, Dublin: CPP & Equality Authority.

Russell, H., and Banks, J. (2011b). *Pregnancy and Employment: A Literature Review*, Dublin: CPP & Equality Authority.

Russell, H., Quinn, E., King-O'Riain, R., and McGinnity, F. (2008). *The Experience of Discrimination in Ireland: Analysis of the QNHS Equality Module*, Dublin: The Equality Authority & the Economic and Social Research Institute.

Russell, H., Watson, D., and Banks, J. (2011). *Pregnancy At Work – A National Survey*, Dublin: CPP & Equality Authority.

Safran, Chana (2006). *Don't Want to be Nice*, Pardes Press.

Safran, H. (2006). *Don't Wanna be Nice Girls: The Struggle for Suffrage and the New Feminism in Israel*, Haifa: Pardes Press.

Sainsbury, D. (1996). *Gender, Equality and Welfare States*, Cambridge University Press.

Saint-Paul, G. (1996). *Dual Labour Markets: A Macroeconomic Perspective*, Cambridge Massachusetts: The M.I.T Press.

Sassen, S. (2006). *Territory, Authority, Rights: From Medieval to Global Assemblages*, Princeton: Princeton University Press.

Saurel, M. J., and Kaminski, M. (1983). "Pregnant Women at Work," *The Lancet* 321 (8322), pp. 475.

Schein, E. (2003). *Kurt Levin's Change Theory in the Field and in the Classroom: Notes toward a Model of Managed Learning*, www.solonline.org/res/wp/10006.html

Selznick, P. (1961). "Sociology and Natural Law," *Natural Law Forum* 6: 84-108.

Sembol, Sarit and Binyamin, Orli (2007). "Structural and Gender Fragmentation of Women's Labour History: The Reduction in Opportunity Structures for Poor Female Employees" *Israeli Sociology (Sotziologia Yisre'elit)* 9 (1) 5-37.

Sen, G. (2000). "Gender Mainstreaming in Finance Ministries," *World Development* 28(7): 1379-1390.

Sevirsky, Barbara (1999). *Equality for Women in the Israeli Welfare State: A Situation Analysis*, Israeli Women's Lobby, Adva Centre, Beit Berl College.

Sevirsky, Shlomo and Connor-Attias, Eti (2001). *Social Situation Report*. Tel Aviv: Adva Centre.

Sevislovsky, S. (1954). "Knesset Echoes—Gossip and Women's Work" *Yedioth Ahronoth*. 30.12.54, pp.5.

Shafir, G., and Peled, Y. (1998). "Citizenship and Stratification in an Ethnic Democracy," *Ethnic and Racial Studies* 21(3): 408-427.

Shakedi, A. (2003) *Words That Try to Touch: Qualitative Research, Theory and Implementation*, Tel Aviv: Ramot.

Shalev, M. (1996). "The Labour Movement in Israel: Ideology and Political Economy," in: E. J. Goldberg (ed.), *The Social History of Labour in the Middle East*, Boulder Colorado: Westview, pp. 131-161.

Shalev, M. (1999). "Have Globalisation and Liberalization 'Normalized' Israel's Political Economy?," *Israel Affairs* 5 (2 & 3): 121-155.

Silberstang, J. (2011). "Learning Gender: The Effects of Gender-Role Stereotypes on Women's Lifelong Learning and Career Advancement Opportunities," *The Oxford Handbook of Lifelong Learning*, p. 370.

Silbey, S. (2001). "Legal Culture and Consciousness," *International Encyclopedia of the Social and Behavioural Sciences*, Amsterdam: Elsevier Science, Ltd., pp. 8623-8629.

Silbey, S. (2003). *Everyday Life and The Constitution of Legality*, Massachusetts Institute of Technology.

Social Exclusion Unit (2004). *Tackling Social Exclusion: Taking Stock and Looking for the Future*, London: Office of the Deputy Prime Minister.

Sover-Heruti, Tali, Bior, Chaim and Weisberg, Hila (2013). "Twenty Thousand Employees Unionize—But Israel is Still not Scandinavia" *The Marker*, 26.12.13.

Stafford, F. P., and Sundström, M. (1996). "Time Out for Childcare: Signaling and Earnings Rebound Effects for Men and Women," *Labour* 10(3): 609-629.

Stein, Chen (2012). Internet site for Attny. Chen Stein: www.hamishpat.co.il/47055/leida

Steyer, Chaya (2006). "The Labour Market," in: Ori Ram and Nitza Berkovic (eds.), In/Equality, Be'er Sheva: Ben Gurion University Press, pp. 385-392.

Stier, H. (1998). "Short-Term Employment Transitions of Women in the Israeli Labour Force," Industrial and Labour Relations Review 51(2): 269-281.

Stier, H., Lewin-Epstein, N., and Braun, M. (2001). "Welfare Regimes, Family-Supportive Policies, and Women's Employment along the Life-Course," AJS 106(6): 1731-1760.

Streek, W., and Schmitter, P. (1985). Community, Market, State, and Association? The Prospective Contribution of Interest Governance to Social Order, Private Interest Governments, London: Sage Publication.

Tahmincioglu, E. (2007). Pregnancy Discrimination is on the Rise, EEOC seeing more complaints, www.msnbc.msn.com/id18742634

Taitz, Sharon (2012). Atty. Sharon Taitz's internet site: www.workrights.org.il/pregnancy-dismissal?gclid=CKqo hubmhLECFRIjfAodlBo1NA

Tamir, Tal and Nagar, Naomi (2007). Women in Israel 2006: Between Theory and Reality, Women's Lobby of Israel, pp. 146-152.

The Committee for the Advancement of the Status of Women (2004). *Dismissal of Pregnant Women at Tel Aviv University* Protocol 151, 28.12.04.

The Committee for the Advancement of the Status of Women (2005). *Indictments by the Ministry of Industry, Commerce, and Employment for Infringements upon the Equal Opportunity at Work Law and the Law for the Prevention of Sexual Harrassment.* Protocol no. 160, 14.2.05.

The Committee for the Advancement of the Status of Women (2007). *"Women's Labour Law" Proposal (amendment no. 39)*, 2007 Protocols (31.1.07).

The Committee for the Advancement of the Status of Women (2008). *Annual Report on "Women's Labour Law" (2007)—Dismissal of Pregnant Employees/ Employees Undergoing Fertility Treatment*, Protocol 109, 19.2.08.

The Committee for the Advancement of the Status of Women (2010). *Dismissals During Pregnancy.* Protocol no. 36, 16.2.2010.

The Committee for the Advancement of the Status of Women (2012). *Yearly report on "Women's Labour Law"— Dismissal of Pregnant Employees*, Protocol no. 135, 12.3.12.

The Committee for the Advancement of the Status of Women and Gender-Based Equality (2014). *Yearly Report on "Women's Labour Law"—Dismissal of Pregnant Employees*, Protocol no. 57, 20.1.14.

Thelen, K. (1999). "Historical Institutionalism in Comparative Politics," *Annual Review of Political Science* 2: 369-404.

Thelen, K. (2004). *How Institutions Evolve: The Political Economy of Skills in Germany, Britain, United States, and Japan*, New York: Cambridge University Press.

Toshav-Eichner, Nirit and Frenkel, Michal (2011). "The State's Protection of Pregnant Employees—the Israeli Case," *Economics Quarterly*, Pichas Sapir Centre for Development, by Tel Aviv University, year 58, edition ½, March-June 2011, pp. 41-65.

Toshav-Eichner, Nirit (2003). *Dismissal of Women During Pregnancy and Fertility Treatments*, Human Resources Planning Authority, Ministry of Labour and Welfare.

Toshav-Eichner, Nirit (2006). *Protecting the Positions of Pregnant Women in Welfare States—A Survey*, Bureau for Research, Planning and Economics, Ministry of Industry, Commerce, and Employment.

Toshav-Eichner, Nirit (2009). *Changing the Rules of the Game in the New Labour World—A Survey*, Bureau for Research, Planning and Economics, Ministry of Industry, Commerce, and Employment.

Trabelsi-Hadad, Tamar (2003). "They Continue to Dismiss Pregnant Teachers," *Yedioth Ahronoth*, 30.5.03

Trubek, D. M. (1980). "The Construction and Deconstruction of a Disputes-Focused Approach: An Afterword," *Law and Society Review* 15(3/4): 727-747.

Tzabar Ben Yehoshua, Naama (2001). "Introduction: The History of Qualitative Research, Influences and Trends," in Naama Tzabar Ben Yehoshua (ed.), *Traditions and Trends in Qualitative Research*, Or Yehuda: Dvir, pp. 13-20.

Tzchor, Maya (2012). Internet site for Attny. Maya Tzchor: www.ovdot.co.il

Tzimuki, Tova and Paz, Sheli (2004). "Without Law and Order, the Yearly Report on Civil Rights Paints a Glum Portrait," *Yedioth Ahronoth*, 1.7.04.

Waitman, Sacha (2007). "Opening Comments," in Pierre Bourdieu. *Sketch for a Self-Analysis*. Tel Aviv: HaKibbutz HaMeuchad, pp. 5-24.

Weber, M. (1949). *Methodology of the Social Sciences*, Shils, E., and Finch, H. (trans.), Glencoe: Free press.

Werum, R., and Winders, B. (2001). "Who's 'In' and Who's 'Out': State Fragmentation and the Struggle over Gay Rights 1974-1999," *Social Problems* 48(3): 386-410.

Williams, J. (2000). *Unbending Gender: Why Family and Work Conflict and What to Do about it*, Oxford; New York: Oxford University Press.

Williams, L. J., and Anderson, S. E. (1994). "An Alternative Approach to Method Effects by Using Latent-Variable Models: Applications in Organisational Behaviour Research," *Journal of Applied Psychology* 79(3): 323.

Williams, W. W. (1980). "Firing the Woman to Protect the Fetus: The Reconciliation of Fetal Protection with

Employment Opportunity Goals under Title VII," *Georgetown Law Journal* 69: 641.

Wirth, L. (2002). *Breaking through the Glass Ceiling: Women in Management*, International Labour office, Luxemburg: 2002.

Women's Labour Law (1990). *Amendment no. 9* , Appendix 1324, from 26.7.90.

Women's Labour Law (2001). *Amendment—Dismissal of Pregnant Employees*, 2001.

Yizre'eli, Dafna (2000). "Genderization in the Work World," in: Dafna Yizre'eli and others (eds.), *Sex, Gender, Politics*, Tel Aviv: Kav Adom, HaKibbutz HaMeuchad, pp. 167-216.

Young, I. M. (2003). "The Logic of Masculinist Protection: Reflections on the Current Security State," *Journal of Women in Culture and Society* 29(1), The University of Chicago, pp. 1-25.

Young, V., and Morrell, J. (2005). *Pregnancy Discrimination at Work: A Survey of Employers in Scotland*, Equal Opportunities Commission.Yuval-Davis, N. (1997). *Gender and Nation*, Sege University of East London.

Zilber, Carmel (1997). "You Deserve It," *Yedioth Ahronoth*, 24.9.97.

Dr. Nirit Toshav - Eichner

www.ingramcontent.com/pod-product-compliance
Lightning Source LLC
Chambersburg PA
CBHW062152270326
41930CB00009B/1511